Barkow Leibinger

Barkow Leibinger
Spielraum

With a foreword by Hal Foster

HATJE
CANTZ

Foreword: Architecture as Instrument
Hal Foster

One origin myth of modern architecture involves the voyaging of German designers like Walter Gropius to North American cities such as Buffalo, where they first saw in situ the industrial structures, such as grain elevators, that they had already proposed as models for functionalist buildings in Europe. The partnership of Frank Barkow and Regine Leibinger is a new variation on this old theme of international encounter: in the late 1980s the American Barkow and the German Leibinger met at the Harvard Graduate School of Design (where Gropius had once presided as chair). Already in the literature on the office this encounter is taken as a primal scene: Frank Barkow, the rangy man from Montana, impressed by the huge infrastructural projects and the great land art of the American West (e.g., hydroelectric dams in the first instance, *Spiral Jetty* by Robert Smithson in the second), meets Regine Leibinger, the sophisticated daughter of the innovative director of TRUMPF, the designer-manufacturer of laser-cut tools based near Stuttgart (which is also where a classic of European modernism, the Weissenhof Siedlung, is located). After training at the GSD under the chairmanship of Rafael Moneo, the two young architects set up a practice in Berlin in 1993, at a time when the new Europe came to represent what the old America once did: an expanded horizon for ambitious building.

However devoted to industrial architecture, modern masters often made signature statements with houses; conversely, in our era when art and entertainment are central to the economy at large, contemporary architects have sometimes become household names through museums. Although Barkow Leibinger have produced both domestic and cultural projects, as well as two landmark office towers, the TRUTEC Building in Seoul (2006) and the Tour Total in Berlin (2012), they are best known for industrial architecture. At the same time Barkow Leibinger are fully aware of how such design has shifted in meaning and motive. On the one hand, the factory is no longer separate from other typologies such as the laboratory; on the other hand, work undertaken there is no longer distinct from other activities such as research and experiment, modeling and computing. So even as Barkow Leibinger "recover essential aspects" of industrial architecture, they have also adapted to its changed parameters, and anticipated still newer ones.[1] If "today technology is representation-less," as Frank Barkow suggests, Barkow Leibinger do not buy into the fantasy of dematerialization that drives the post-Fordist ideology of "light construction."[2] In effect, they see industrial architecture as a set of operations involving materials and techniques both new and old, and they develop these operations in architectural terms, often mimetic of industrial ones, that are "repetitive, serial, and additive."[3]

Distinctive though they are as an American-German partnership, trained in the one country and based in the other, Frank Barkow and Regine Leibinger are also representative of a generation that is sometimes called "post-critical." Yet this term is inaccurate, because, although this generation is not reliant on a priori theory, as an architect like Peter Eisenman often was, neither is it dependent on imagistic scenography, as architects like Robert Venturi and Denise Scott Brown, the postmodern opponents of Eisenman, often were. At the GSD under Moneo, Frank Barkow and Regine Leibinger learned to navigate between the Scylla and Charybdis of applied theory and applied images alike.[4] Just as important, as they developed, they steered clear of two younger sirens that might have proved more seductive. In many ways the theoretical formalism represented by Eisenman morphed into the digital formalism promoted by Greg Lynn, while the scenography represented by Venturi and Scott Brown hardened into the "fetish ornaments" promoted by Zaha Hadid.[5] If the former tendency has largely surrendered the tectonic clarity of much modern architecture, the latter has mostly exacerbated the imagistic superficiality of much postmodern architecture. Barkow Leibinger have resisted both developments: in their view, new materials and techniques hardly nullify considerations of structure—on the contrary—and architecture as a sculptural object is no advance over building as a flimsy sign.

What, then, is the third way that Barkow Leibinger have pursued? Ten years ago some members of their generation spoke of a "new pragmatism," while others insisted on a "design intelligence" that was "projective" rather than "critical." Both notions pointed to a renewed commitment to practice, not an aversion to theory or representation per se but, rather, an advocacy of knowledge that is intrinsic to architecture, that emerges from its distinctive protocols of research, experiment, calculation, and execution. Barkow Leibinger favor a slightly different term, "design performance," which can be taken to indicate an architecture that meets the highest standards of industry (or any other client), to be sure, but that is also performative in another sense—inventive, even playful. This is a cohort that, not concerned with a signature style, is responsive to given conditions of client, program, and site, and that is alert to how advances in technology and engineering can be turned to architectural ends.

"For me it always has to be comprehensible and it has to be appropriate," Regine Leibinger remarks. "Those are key terms for [our] architectural approach."[6] That approach is an ethical one too; certainly it was for the early advocates of modern architecture. The common term for this modern commitment was "transparency," which etymologically means "an appearing through." For the most part this value operated by analogy: if the materials, structure, and construction of a building were made clear, then, it was thought, other aspects of life often shrouded in secrecy—social relations, economic operations, political decisions—might also be drawn into the open, into the clear light of democratic understanding. That analogy, which was active in modernist art too (where the common phrase was "truth to materials"), was never a strong one, and today it is flouted by many architects whose production of atmospheric and affective effects mostly abets the obfuscation that now dominates these other realms (again, the social, the economic, and the political).[7]

This is why it is so important that Barkow Leibinger insist on "legibility," the term they prefer over "transparency." Again, the legibility they seek is hardly that of a postmodern *architecture parlante,* yet neither is it simply that of a modern structural transparency, the assumed self-evidence of construction in brick, concrete, glass and steel, and so on. If much technology is "representation-less" today, Frank Barkow and Regine Leibinger do not leave it there, in its own black box; they work to put various techniques into action and, in doing so, not only to demonstrate them but also to transform them in ways that are appropriate to present conditions. A Barkow Leibinger mantra has it that "tools shape materials that make forms, not the other way around," a sequence that reverses the usual order of design.[8] Here they acknowledge the importance of the symbiotic relationship they have enjoyed with TRUMPF, a strong client that led Barkow Leibinger to consider "how digital fabrication technologies can be used to make buildings."[9] Yet they have also worked with other fabricators and engineers to incorporate new materials and techniques into the design process. In this manner, as they look ahead to the advanced world projected by, say, TRUMPF, Barkow Leibinger also look back, beyond modern architecture, to the materialism of manufacture advocated by Gottfried Semper (their interest in "carpeting," for example, recalls his fascination with textiles). The outcome is a distinctive "atlas of fabrication," in which materials and techniques are legible in the structures and spaces that result, in ways that unite design and program as well as construction and site.

Another Barkow Leibinger motto is *Kein Stil, sondern Haltung,* which can be translated roughly as "Position over Style." "Position, in our case," they add, "favors process over preconceived form," and by "process" they mean specific operations performed on specific materials that are deemed appropriate for a given project.[10] Forty-seven years ago, discontent with the pictorial effects of a Minimalist Art that contradicted its own program of literal transparency, Richard Serra also developed a set of specific operations to be performed on specific materials, a protocol laid out in his famous *Verb List* (1967–68): "to roll, to crease, to fold . . ." These tasks governed his first mature works: sheets of lead rolled, folded, torn, or otherwise manipulated; molten lead splashed along the base of a wall and peeled back in creased rows; slabs of concrete stacked on top of one another or sheets of lead propped up against each other; and so on. In their exhibition catalogue *An Atlas of Fabrication* (2009) Barkow Leibinger present a "list of actions" of their own: "2D-Cutting, Casting, Cutting/Stacking, Bending, Punching, Welding/Inflating, 3D-Cutting (Revolving), Anticipating."[11] Although these operations, sometimes separate, sometimes combined, are often sophisticated in technical terms, they are usually simple when it comes to legibility. Like Serra, Frank Barkow and Regine Leibinger think of practice as a matter not only of experiment and execution but also of demonstration and disclosure.

Take cutting and rotating, as performed in the façade of the office building in Seoul, for example, or in the roof of the TRUMPF canteen in Ditzingen. In the first instance, Barkow Leibinger had glass panels cut at irregular angles and fitted into two- and three-dimensional steel frames in a way that produced standard types; they then rotated these extrusions through 180 degrees in such a way as to create "a huge amount of variation and nuance within the façade."[12] In the second instance, Barkow Leibinger had glulam wood cut into irregular cells and set again in steel frames in such a way that formed "a kind of infill webbing"; again the result was both varied and nuanced not only in appearance but also in function, since the cells could be "programmed as skylights, acoustic panels, or artificial lighting."[13] Even as the simple operations remain legible, the complex outcomes become resonant: the Seoul façade suggests a giant kaleidoscope, while the TRUMPF roof evokes a canopy of leaves.[14] In this way Barkow Leibinger make both materials and techniques respond to human invention and natural reference, which is to say that, just as they do not allow technology to be a black box that mystifies us, they also do not project it as a "second nature" that dominates us.

Another connection to Post-Minimalist Art might be mentioned here, one that involves not only a protocol of process but also a sensitivity to site. Again like Serra, Barkow Leibinger understand work as embedded in a particular context, to be experienced there, bodily, under particular conditions. This is evident enough in the TRUMPF campus, for example, but even more in the Potsdam Biosphere, where the site helped to generate a structure that in turn articulates the site. Here the critique of "image making" is one with a commitment to "space making": buildings are not boxes dropped in an abstract space but rather interventions that extrapolate, demarcate, and activate a specific field.[15] One of the strong suits of the Barkow Leibinger generation is to redefine architecture and landscape in mutual terms, yet even more is at stake here for Frank Barkow and Regine Leibinger: a conception of architecture as an instrument to probe a site à la Serra, even to map a condition "where nature and technology are always in flux" à la Robert Smithson.[16] In effect, just as Post-Minimalists like Serra and Smithson critiqued Minimalist Art, so Frank Barkow and Regine Leibinger critique "Minimalist" architecture today, which, again, in its pursuit of atmospheric and affective effects, has tended not only to obscure structure and space but also to overwhelm subject and site.

Although Barkow Leibinger sometimes refer to architecture as "engineered structure," they always turn whatever engineering they employ to architectural ends.[17] In this way they avoid another great hazard in contemporary design, that of hypertrophic engineering presented as architectural art, which usually means architectural spectacle (e.g., Santiago Calatrava). Often enough, both materials and operations in the Barkow Leibinger repertoire are neither novel nor high-tech; some are not only traditional but also almost primordial in origin (e.g., wood, casting).

In the end Barkow Leibinger are *bricoleurs* as much as they are engineers. The *bricoleur,* Claude Lévi-Strauss writes in a famous definition, treats "a collection of oddments left over from human endeavors"; he or she "makes do with 'whatever is at hand,' that is to say, with a set of tools and materials which is always finite and is also heterogeneous."[18] Although sensitive to the materiality of these odds and ends, the *bricoleur* treats them as signs in which the signified turns into the signifying and vice versa, even as "operators" that "represent a set of actual and possible relations."[19] This is the case with Barkow Leibinger. Often they are inspired by found images and objects—a micro-photograph of a leaf, a snapshot of a stack of wood, a left-over piece of bubble wrap, an old toy like the Slinky (this cylindrical coil of wire is a miracle of tectonic elasticity), a picture of the sinuous brick walls designed by Thomas Jefferson for the University of Virginia campus, and so on. Sometimes they even make "frame-molds out of interesting junk lying around the office."[20]

This interest evokes a key aspect of Brutalist architecture as defined by Reyner Banham almost sixty years ago: "valuation of materials for their inherent qualities 'as found'." In fact, the two other elements in his definition of Brutalism also resonate with Barkow Leibinger: "formal legibility of plan" and "clear exhibition of structure."[21] "To make our mechanisms speak with our spaces is our central problem," Alison and Peter Smithson, the central protagonists of Brutalist architecture, once wrote, and Barkow Leibinger would agree.[22] "Brutalism tries to face up to a mass-production society," the Smithsons declared, "and drag a rough poetry out of the confused and powerful forces which are at work."[23] Barkow Leibinger update this ethical attitude of committed address for "a mass-customization society"; their architecture, which they label "prêt-à-porter," also extracts a rough poetry out of the complex forces of our time. In many ways Brutalism was an attempt to reclaim the values of the modern architecture of Ludwig Mies van der Rohe and Le Corbusier against its "degradation" as so much stylistic "veneer" after World War II.[24] Barkow Leibinger occupy a similar position in relation to an architecture given over to digital formalism and fetishistic ornamentation.

"The work of Barkow Leibinger comes to us from inside architecture," George Wagner has written, and it is true: theirs is a reflexive language, one developed recursively through building.[25] It is a language they always revise in accordance with the constraints of the program and the conditions of the site, and it is a language they always extend through other activities such as competitions and master plans, prototyping and archiving, teaching and exhibiting. It is a language in which architecture is an instrument, as complex or as simple as the case requires.

This brings us back to "design performance," from which I want to draw a final implication. There is always an element of inspired performance in *bricolage*. And as the greatest philosophers in German aesthetics tell us, such play (*Spiel*) is also essential to art; it opens up a realm for an imaginative response to any question. In the end, this is what Barkow Leibinger offer us all: *Spielraum,* room for play, space for invention.

1 Frank Barkow and Regine Leibinger, "Beyond Ground Zero: A Conversation with Frank Barkow and Regine Leibinger," interview by Jan Otakar Fischer, in *Barkow Leibinger: Werkbericht, 1993–2001,* ed. George Wagner (Basel, 2001), p. 23.

2 Ibid., p. 24; see Terence Riley, *Light Construction* (New York, 1995).

3 Barkow and Leibinger 2001 (see note 1), p. 22.

4 In this respect Barkow Leibinger also acknowledge the guidance of Robin Evans at Harvard University, who, for all his interest in the representation of architecture, insisted above all on its *experience*.

5 Barkow and Leibinger 2001 (see note 1), p. 26.

6 Ibid., p. 21.

7 See Hal Foster, *The Art-Architecture Complex* (London and New York, 2011).

8 Frank Barkow and Regine Leibinger, *Barkow Leibinger: An Atlas of Fabrication* (London, 2009), n.p.

9 Ibid. The gatehouse at the TRUMPF campus in Ditzingen was the first Barkow Leibinger building to incorporate TRUMPF technology in the overall strategy.

10 Frank Barkow and Regine Leibinger, "Peripheral Vision," in *Barkow Leibinger Architects,* ed. JaeHong Lee (Seoul, 2007), p. 11.

11 Barkow and Leibinger 2009 (see note 8), n.p.

12 Ibid.

13 Ibid.

14 Or perhaps a canopy of crystals. There is a way in which Barkow Leibinger here participate in the current shift in architecture from a biological paradigm to an environmental, even geological, one. See Stan Allen and Marc McQuade, *Landform Building: Architecture's New Terrain* (Baden, 2011).

15 See Aaron Betsky, "From Field to Form, With an Attitude," in Lee 2007 (see note 10), pp. 16–23, esp. p. 16.

16 Barkow and Leibinger 2001 (see note 1), pp. 21, 20.

17 Similarly, Serra, who sometimes sees sculpture as "engineered structure," always turns engineering to sculptural ends.

18 Claude Lévi-Strauss, *The Savage Mind* (1962; Chicago, 1966), pp. 17, 19.

19 Ibid., p. 18.

20 Barkow and Leibinger 2009 (see note 8), n.p.

21 Reyner Banham, "The New Brutalism," *The Architectural Review* (December 1955), pp. 354–61, reprinted in *October* 136 (Spring 2011), p. 23.

22 Alison and Peter Smithson, *Without Rhetoric: An Architectural Aesthetic 1955–1972* (Cambridge, MA, 1974), p. 14.

23 Alison and Peter Smithson, "The New Brutalism," *Architectural Design* (April 1957), p. 113, reprinted in *October* 136 (Spring 2011), p. 37. See also in the same issue Hal Foster, "Savage Minds (A Note on Brutalist Bricolage)," pp. 182–91.

24 Theo Crosby, "The New Brutalism," *Architectural Design* (January 1955), reprinted in *October* 136 (Spring 2011), p. 17.

25 George Wagner, "Matters of Fact," in *Barkow Leibinger: Werkbericht, 1993–2001,* ed. Wagner 2001 (see note 1), p. 11.

The phrase "Revolutions of Choice" signifies architectural opportunity driven by the rise of digital (and analogue) capabilities and competences, but it also means something more essential: architects longing for the agility, authority, and ability to predict and control the very nature of architectural making that arises from our imagination. But, we might ask, how can we better mediate between the tools we use, and how might they inform an architectural outcome?

To say that Barkow Leibinger is a material practice is to say, as expressed in their manifesto for the Architecture Biennale in Venice in 2008, that "architectural ideas and materials are inextricably intertwined. Put another way, architecture is a physical substance, and the point of conceptualization is to figure out how to treat that material."[1] This has been both a salient aspect and the origin of the practice's methods, which continue to evolve. One crucial motivation for working directly with actual building materials (new and old), and preferably at the scale of one-to-one, has been the desire to circumvent, as much as possible, the problems that representations (drawings and models) pose for architects. This is because such renderings guide the construction of buildings but do not simulate their visual and spatial effects experientially. Rather, mockups, prototypes, installations, and one-to-one elements offer representational alternatives that mediate between an initial idea and a building. Viewing such representations in this way underscores the belief that ideas arise as much from the things you make as from any preconceived conceptualization.

This belief assumes that design follows technology. Its adherents make use of techniques that include a wide spectrum of tests, experiments, trial and error, success and failure. Their working method is rather experimental and nonlinear, following an evolving process that forms a core body of knowledge and expertise that enables the architect to determine the building systems that constitute the buildings he makes. In this way the architect becomes his or her own expert, producing prototypical building components, which replace or supersede the standard building catalogue. It is this atmosphere of experimental freedom—semi-autonomous from the demands of project and building deadlines and construction limits—that allows the practice to thrive and to evolve. At perhaps no other moment than during the research and design phase is the opportunity greater for all a project's trajectories, including aesthetics, performance, sustainability, and economic viability, to intercept and inform each other, according to the architect's orchestration.

1 *Out There: Architecture Beyond Building, 11th International Architecture Exhibition La Biennale di Venezia,* ed. Aaron Betsky, exh. cat. La Biennale di Venezia (Venice, 2008), p. 15.

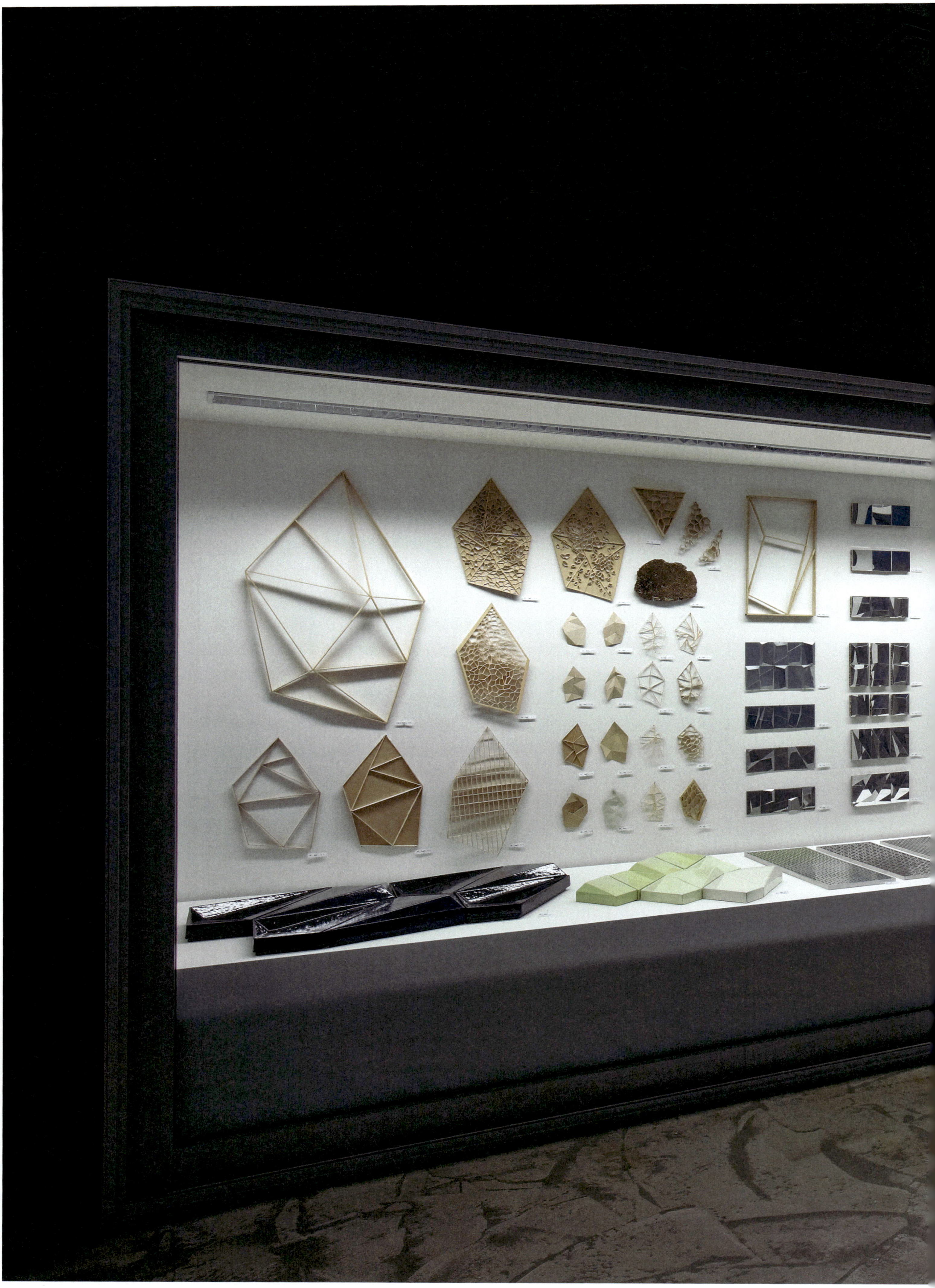

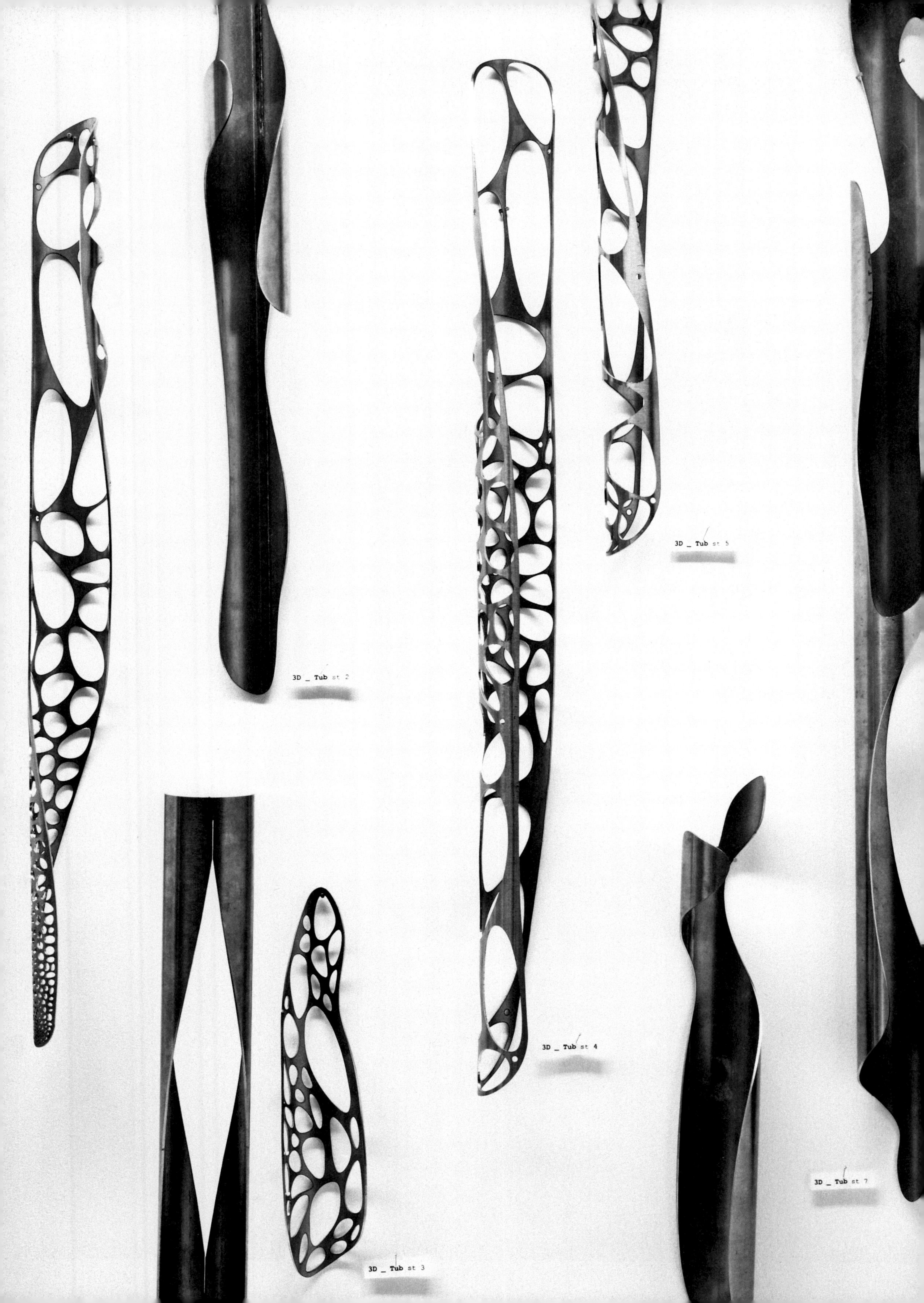
3D _ Tub st 5
3D _ Tub st 2
3D _ Tub st 4
3D _ Tub st 7
3D _ Tub st 3

Tube Studies

With the invention and production of the TRUMPF Tubematic Laser (cutting machine tool) a number of applications became immediately apparent to Barkow Leibinger beginning in the early 2000s. Student interns went to TRUMPF's research center in Stuttgart to test the limits, capacities, and economics of this machine and began producing experimental "off-cuts."

These off-cuts led to a prototypical array for the exhibition *Re-Sampling Ornament* at the Swiss Architecture Museum in Basel: a circular array of vertical, fifty-millimeter stainless steel tubes, which were scroll cut and varied in scale and pattern. Several of the tubes were mechanized and rotate such that they articulate light and pattern, kinetically anticipating an aesthetic and performative façade screen.

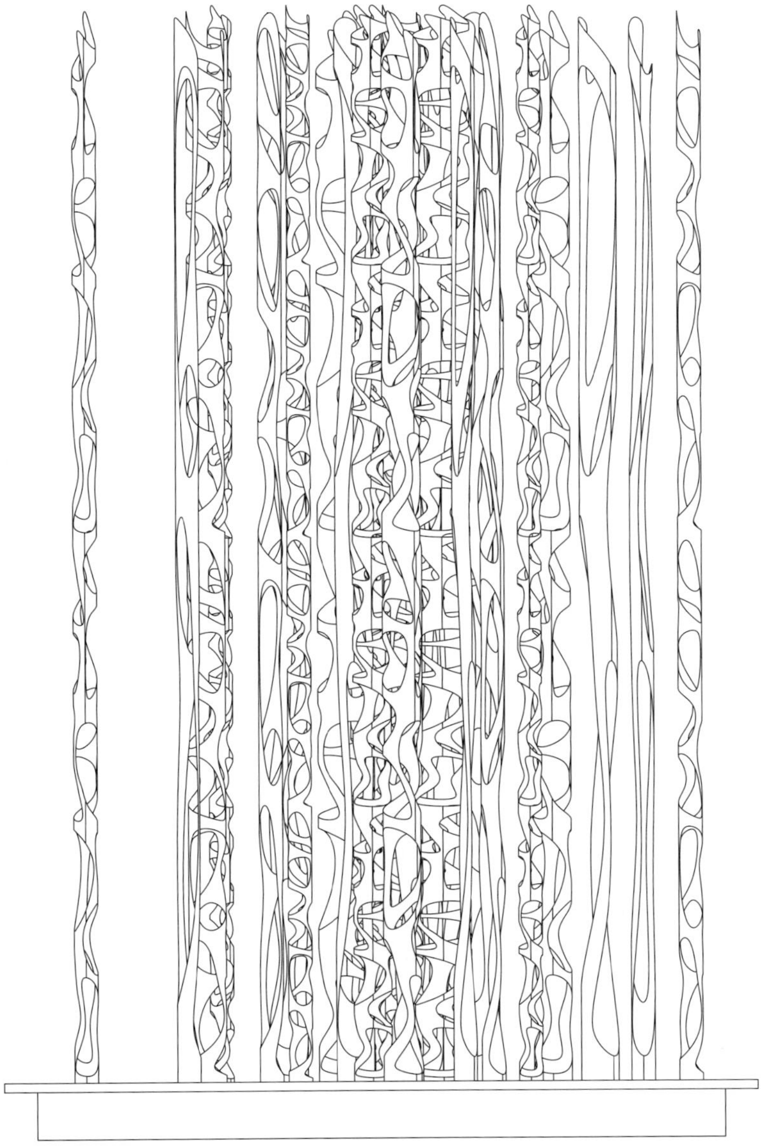

This prototype found an application in a penthouse in Berlin for a tubular screen that controls daylight and produces an ornamental surface effect. This façade system was modified later for the Scenario building near the historical Weissenhofsiedlung (Weissenhof housing settlement) in Stuttgart, where large-scale tubes of core-ten steel are cut in spiral sections, generating an ornamental sun screen that represents a veil or curtain of intense material depth for the fashion wholesalers located within.

For the eleventh Venice Biennale, "Out There: Architecture Beyond Building," Barkow Leibinger constructed an array of tubes fitted into a CNC-cut wooden platform much like a pegboard. This installation-scaled project created an artificial, interactive garden whose clusters of scrolled tubes offered endless possibilities for configuring the space for the visitors in the Arsenale exhibition hall. This research area showed some of the limits and possibilities, ranging from experimentation to architectural application, derived from one tooling system.

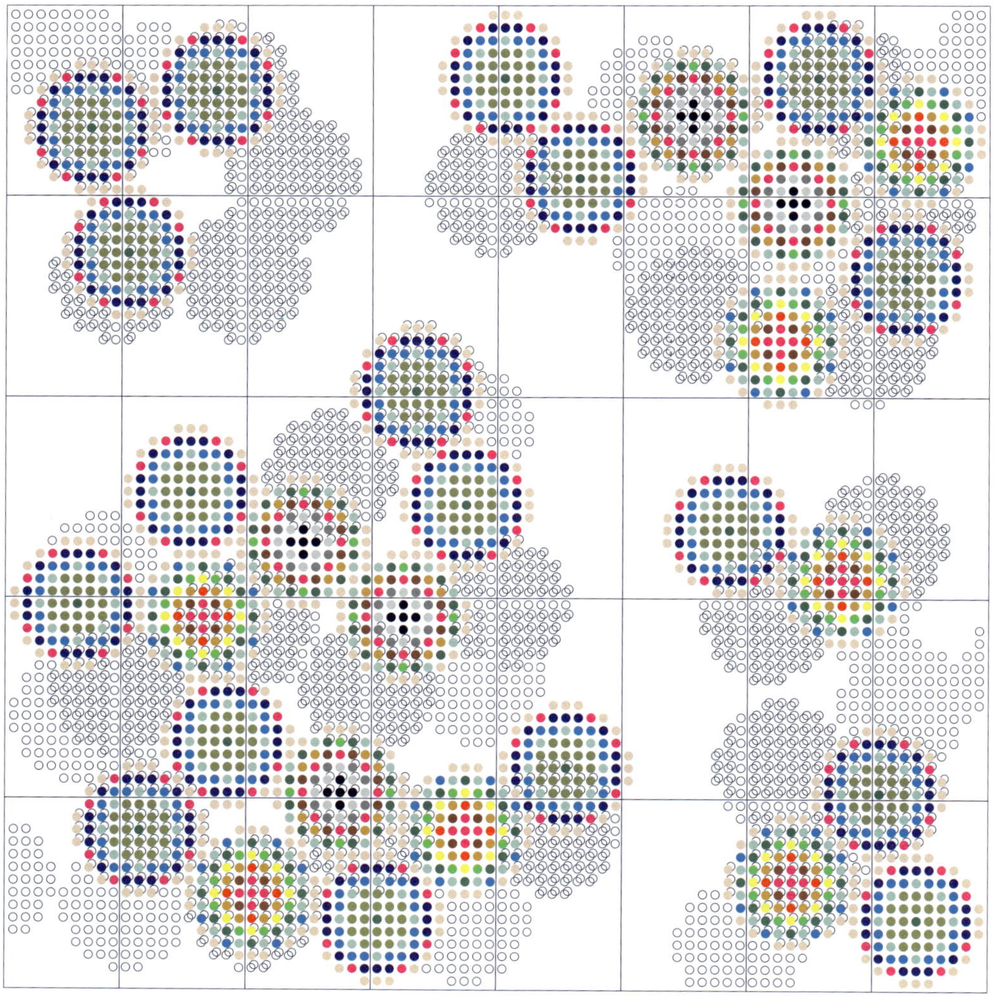

Light Structure
Installation, 2009

“Light structure” is a concept for lighting elements that utilize Barkow Leibinger’s capability for digital fabrication. Fifty-millimeter Plexiglas tubes are laser-cut (by the A.L.L. company in Munich) to form topographical surfaces that are top-lit by LEDs, causing the cut and polished edges to glow. The tubes, bundled into clusters of various sizes, accumulate in a cellular fashion to produce larger and more complex forms. When arranged together in a single space their organic surfaces constitute a vertical, topological re-mapping of the ceiling of a gallery. Lit from above the material is in effect dematerialized and creates soft, ephemeral forms.

“Scripting” (Visual Basic .NET) and parametric software enables the geometry of the cut tubes to remain tangent to one another, so that, seen from below, they appear as a continuous plane of glowing rings. The digital commutations also ensure that each cut produces two fully usable parts, avoiding material waste in their production (zero waste of a recyclable material). Twenty-five cut variations produce fifty tube types that can be configured in multiple arrangements avoiding modular repetition. Exploiting the colors of the transparent tubes, which are either clear or tinted, helps to reinforce the idea of the piece as a landscape composed of vertical elements. This research supported several outcomes, including an installation at Hans-Peter Jochum’s gallery in Berlin and a one-to-one prototype chandelier for a bank’s VIP lounge.

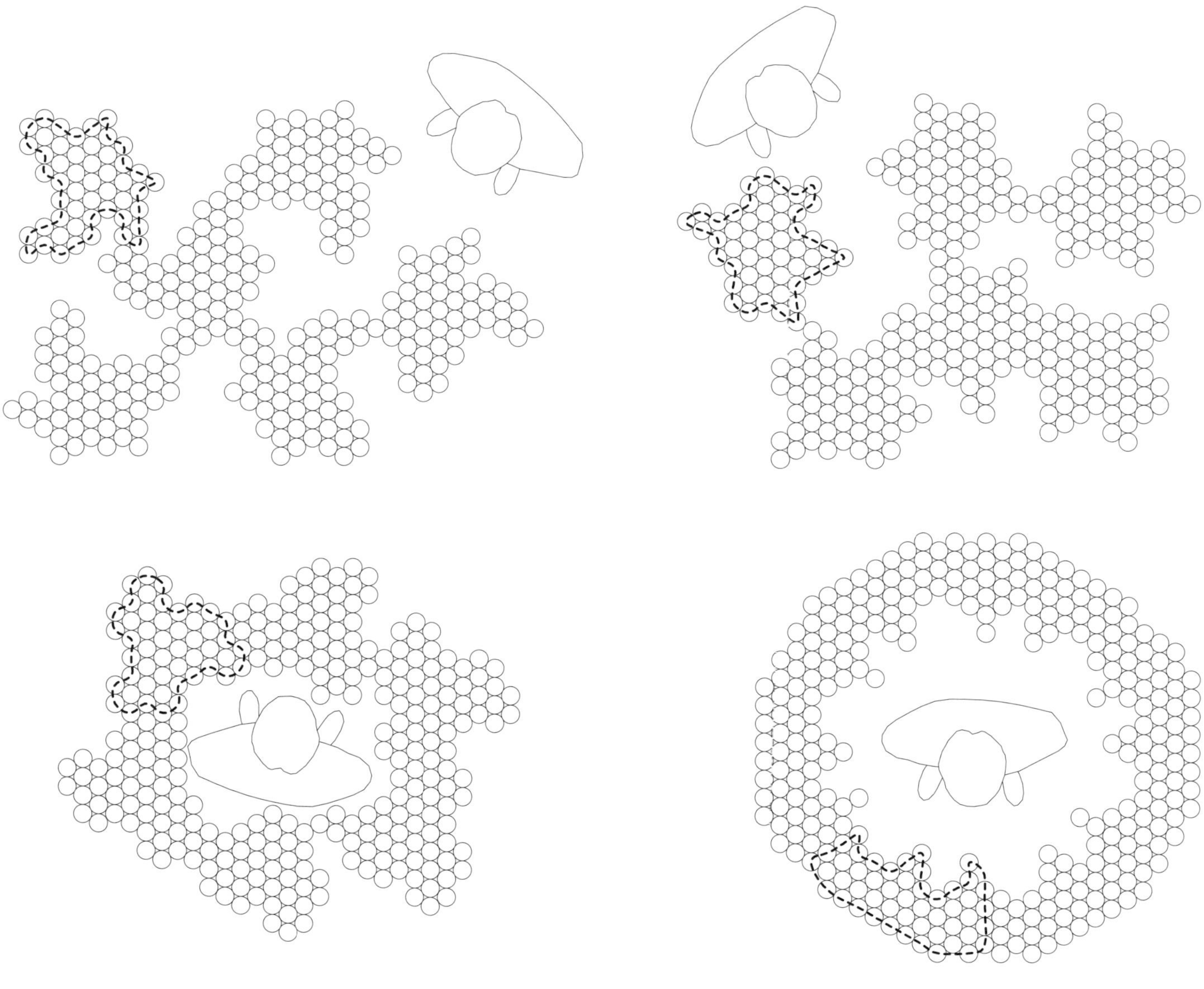

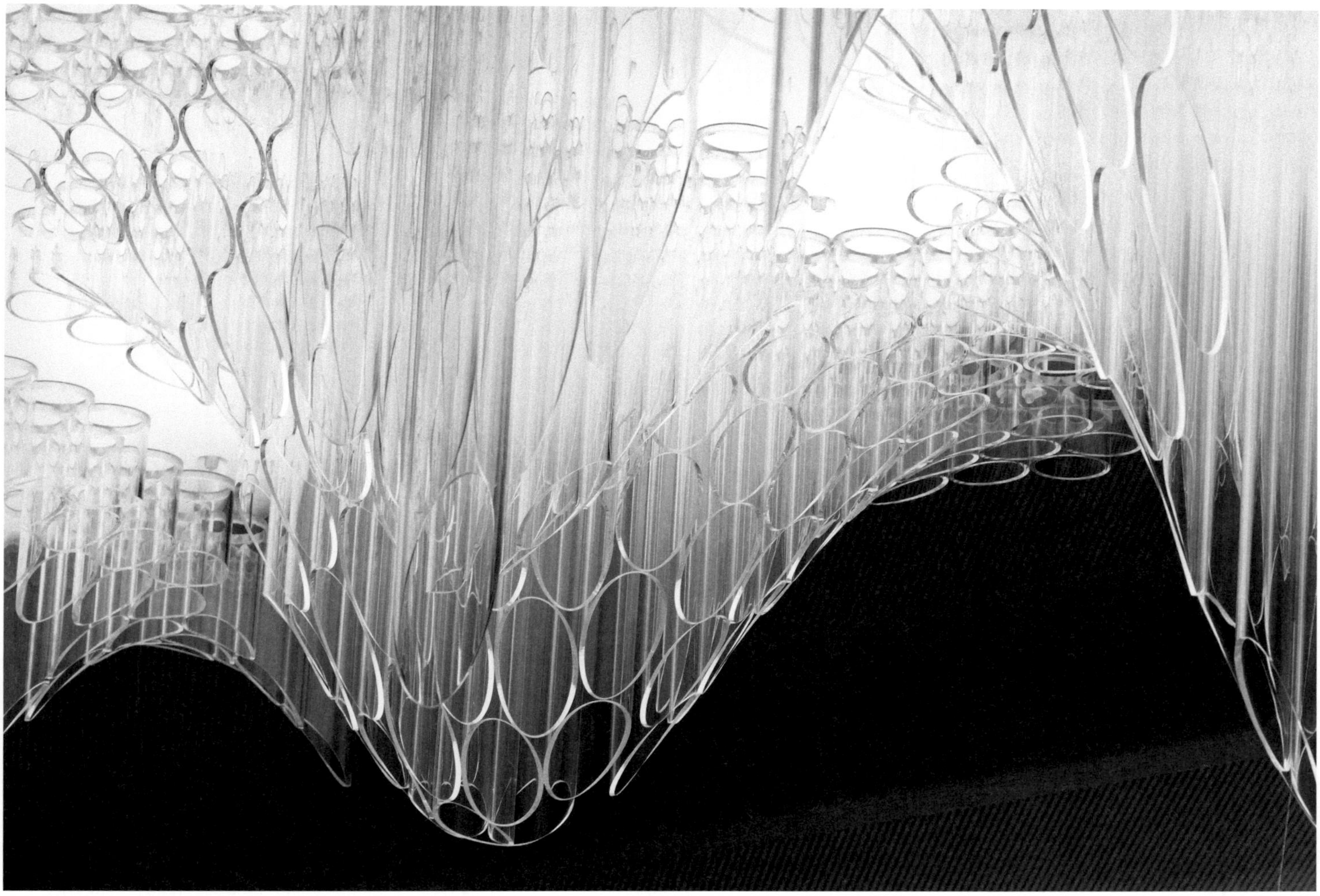

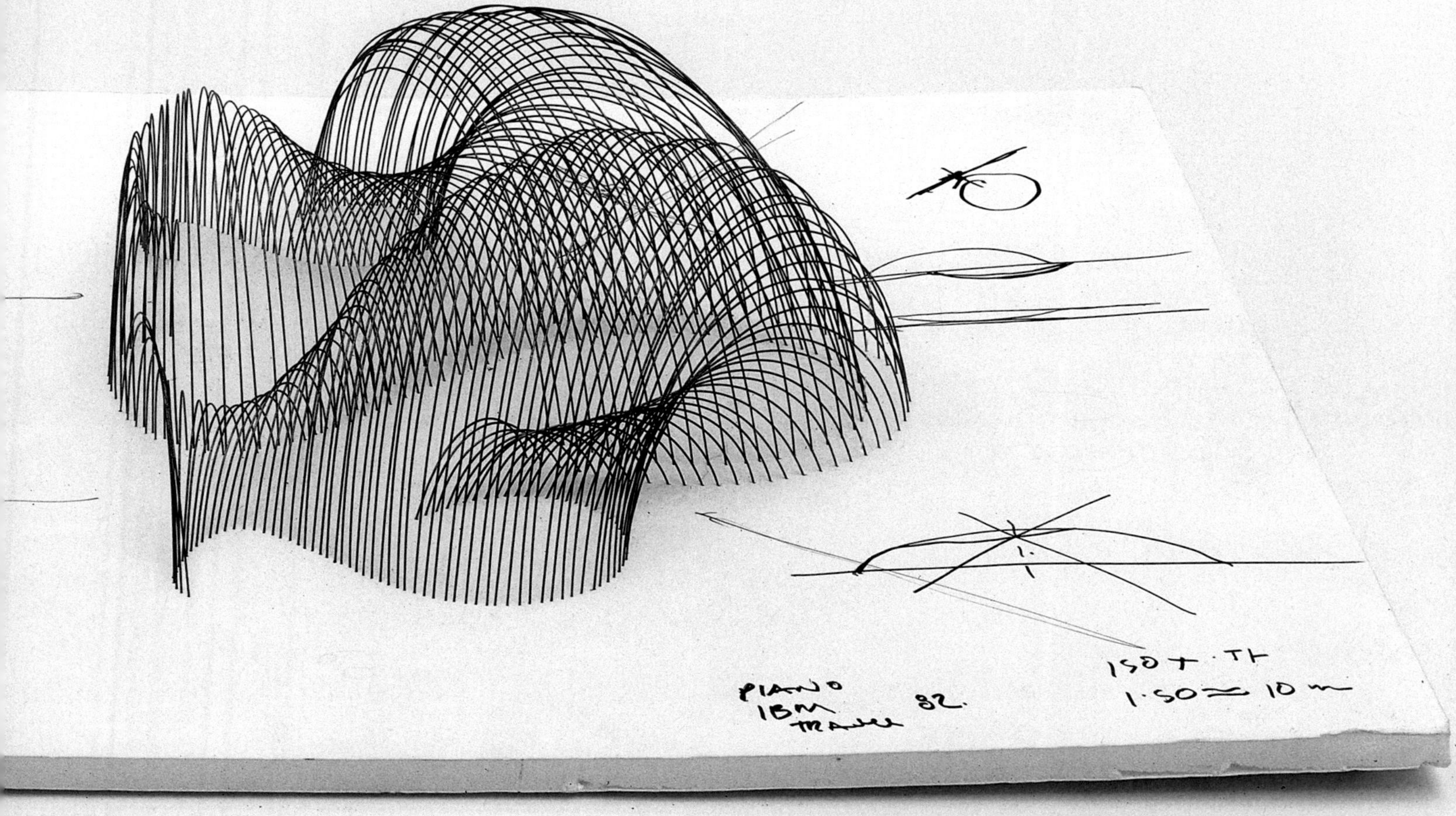
PIANO
IBM
82.
1·50 ≃ 10 m

DAM Pavilion
Design Study and 1:1 Mockup, 2009

The DAM architectural pavilion is neither a building nor exclusively an experiment. It hovers between the speculative and the programmatic. It is a provocative prototype for testing the limits and capacities of speculative work. With this in mind a temporary pavilion was developed with the structural engineer Werner Sobek for the Deutsches Architekturmuseum (DAM) in Frankfurt am Main on the occasion of their twenty-fifth anniversary. In collaboration with material and production sponsors a pavilion was conceived for the garden of the Museum für Angewandte Kunst Frankfurt.

Working with Bayer Makrolon, Beton Kemmlit, MBM Construction, and 3M (Velcro fasteners) the material and fabrication partners determined real physical possibilities and limitations that provided an initial starting point. By observing and speculating on the possibilities these systems offered, we discovered the technique of using digitally bent, steel tube profiles for constructing an arched enclosure with differentiated radii.

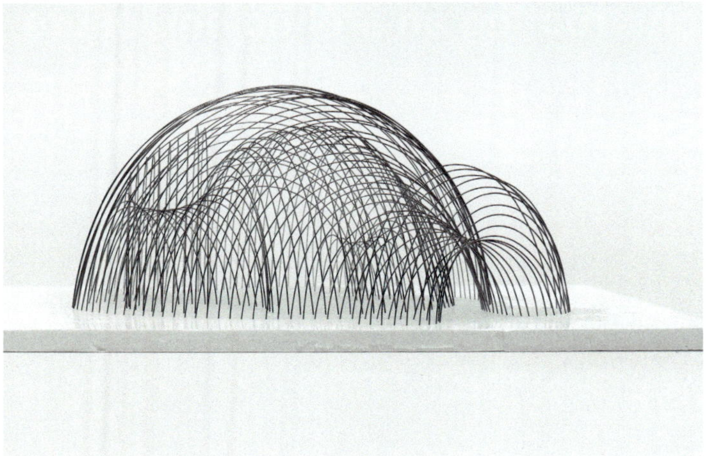

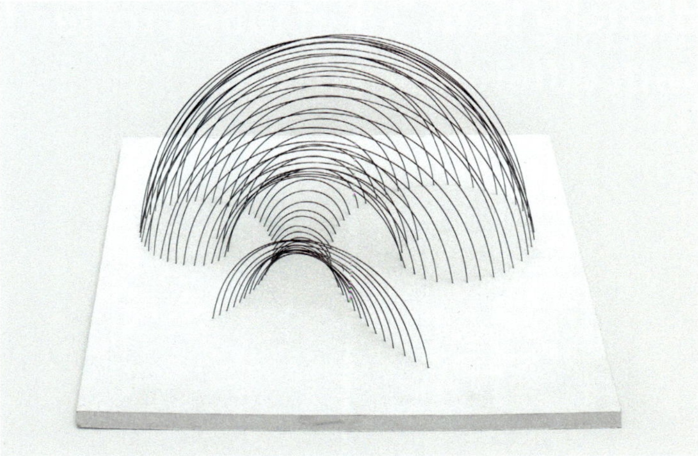

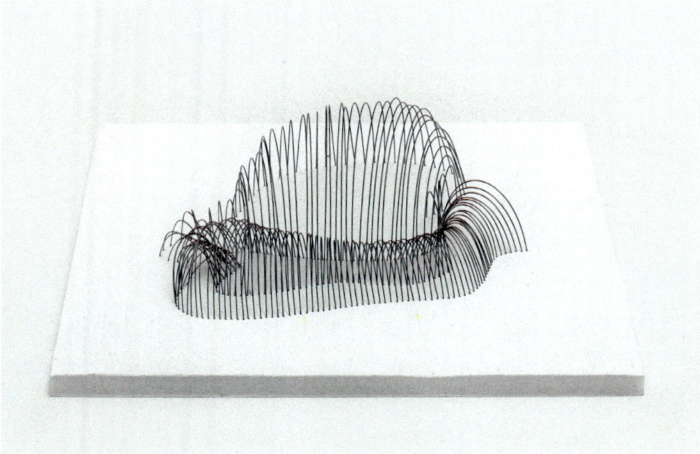

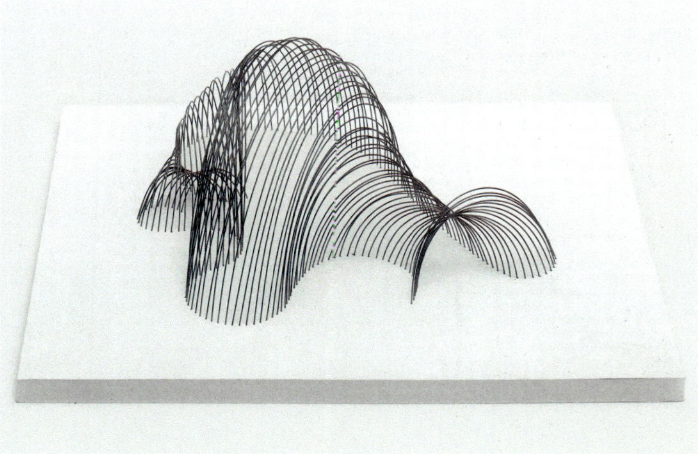

Here, a thirty-millimeter tube stabilizing the structure is attached to the base of precast concrete foundation planks and crisscrossed with each unique, eighty-millimeter tube-arch. Using scripting software a limited number of (twelve) makrolon shingles that overlap were deteremined, offering both weather protection and natural ventilation during the summer exhibition period. Sobek developed a Velcro point-fastener to attach the shingles to the structure, allowing for quick construction and easy adjustability. These shingles were then coupled with a photovoltaic dot-pattern that is parametrically positioned to enable optimal sun shading and solar gain. This process was demonstrated at the 2009 exhibition *Der Pavillon* at the Deutsches Architekturmuseum by building a one-to-one mockup of five arches with cladding of a pavilion segment.

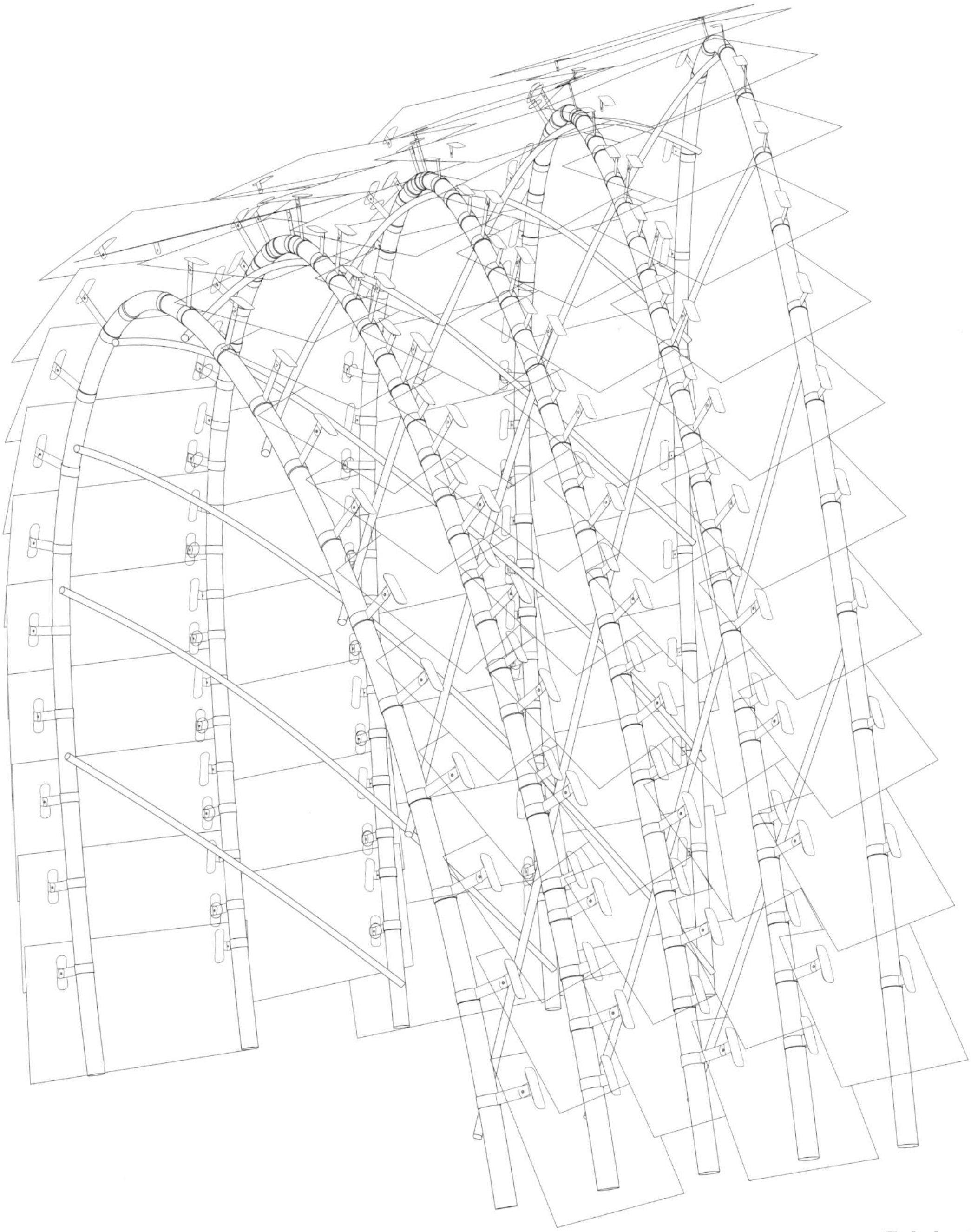

Thicket
Installation, 2014

An installation for the *How Soon Is Now* group exhibition at the Judin Gallery, Berlin, anticipates a near future of increasing material efficiencies, scarcities, and performances. This prototype is a tessellated thicket. In this one-to-one scaled installation, the boundaries between physical materiality and space-making are blurred where an ephemeral poché of bundled rods defines a series of spaces and passages between them. *Thicket* also begs a comparison between our artificially contrived one and those found in nature as in: to be lost in a thicket, a kind of labyrinth.

The bundles are self-stabilizing structures that define space, and as a prototypical system it is infinitely configurable and could define a space, a pavilion, with a roof and floor; the exhibition offers simply one such possibility. The logic of the prototype is an accumulating one where 2 by 2500 millimeter (super thin) rods are gathered and bundled to form an 8 by 8 centimeter cluster of four rods that add up 25 bundles (a component) that consists of 100 rods, and so on, generating a flexible matrix like a mosaic. The individual part, the 2-millimeter rod, is CNC bent, an existing technology to make wire coat hangers, in order to allow them to configure and combine with like (identical) rods. The rods are clipped together quickly and simply with plastic zip ties.

Space Frames
Design Study, 2008

In conjunction with an invited competition for a new art museum, the Kunsthaus Zürich (2008), a research project was embedded investigating the use of space frame construction for exterior, load-bearing façades for the museum.

As a starting point, modern historical precedents were considered, such a I. M. Pei's Kennedy Library in Boston, Louis Kahn's Yale University Art Gallery in New Haven, Anne Tyng's Philadelphia City Tower, and Buckminster Fuller's geodesic domes. Several material space-frame versions (e.g., steel, precast concrete, and timber) were tested and parametrically differentiated based on structural loading efficiencies. A second consideration was the application of digital fabrication techniques (e.g., laser welding and the cutting of steel) in order to achieve such a project.

BE _ Spa _ st 2
BE _ Spa _ st 6

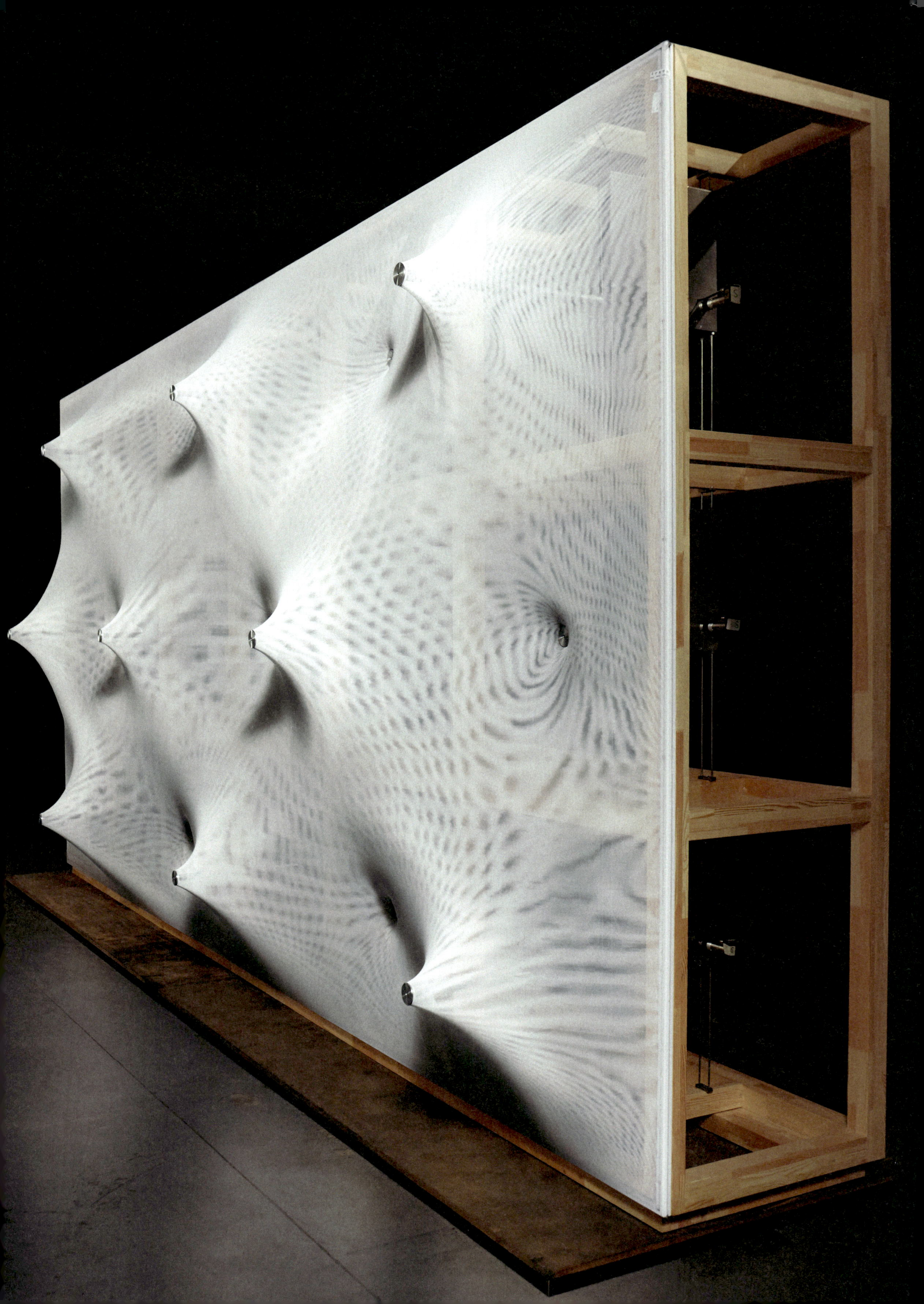

Kinetic Wall
Prototype, 2014
La Biennale di Venezia
14th International Architecture Exhibition—Fundamentals

The "Kinetic Wall," a prototype created for the fourteenth International Architecture Biennale "Fundamentals" in Venice, revisits the utopian dream of an architecture that can move, kinetically, as first introduced in the twentieth century as part of the larger modernist project. This addition to the biennale culminates a historical evolution of wall making (ranging from stone, brick, and wood to glass partitions, fire shutter, and so on) in the context of the "Wall Room" at the *Elements of Architecture* exhibition in the Main Pavilion in the Giardini.

Surface (wall) movement is activated by a series of motorized points, which extend telescopically and retract to convert an elastic (stretched), translucent synthetic fabric into a topographical section of peaks and valleys. This movement transforms the exhibition visitor's corridor between the Kinetic Wall and the adjacent (glass) partition wall into a differentiated, arch-like space. The limited and changing width of the passage generates an immediate, intimate, and corporeal experiential relationship with the viewer/visitor. A digitally controlled choreography enables endless surface patterns, which emerge slowly, then recede and change. This visual, surface effect is further enhanced by the two layers of gridded fabric that, when shifted over each other, produce a moiré effect, a second scale of movement that is translucent and ephemeral.

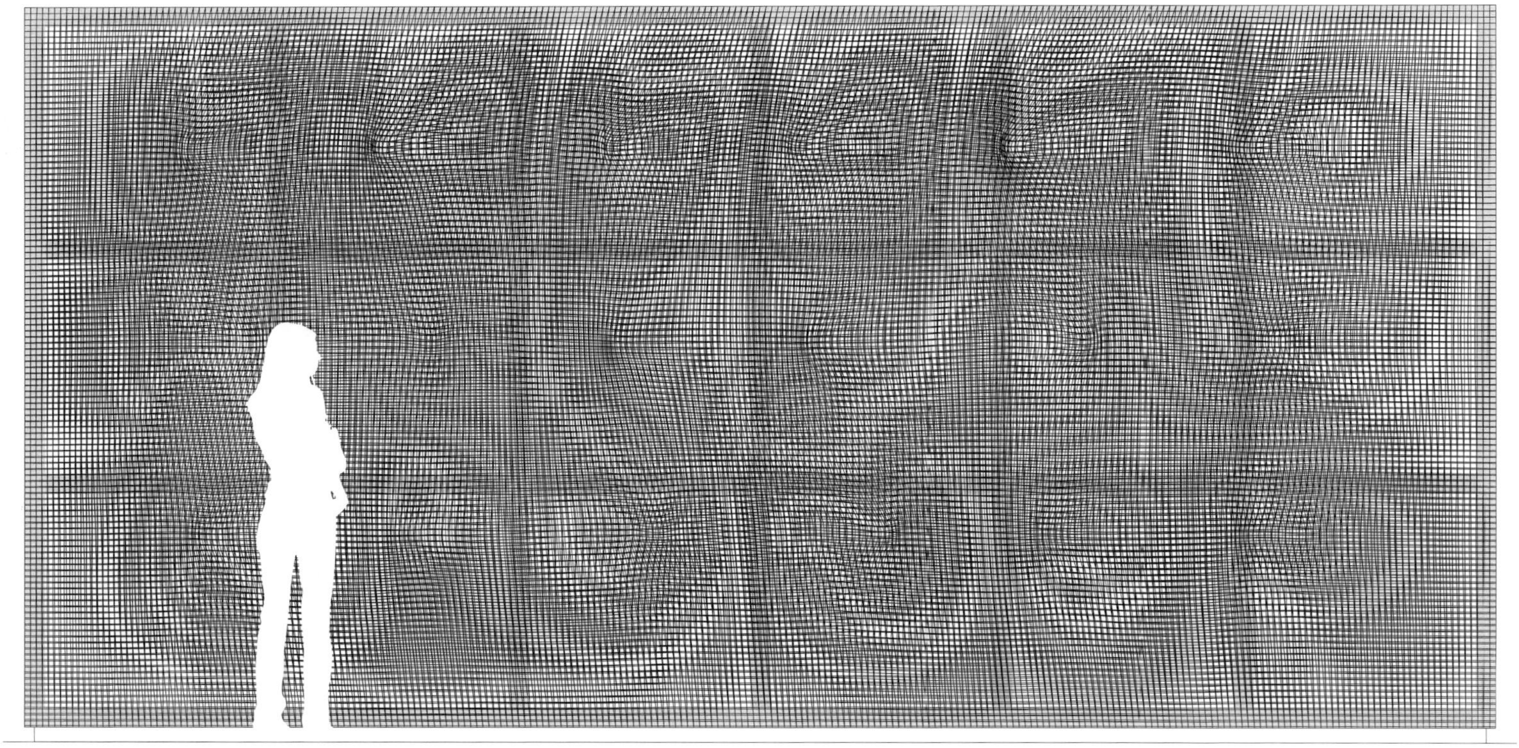

The fabric skin is supported by a space frame containing a mechanical plenum that produces a new kind of malleable poché—a material thickness. The lightweight, laminated timber scaffolding (space frame) is an anchoring framework for the fabric and houses the mechanisms that activate the surface. The wall has an apparent front and back but such that both sides of the skin are visible simultaneously. A Kinetic Wall offers an alternative future, an architecture that is materially and spatially dynamic, and comprised of both natural and synthetic, as well as recycled materials.

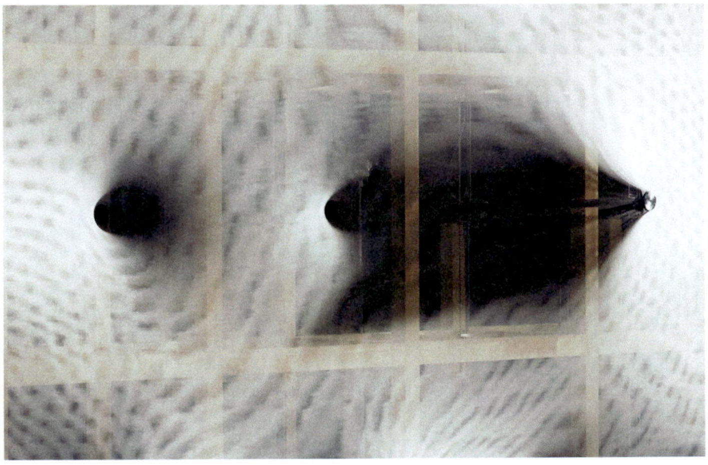

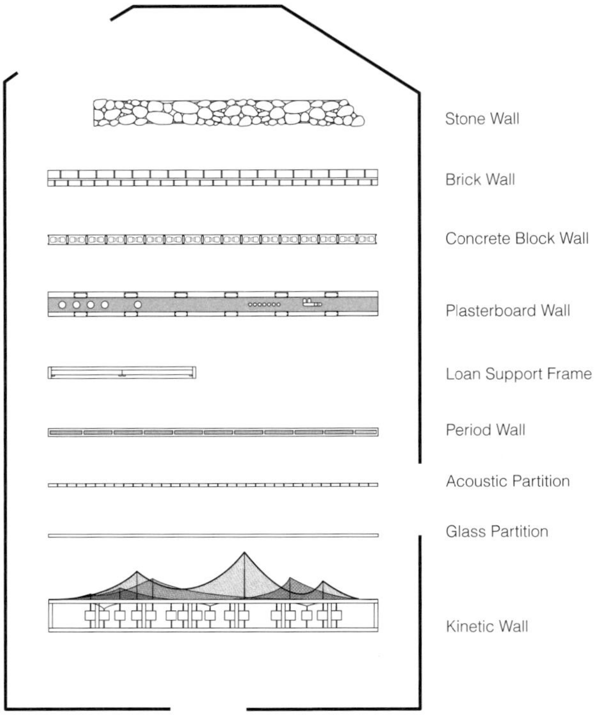
Stone Wall
Brick Wall
Concrete Block Wall
Plasterboard Wall
Loan Support Frame
Period Wall
Acoustic Partition
Glass Partition
Kinetic Wall

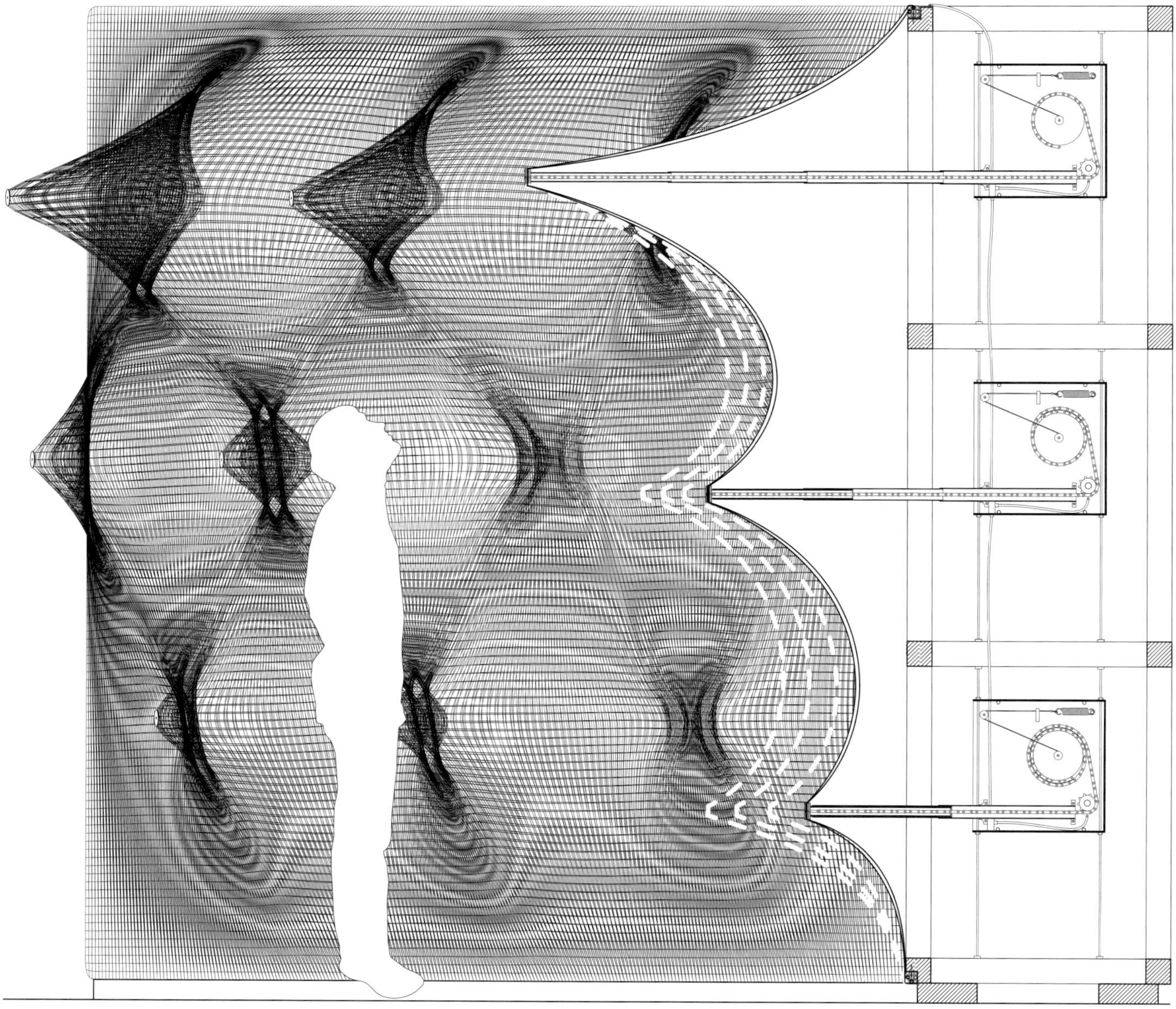

...walls provide str re and e space: the
wall, separating r om gro and the contin
partition wall, orga ng mov within the re
container. The form s seem as stable as
need for shelter; t tter as
of sociability... the ition is
With the advance chnolo
temporar or flimsy
and plumbing, ins
protection technol and se – even as ou
becomes increasi bare,
Seen in time-lapse history
plans would be th story of
as new segmentat of spac
forms of society. T ingle-c
hud shared ace, giv
con ons of s within
of dualism
e dem or open space
declara of war on the

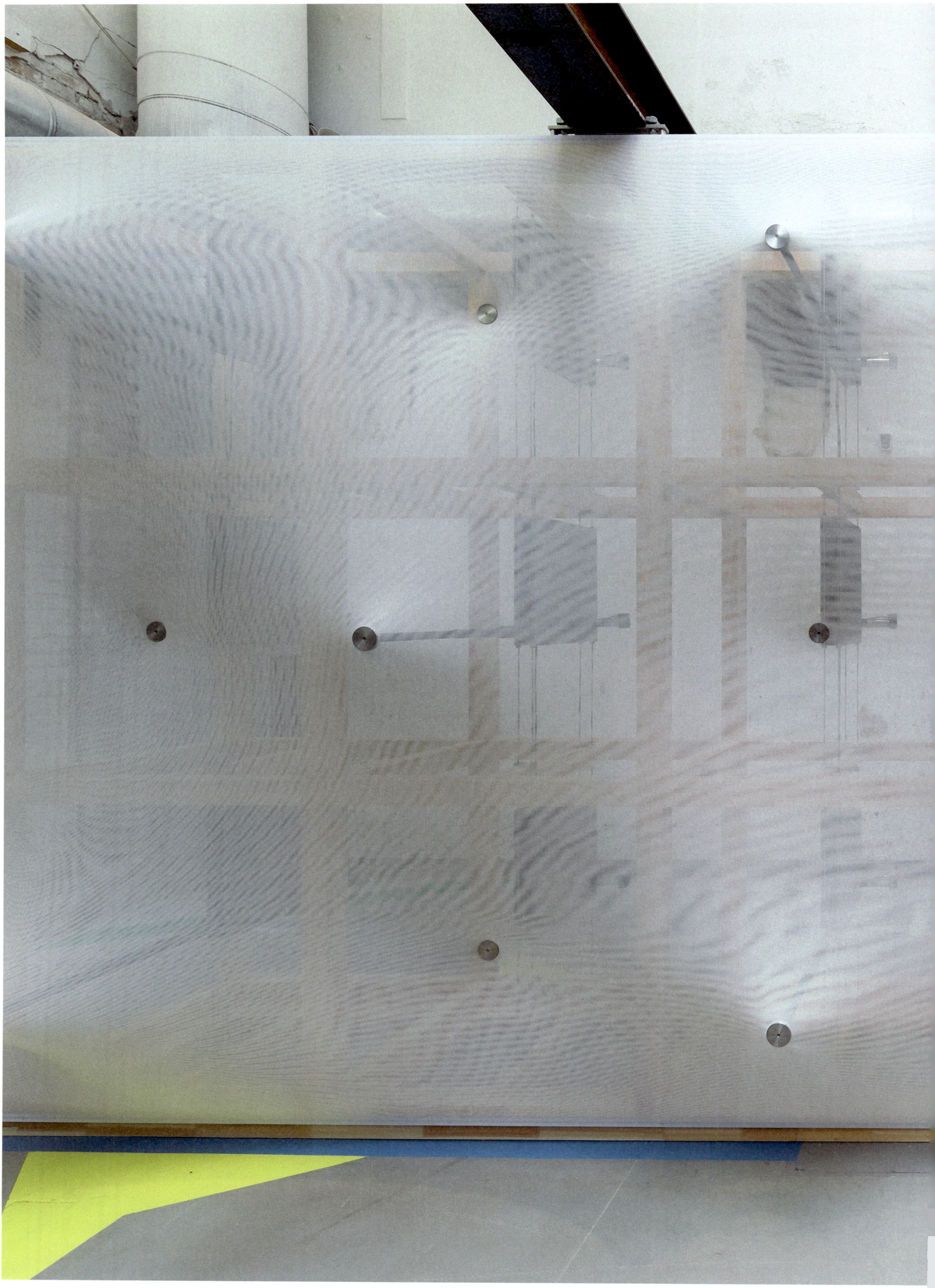

Marrakech, Seoul, and Berlin: Barkow Leibinger in Context
Carson Chan

Barkow Leibinger's observers know them for the way material logic has guided and informed their work. For Aaron Betsky, their buildings "push and pull" received elements of construction[1]; Anthony Vidler sees them as innovators of surfaces.[2] Barkow Leibinger's buildings are said to display a thought process rationalized through material; they communicate with materials and form narratives with their physical properties the way a writer does with words and sentences. Visually, "you cannot immediately identify a Barkow Leibinger building in terms of language," Regine Leibinger once explained. "You can probably see a certain *Haltung* (attitude) in the work."[3] Two examples help to illustrate this: two of their pavilions (2001, 2004) in Grüsch, Switzerland, between the foothills of Chur and Vaduz, are composed of shear walls used statically as tension members—in this way the construction, which spans a great area, allows for an open floor plan. By contrast, the roof of the gatehouse (2007) built for the technology firm TRUMPF in Ditzingen is entirely constructed out of sheet metal using the laser-cutting and welding technologies developed by the same company. Its roof doubly calls out its own construction as it both cantilevers twenty meters across the street and is systematically perforated to reduce its weight to meet the various static requirements across its length.

Deploying the building—its material and structural design—as a performative statement about architecture is a familiar feature of Barkow Leibinger's work, but for a more recent series of their projects, analysis through a sociohistorical lens rather than a material one yields a new, productive, and unexplored conceptual framework for considering their work. Many of the firm's past projects exist outside of urban centers, giving them a measure of freedom, if not a justified cool in the treatment of cultural specificities in their designs. Barkow Leibinger's aforementioned pavilions in Switzerland are located at the edge of Grüsch, a village of chalets in the alpine Prättigau Valley. The southern edge of TRUMPF's campus lies at the southern edge of Ditzingen—looking beyond, farm fields extend to the horizon. Whereas these projects—along with the fortress-like Biosphere in Potsdam (2001) and the TRUMPF staff cantina, with its iconic cellular roof, in Ditzingen (2008)—are often read according their formal attributes, structural innovation, and material experimentation, urban projects such as the temporary installation *Loom-Hyperbolic* in Marrakech (2012), the TRUTEC Building in Seoul (2006), and the Tour Total in Berlin (2012) draw out the deep, yet oft-overlooked, social resonances in the office's work. Key to this reading is a close analysis of the public interface these urban projects offer, the ways in which they address a site in both social and physical terms, and, in the case of Tour Total, a brief urban history of Berlin, where Frank Barkow and Regine Leibinger started their office in 1993. Just as Yve-Alain Bois sees Richard Serra's large-scale works as sculptural experiences created by the dialectic of walking and looking, these projects similarly produce meaning through one's physical encounter with them, or they at least demand one's presence before revealing their full engagement with their surroundings.[4]

The *Loom-Hyperbolic,* Barkow Leibinger's contribution to the fourth Marrakech Biennial in 2012,[5] was as much about the spatial performance of material as it was about embodying and accentuating local cultural contexts. Here, more than half a century after the advent of Moroccan independence from France in 1955, the visual arts, their production, their presentation, and access to them, are a matter still fraught with postcolonial tensions. Maurice Tranchant de Lunel and Prosper Ricard, the first two directors of the Protectorate Fine Arts Administration in occupied Morocco, established schools to codify techniques, as well as motifs, for skills such as carpet weaving, pottery, silk dying, and illumination.[6] Institutionalizing traditional art forms, whose production was often mechanized in the process, allowed the French to maintain their Western projection of Moroccan authenticity while fulfilling quotas of goods for the French market. In this way, Moroccans were restricted from fully engaging their own heritage. In Morocco, the relationship between the arts and their technical production was, and still is, a matter that intermeshes political agendas with cultural patrimony.

Inspired by Moroccan weaving techniques during a research trip to Marrakech in the fall of 2011, *Loom-Hyperbolic* combined Barkow Leibinger's research on moiré patterns and production techniques into an architectural experience. The firm documented Moroccan designs and architectural forms in Marrakech and processed them through algorithmic software, producing drawings that were then interpreted by Marrakshi craftsmen. Installed directly next to the Koutoubia mosque in the medina, on around 400 square meters of a former mosque's exposed foundation, *Loom-Hyperbolic,* when viewed from afar, looked like an orderly array of white tents, pitched next to the minaret. As one came closer, however, the tents dissolved into individual strands of white yarn. Closely strung over rows of wooden poles formed into peaks and valleys, the yarn surfaces—like the warp threads of an outsized loom—aligned and overlaped, creating varying opacities and interference patterns as visitors walked around and through the installation. Under the peaks, one had the sense of being in a transparent tent. From above, one gained an overview of the installation's component structures: its rhythms lined up with that of the mosque's foundation. In other words, the work's appearance shifted depending on where the viewer stood. To apprehend its logic was to physically move in and around the work.

The Koutoubia mosque is one of Marrakech's most recognizable landmarks; surrounded by hawkers and tour buses, it stands like a rock in a stream of people and animals moving in and out of nearby souks. The iconic stature of the Koutoubia's seventy-seven-meter-tall minaret is protected by city ordinances that prevent high-rises from being built in its vicinity. In situating their installation directly adjacent to this monument, Barkow Leibinger prompted locals and tourists alike to actively consider public space as a place for not only commerce and entertainment but also for artistic contemplation and discourse. Moving around *Loom-Hyperbolic*—dodging crowds and traffic—was to become alive to the systems of the city surrounding it. Morocco does not have contemporary art museums, and the galleries exhibiting contemporary art in Casablanca, Rabat, and Marrakech remain just as much reserved for the foreign and Moroccan elite now as they were during French rule. To exhibit art in a public space in Marrakech is an act of creative transparency and intellectual generosity, but exhibiting contemporary work by foreigners, freely and in the town's center, is to challenge the social status quo, a stance that lays bare the politics of how, by whom, and for whom access to culture is offered.[7]

It is not very often that architecture participates so directly and visibly in the politics of cultural history as was the case with *Loom-Hyperbolic*. Barkow Leibinger's office tower in Seoul is famous for its crystalline, glass façade, and, as one of the first buildings to be completed on the *tabula rasa* of a new urban district, it seems at first to confirm the neoliberalist ideals that drive so much of today's urban expansion projects, particularly in Asia. Indeed, the TRUTEC Building is a high-rise construction with a shiny glass curtain wall—a descendent of the glass towers that emerged from the open markets of Wall Street in the 1960s. While recognizing the origin of the glass office tower type is certainly important, examining the TRUTEC Building geopolitically reveals it to be an object that problematizes facile assumptions and offers a shrewd critique of the context from which it sprang.

Ilhyun Kim's essay about the TRUTEC Building site reminds us that Seoul has been shaped by two major forces of the twentieth century—urbanization and war.[8] In Korea, urbanization began after the country opened its ports to the world in the 1870s, and by the mid-twentieth century, after the Japanese occupation and the Korean War, South Korea was all-embracing of urban and infrastructural growth. The capital city soared upward and outward, and its population increased more than sixfold in less than fifty years, causing massive infrastructural problems.[9] Urbanization also produces waste, and by the late 1970s, just south of where the TRUTEC Building stands, waste was being dumped on to Nanjido, an island on an estuary of the Han River, at such a rate that trash piled up more than one hundred meters high. This period of intense growth was weighed down by North Korea's watchful presence just a few hours' drive from Seoul. Although the two Koreas have in fact been separated by a four-kilometer-wide Demilitarized Zone (DMZ) since the 1953 armistice, this border nevertheless remains one of the most armed, and volatile, in the world. A stopgap to prevent violent conflict, the DMZ is a geopolitical feature that has maintained a sixty-year-long ceasefire. In Seoul its presence is perceived like a pressure cooker left on; it is a lingering vexation caused by unfinished business whose resolution is dangerously overdue.

The "Digital Media City," or DMC for short, on the other hand, is a 570,000-square-meter swath of reclaimed land in the northwestern reaches of the city. Since 2002 the city has been actively transforming this area, once part of the Nanjido landfill, into a mixed-use district with offices, residential towers, retail, and various cultural amenities, including a new film museum. As its name itself suggests, the DMC is Seoul's wager on an expanded IT industry. Also built on the landfill is the World Cup Park, the largest green space in the city; it was in this techno-utopian context that Barkow Leibinger was tasked with building an office tower. Besides its history as reclaimed land and status as a new development, the DMC had little context to offer, as few others had broken ground in 2004 when Barkow Leibinger began the project.

The TRUTEC Building is a fifty-four-meter-tall office tower that draws attention to itself by visually fragmenting its surroundings. In the DMC, glass high-rises are the status quo; on a clear day the entire area appears washed in a blue haze of sky reflected on and off the towers. The TRUTEC Building is wrapped in a silvery, reflective-glass curtain wall, and, strikingly, half of its surface is articulated in origami-like folds, breaking up the surrounding area on its façade into a Picasso of its former self. As with Cubist paintings, to look at the building is to see the sky, the ground, the distance, and shards of oneself—above, below, inside, outside, in front and behind, all at once; like *Loom-Hyperbolic,* the building's appearance differs depending on where one stands. As one moves around it, the sun glares off its many surfaces like paparazzi flash bulbs. The TRUTEC Building's façade is an optical tool for delaying spatial comprehension, demanding attention from and bringing focus to our usually distracted gaze. The folded glass panels follow a loose pattern that breaks now and again, giving the office building a sense of agency, subjectivity, and randomness uncommon to its typology. So much is simultaneously presented that making sense of the reflected views becomes impossible; to facet the mirror façade like a jewel is to accept the deception of accurate representation, and the imperfections of reality. As if intuiting the geopolitical history latent in the DMC, Frank Barkow explained that "a mirror façade is always inherently distorted: it's never fully flat."[10] To elaborate on this condition within the TRUTEC Building's design suggests a conscious distancing from corporate, postwar, late-modernist ideology.

To be completed by 2015, the DMC, as its name suggests, is meant to be an urban response to the intangible yet pervasive presence of digital media in the last two decades. According to its website, the development is meant to contribute to the parallel growth of interest in Korean culture at large, or the so-called Korean Wave.[11] Two blocks west of the TRUTEC tower is the triangular-shaped Millennium Park, and in 2010 a large piece of public art called *Millennium Cell,* jointly created by the artists Joem Soo Na, Young Ho Yoo, and Bei Kyoung Lee, was unveiled. Like the TRUTEC tower's façade, this sculpture is highly reflective. Composed of polished steel balls stacked twenty-three meters high, *Millennium Cell* captures the world on the surface of its mirrored spheres in "the everlasting essence of media and technology."[12] At the base of the sculpture is a three-meter-wide circular LED screen set in a well-like base. The screen perpetually shows the sky above the city of Montevideo, Uruguay, which is exactly on the opposite side of the globe from Seoul. In the face of such unabashed displays of grandeur and self-affirming claims to technological reach, the TRUTEC Building stands as an open question, a subtle yet potent caveat—its façade throws back the ordered world anew, transformed.

It is too soon to tell if Seoul will be successful in branding its new district as the seat of Korea's technological future. Casting buildings in particular roles, as with casting performers, does not guarantee those roles will be acted out. Comparably, post-reunification Berlin has likewise taken on many roles: The West's long-lost cousin (Mitte), the ex-commie (Friedrichshain), the free-spirited pioneer (Prenzlauer Berg), the nostalgic revisionist (Treptow), the poor but sexy bohemian (Kreuzberg), and so on. During the Cold War, Berlin was the world's main stage for East-West ideological one-upmanship. When, in 1952, East Berlin began construction of their Soviet-style Neoclassical housing estates on Stalinallee (now Karl-Marx-Allee), the West responded in 1957 with the Hansaviertel housing towers authored by their own modernist greats. When the Hamburg media giant Axel Springer had a seventy-eight-meter-tall tower built for its Berlin headquarters directly next to the Berlin Wall in 1966, the East retorted with a series of housing towers two years later (the tallest also measuring seventy-eight meters high). Built close to the Axel Springer building on the other side of the wall, these towers, the so-called *Springer-Decke* or "Springer cover," blocked views of this symbol of Western values and free press—the sides facing West Berlin were designed without windows or balconies.[13] The Park Inn Hotel building was completed in 1970 at Alexanderplatz, the center of East Berlin, and at 125 meters it remains one of the tallest buildings in the reunified city.[14] Compared to Frankfurt, or other European capitals like London or Paris, Berlin's tall buildings are few, relatively short, and found peppered, not grouped, throughout the city. When Barkow Leibinger's Tour Total was completed in 2012, directly across from Berlin's main train station and at a height of sixty-nine meters, it added another chapter to an ongoing, heated, urban-scale dialogue.

Just north of Huboldthafen, Berlin's former industrial river port, and the Hauptbahnhof, the city's main rail hub since its opening in 2006, a stretch of land about three-quarters the size of the DMC is being developed into a generic combo of residential, office, and retail usage called Europacity. At the time Tour Total was completed it was the only structure realized in Europacity. Before other buildings are erected, it will be the first and only large structure visitors and residents see when they exit through the station's main access on Invalidenstrasse, or emerge from the Tiergarten Tunnel by car. Standing seventeen stories tall, Tour Total is a precast, white concrete rectangular volume atop a colonnaded base, its height amplified by a grid of vertical windows that cover its entire surface. At first glance, Tour Total—a boxy volume punctured regularly by undifferentiated windows—looks like many other buildings typical to post-reunification Berlin. The fourteen-story Motel One, located 500 meters away, across from the train station, and completed in 2011, features a similarly oblong vertical grid of windows on white concrete—in fact, just like all the other Motel One buildings by Nalbach Architekten across Germany. Its narrow, vertical windows produce a vague air of the past, alluding to a time before the industrial plate glass production of the 1950s enabled the realization of large glass surfaces. In homage to the "Golden Twenties," the towers of Hilmer & Sattler und Albrecht's Beisheim Center complex (2003), along with Hans Kollhoff's brick-faced tower (1999) on Berlin's Potsdamer Platz, all made use of the same vertically organized windows to visually harken back to the early high-rises of Chicago and New York, perhaps dissipating the poisonous weight of Germany's recent history into the vast oceans of a collective imagination of a distant past.[15]

A second look at Tour Total reveals its uncanny distinction. All the cast-concrete vertical elements of the façade are chamfered on the bias and hung in a diagonal pattern so as to create subtle plays of color and contour. Like both the *Loom-Hyperbolic* and the TRUTEC Building, Tour Total's physical attributes appear to shift as one moves around it. Seen frontally, from afar, and on an overcast day, the building looks flat; only its subtly zigzagging silhouette distinguishes it from the mock façades printed on canvas, commonly hung on scaffolds in Berlin's empty lots to give the impression of a finished building. On a sunny day, and particularly when seen at an oblique angle, the building's vertical lines appear skewed in different directions. A diagonal pattern of dark, wave-like bands washes over its lateral surfaces; the dark rectangles of the windows seem to have no right angles; the white concrete verticals separating them appear to widen and then shrink together like the verticals of a Rudolf Steiner typeface. At night, when the interior lights are on, Tour Total, with its obstinately regular window grid, looks like any other office tower. But when its exterior lights were also turned on at the building's opening reception, the structure shattered into long, diamond-shaped spears of black and white. On approach, the angled vertical edges become more pronounced. The double-height columns of the ground floor colonnade seem to bulge and wobble as one moves around them. From here, Tour Total resembles Motel One the way one's reflection might appear in a fun-house mirror—the deformed reflection provokes us to verify what is and what is not.

If the Motel One building (and other nearby budget hotels, such as the InterCityHotel and the Meininger Hotel, that have also caught on to the vertical window trend) symbolizes the knee-jerk economic imperatives that have triggered developments like Europacity, then Tour Total stands conspicuously as its destabilizing critique. And if Tour Total had in fact been conceived as a critical stance toward Berlin's urbanism, it could not be better positioned for the task. Europacity is located one block west of the former Berlin Wall's death-strip (*Todesstreifen*)—the fortified area between the West and East German border walls, not unlike the DMZ. By virtue of its location next to where the Berlin Wall once stood—indeed the border between the former Western and Eastern world ideologies—it cannot but continue the architectural dialogue started by the construction of Stalinallee in 1952.

From city maps dating back to the mid-eighteenth century we know that this area had never been heavily developed, but south of Invalidenstrasse, at the present-day location of Humboldthafen, was to be Adolf Hitler's Grosse Halle (Great Hall): the "Eighth Wonder of the World," and the pinnacle of his colossal North-South Axis. In 1937, four years after the National Socialist party took over the Weimar Republic, Hitler and his chief architect, Albert Speer, forged their plans to transform Berlin into the new *Welthaupstadt* (world capital) Germania. Though the city was to be "reprovincialized," monumental buildings, public spaces, and grand axes were designed to display the immensity of the Third Reich's power to the world and to itself. The functions of the new metropolis were to be manifested as monumental granite palaces, strung along a five-kilometer avenue. Starting just west of the Tempelhof airport, this axis extends northward, past Hitler's chancellery, through a vast square (about half a kilometer in both length and width), before reaching the Grosse Halle, a gargantuan congress hall for an audience of 180,000 people.[16] The Grosse Halle was inspired by the Pantheon in Rome. It was to have a height of 290 meters and an even greater width, and its forty-six-meter-wide oculus alone would have been bigger than the Pantheon's dome. Germania resembled Berlin in neither scale nor scope: just the Grosse

Halle's seventy-four-meter-high base itself would have been five meters taller than Tour Total, the entire Europacity site was to be a giant rectangular reflection pool.

Tour Total's location on the corner of Heidestrasse and Minna-Cauer-Strasse is only meters from the North-South Axis if it had been extended northward. Though the building's windows are slender, the offices on the upper levels offer unrestricted panoramic views of Berlin. At the pinnacle of the planned triumphal axis of a previous era, and adjacent to the former interior borders of a more recent one, the view from Tour Total is shaped by the histories that have indelibly marked the city's past. Looking south from here one sees Berlin today—the bends of the Spree, the streams of humans around the Hauptbahnhof (with Motel One across the street), the dense green of the Tiergarten, the glassy gleam of Potsdamer Platz—and, imagining for a moment the Third Reich's vision realized, what the city did not build becomes a positive reminder, a measure, of what it could be.

In February 2009 Barkow Leibinger opened an exhibition at the Architectural Association in London called *An Atlas of Fabrication*. The school's website explains how 3D-laser-cut aluminum tubes, quilted layers of sheet metal, and glass pieces of varying reflectivity from the Berlin office were exhibited to demonstrate how "architectural ideas and materials are inextricably intertwined."[17] Adding a geopolitical dimension to Barkow Leibinger's material atlas, as in these instances of narrating the various contextual frames informing the *Loom-Hyperbolic,* the TRUTEC Building, and the Tour Total, allows us to see not only how materials intertwine with architectural ideas but also how architectural ideas, materially manifested as buildings, are intimately involved in the inscribing of history.

1 Aaron Betsky, "From Field to Form, With an Attitude," in *Barkow Leibinger Architects* (Seoul, 2007), p. 16.
2 Anthony Vidler, "New Skins for a New Age: Class Culture in the Work of Barkow Leibinger," in *Barkow Leibinger: Reflect*, ed. Andres Lepik (Ostfildern, 2007), p. 26.
3 Barkow Leibinger, "Barkow Leibinger in Conversation with Barry Bergdoll and Andres Lepik," in Lepik 2007 (see note 2), p. 67.
4 Yve-Alain Bois, "A Picturesque Stroll Around 'Clara-Clara'," *October* 29 (Summer 1984), pp. 32–62.
5 The fourth Marrakech Biennale was curated by Nadim Samman and me.
6 Katarzyna Pieprzak, *Imagined Museums: Art and Modernity in Postcolonial Morocco* (Minneapolis, 2010), pp. 5–6.

7 Most notably, art students from the art school in Casablanca opened a public painting exhibition in the Jemaa el-Fnaa in 1969.

8 Ilhyun Kim, in Lepik 2007 (see note 2), p. 33.

9 In 1955 Seoul's population was 1.6 million; it grew to 10.3 million by 1999 and remains around this level today. Source: Seoul Metropolitan Government, *Seoul Statistical Yearbook* 2000 (Seoul, 2000).

10 Lepik 2007 (see note 2), p. 72.

11 Introduction to DMC: digital media city (website), http://dmc.seoul.go.kr/eng/en_about/en_project/en_introduction/en_introduction.do (accessed October 31, 2013).

12 "Millennium Cell," MillenniumEye (website), http://millenniumeye.co.kr/en/cell.html (accessed October 31, 2013).

13 Jörg Niendorf, "Begehrte Platte," *Frankfurter Allgemeine Sonntagszeitung*, July 7, 2013.

14 The Treptowers were built in 1998 and have the same height.

15 Claire Colomb, *Staging the New Berlin: Place Marketing and the Politics of Urban Reinvention Post-1989* (London, 2012), pp. 159–65.

16 Léon Krier, *Albert Speer: Architecture, 1932–1942* (New York, 2013), pp. 75–83.

17 "An Atlas of Fabrication," Architectural Association School of Architecture, February 28, 2009 (website), http://www.aaschool.ac.uk/PUBLIC/WHATSON/exhibitions.php?item=23 (accessed December 11, 2013).

Building envelopes constitute compelling sites for contemporary architecture. A large degree of freedom continues to emerge where skins are relatively liberated from the demands of useable floor areas, core efficiencies, and, occasionally, structure. Program typologies that underscore this autonomy, such as office or industrial buildings that favor flexibility, light and air efficiencies, and interior changeability, demand a neutrality that further emphasizes the relative independence between the skin and the interior of a building. In embodying (and relaying) formal and performative characteristics a façade mediates between exterior and interior, public and private, and determines energy performance. Envelopes control natural light, ventilation, and acoustics. This also means that façades are the first threshold for controlling the use and expenditure of energy in a sustainable manner. As such, envelopes are sites for intensive technical and aesthetic architectural responsibility. A façade is normatively (along with scale and massing) that component of a building that best assimilates it into its context or through which it resists adapting to its surroundings.

The works presented here exhibit a range of façades, from curtain wall solutions to load-bearing and hybrid versions. These differences are expressed by and made legible in the buildings where structure coexists with a façade solution or exists independently from it. Yet, despite such differences, every façade is a threshold that possesses a spatial component: it is a territory to be occupied bodily, as well as one whose depth controls light and atmosphere. It has a material presence, as in the concrete folds of the Tour Total or in the kaleidoscopic TRUTEC Building. In comparison to the mid-century curtain wall constructed of steel and glass and with a minimal depth that emphasized flatness, the surfaces presented here are spatial. That is to say, they are developed with depth as a strategy to control the environment but also as something that is spatially and sculpturally thickened. They are conceived as fully three-dimensional surfaces that are spatial, performative, iconographic, and physical.

Such envelopes manifest an inherent reversibility: they affect a building's image as an urban object, and they are experienced from the interior as a kind of lens. In the examples here the façade is part of a tectonic system that resonates throughout the entire building.

Tour Total
Berlin, Germany, 2012

The Europacity is a master plan for a new urban district spanning forty hectares directly to the north of the main train station (Hauptbahnhof) in Berlin for housing, hotels, and office use. The first building in this plan, for the French energy company Total, was completed in fall 2012. The Tour Total is a solitary high-rise giving the company a clear identity and location for their headquarters in Germany and 500 employees.

Separated from the typical historical block height of twenty-two meters the new tower is shaped volumetrically to respond to the orthogonal grid of the Heidestrasse and the radial one of the Minna-Cauer-Strasse by gently bending and thus creating a concave and convex façade. A single core punctuates the floor plan with a day-lit elevator lobby and well-lit perimeter offices. A two-story arcade at the building's base responds to programs (lobby and bistro). A second-phase office building, now underway, will complement and complete a pedestrian promenade along the west arcade.

TOTAL
Alles im Lot.
Zeit.
Budget.
Qualität.

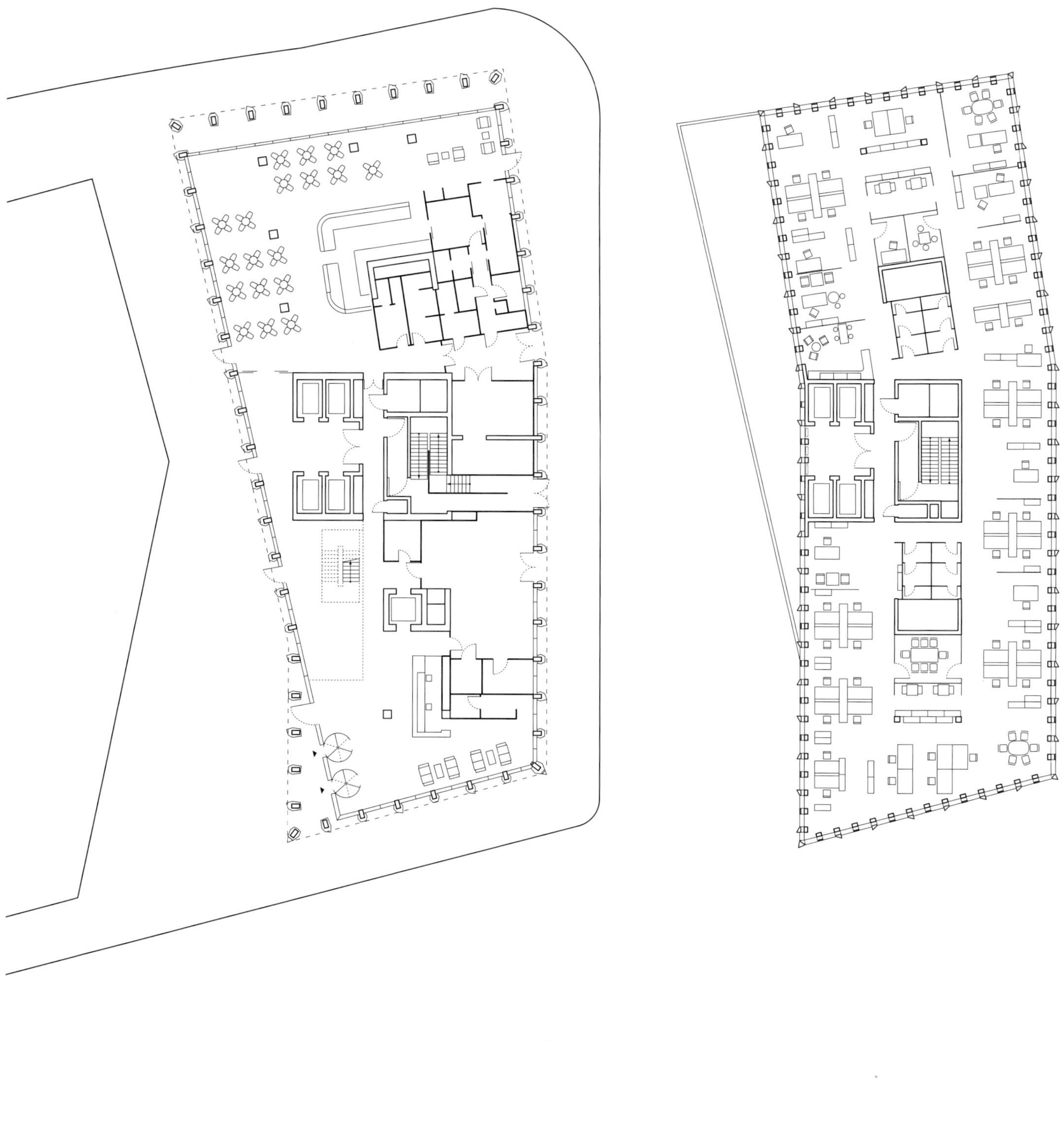

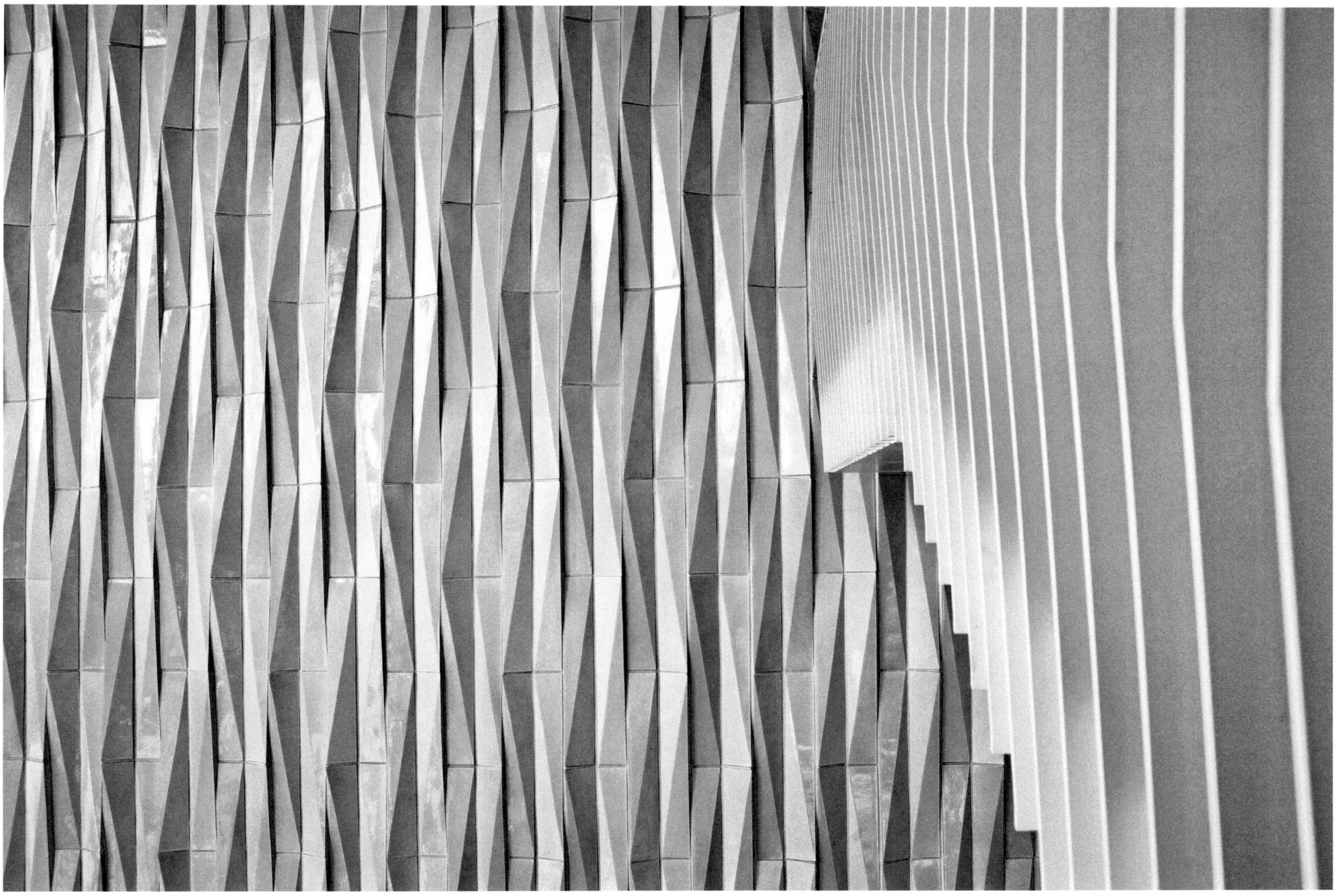

The load-bearing façade, a 135-centimeter-thick gridded frame, responds to the typology of historical Berlin. Constructed of precast concrete, the façade is the primary site for energy control, with its opaque surfaces (the frame) outfitted with insulated surfaces 60/40, exterior sunscreens, triple glazing, and operable floor-to-ceiling windows. The façade grid uses the surface depth and sculptural quality to emphasize the verticality of the building. A geometric pattern—double-story T-elements with a K-shaped fold—which repeats itself diagonally, wraps around the corners of the building like a thick, curtain-like cladding.

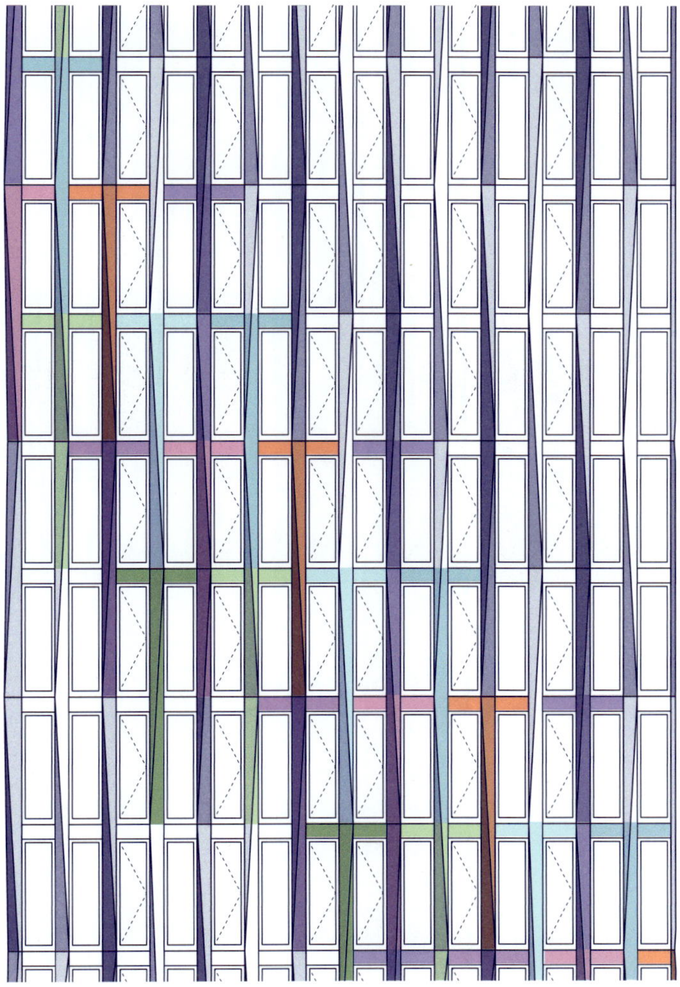

TOTAL
EXEDRA

MS
호텔 코리아

TRUTEC Building
Seoul, Korea, 2006

Located in the Digital Media City, an anonymous office tech park, in one of the last remaining open sites in the north of Seoul, this fifty-five-meter-tall building is a steel-framed structure comprised of eleven stories of office and showroom spaces. Since the site offered no discernable context to respond to (other than building code and zoning) the façade became a primary tool for developing the building. A twentieth-century history of mirrored curtain wall façades was considered: here the question was posed whether the imperfections observed in a flat, reflective curtain wall could be exploited to produce a kaleidoscopic visual effect.

GS 건설

This approach became a tool for assimilating the architectural object of the building into an unpredictable and emerging context, while also allowing the façade to be effected by change, such as the shift from day to night, moving traffic and pedestrians, or weather. Here, an enormous amount of visual complexity could be achieved within a shallow, twenty-centimeter depth by alternating a two-dimensional window bay type and a three-dimensional bay, which could produce another when flipped 180 degrees.

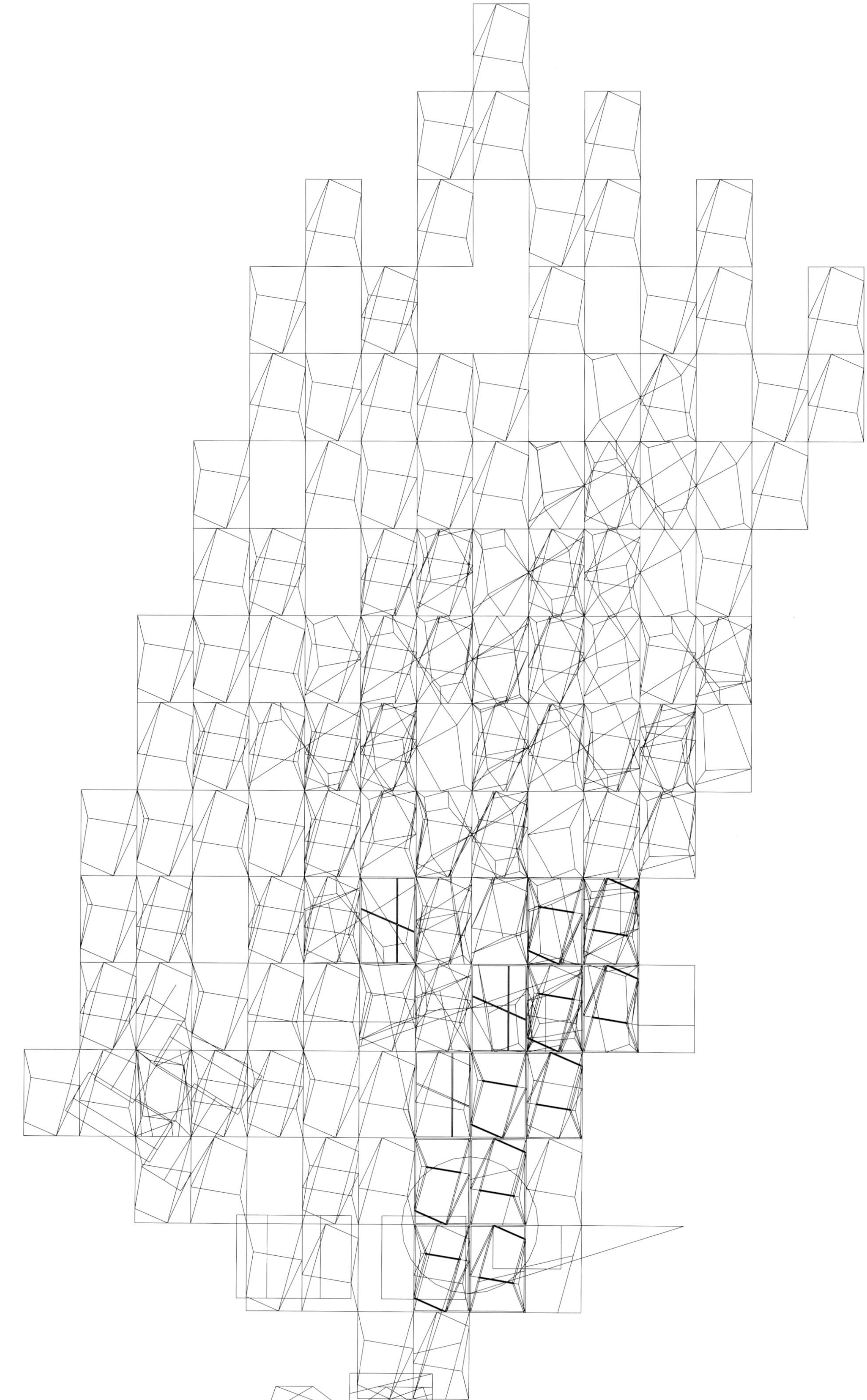

Reciprocally, from the interior, window bands act as panoramic lattices combining transparent and translucent glass, framing multiple views and orientations. This way the building acts as a phenomenal filter, effecting both how one sees from it and how it is seen as an object in the cityscape. It offers a visual and liminal space between the public exterior and private interior.

The other significant decision was to offset the building core to the eastern, lightless corner of the building. On the exterior the core is clad in a dark zinc shingle. This location of the core allows for large, deep swaths of rentable spaces within an almost column-free interior.

Programmatically the ground floor is given to a double-height, column-free showroom (for German high-tech machine tools) and a lobby infilled with a partial, first-floor mezzanine. The second and third levels offer additional showrooms, while the upper seven levels are given over to office space. The façade extends upward to a twelfth-floor roof garden designed as an open-air courtyard between the core and the skin.

A large, triangular indentation, exaggerating the folding system, marks the formal entrance to the building. This offset entrance also sets up a strong connection to the park located diagonally across from the building.

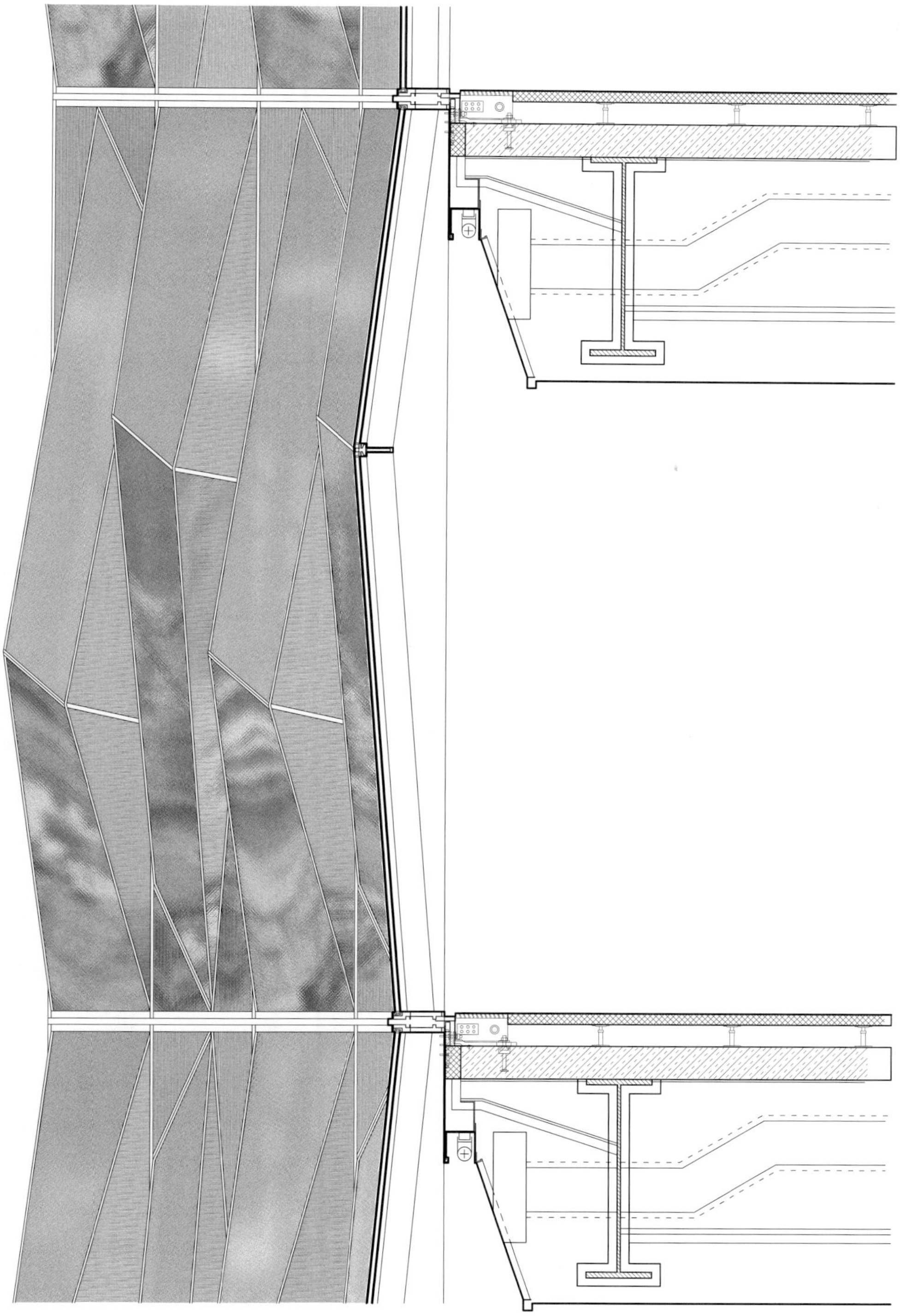

TRUMPF

Production and Office Facility
Baar, Switzerland, 2001

The addition to an existing high-tech laser manufacturing company in Baar, in the Swiss Canton of Zug, contains a new production and office facility. It is organized as three volumes telescoping like a set of drawers out of the sloping site. The largest volume, a two-story production hall, is situated at the highest elevation, retaining itself against the mountain slope. The second volume containing the lobby, core, and office spaces slips out of the larger production volume. The third and smallest building volume consists of an exterior stair-tower in the north elevation. The two principle building volumes are differentiated, not only in their scale and function but also by the materiality and articulation of their folded exterior façades.

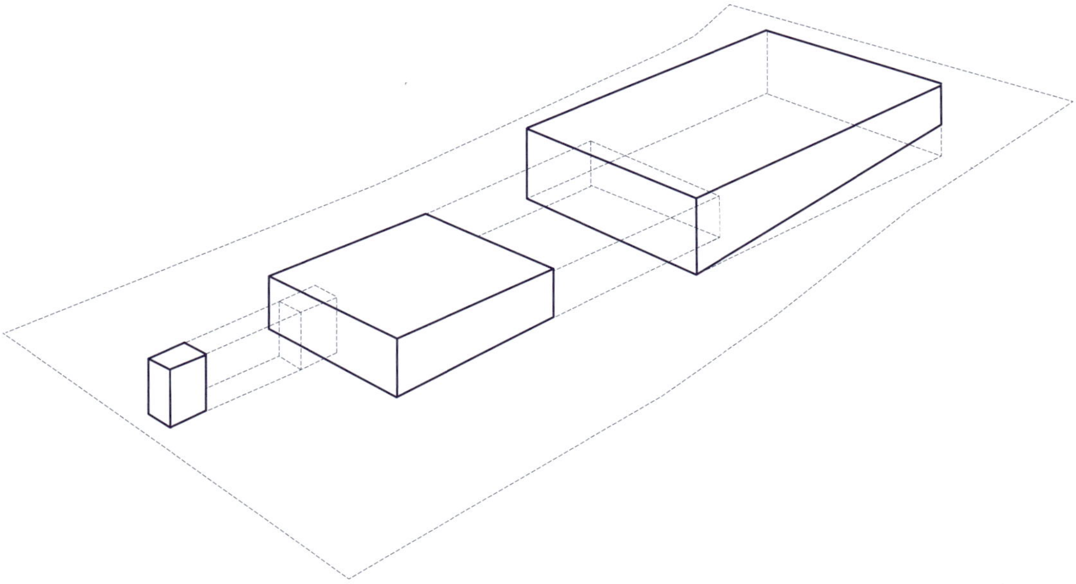

The folding exterior skin gives the façade a certain depth and spatiality while forming a circulation zone between the exterior curtain wall and the outermost column grid. The exterior skin of the production hall is formed by a steel frame clad with copper, standing seam sheeting, glass, or aluminum panels on pivoting hinges.

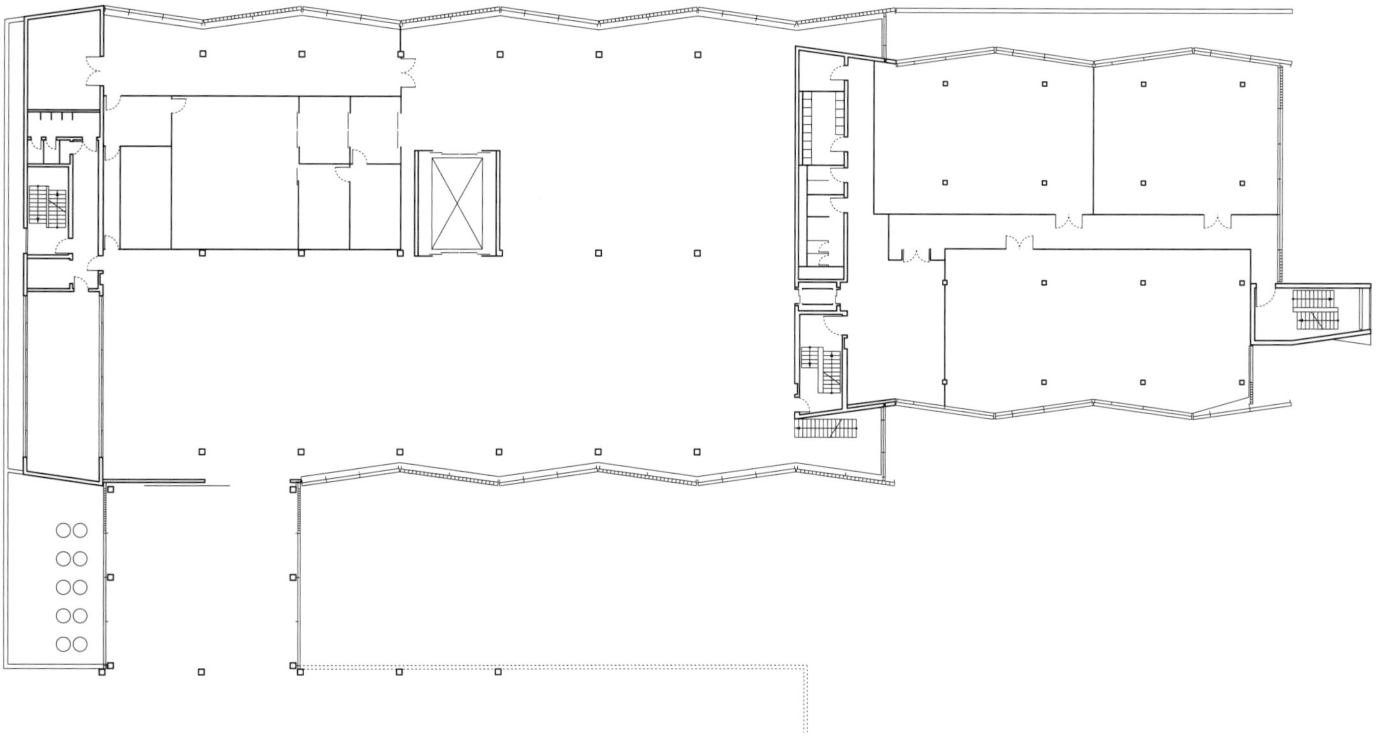

The framing system in the office volume is clad with aluminum panels and transparent or translucent glass. The translucent surfaces consist of a double-glazing system, which sandwiches an aluminum honeycomb in order to reflect daylight deep into the office spaces. Pneumatically inflated, stainless steel sheet metal forms an ornamental radiant heating system on the lobby walls.

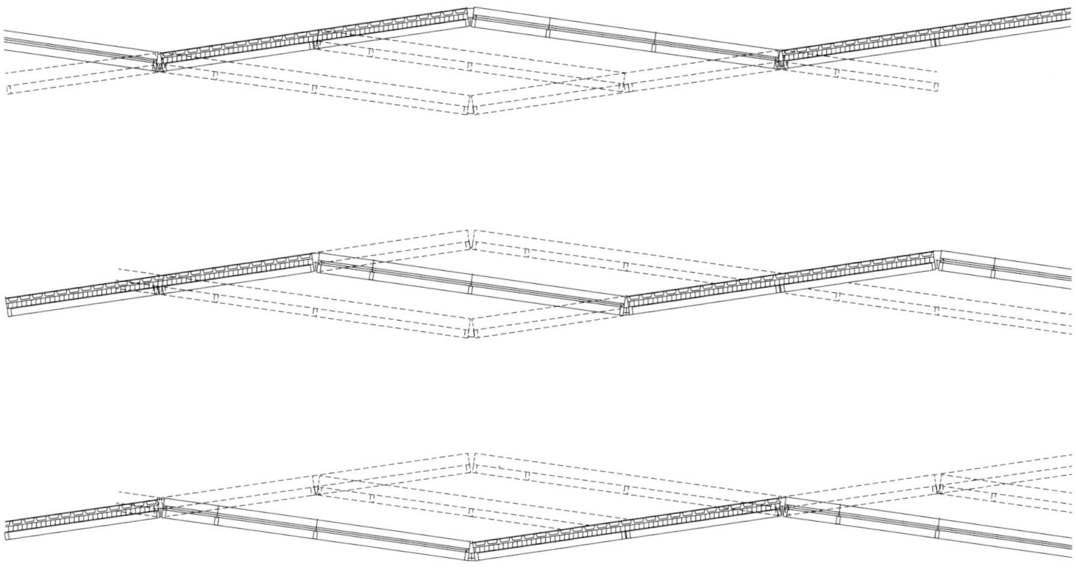

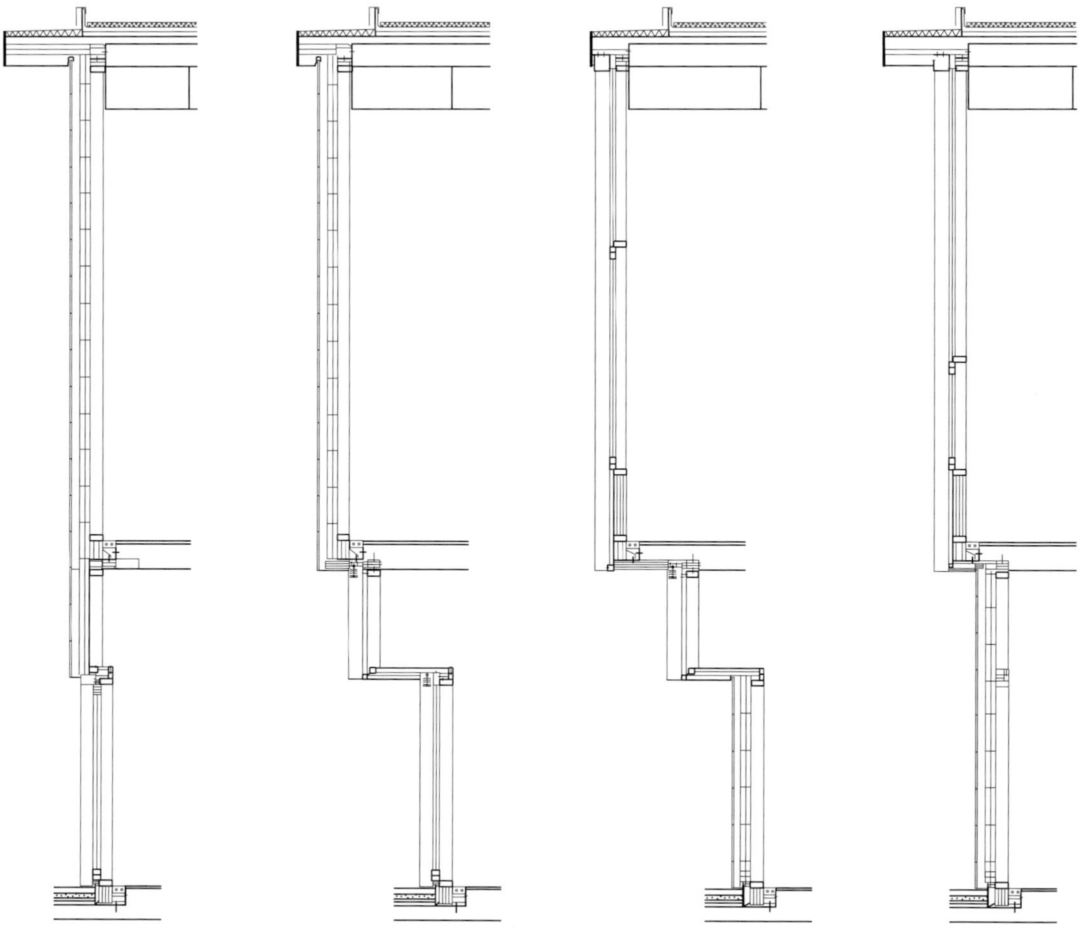

Laser Factory and Development Center
Ditzingen, Germany, 1998–2000/2007–09

The laser factory extends into the existing agricultural landscape from east to west, parallel to the adjacent autobahn, gradually stepping up the rising slope of the ground. The factory is situated on existing agricultural parcels, which offer a flexible patchwork of territory to be converted into industrial uses. The roofs of the factory fold and weave in response to the landscape, creating a series of diamond-shaped roof openings, which illuminate the workspaces below.

A tunnel to the existing plant connects to the new circulation spine, a spacious, double-height route for pedestrians and machines. Both are top-lit. The façades are comprised of standing seam zinc or precast concrete panels. The roof is made of steel trusses clad with a standing seam aluminum skin.

A new development center added in 2009 continues the geometry and language of the existing production halls. In the new expansion the dynamic roof form now shelters two functions: production and office areas, the latter of which are conceived as open, loft-like spaces. A split-level organizational strategy between the individual office lofts enhances the visual and communication capabilities and interaction between teams.

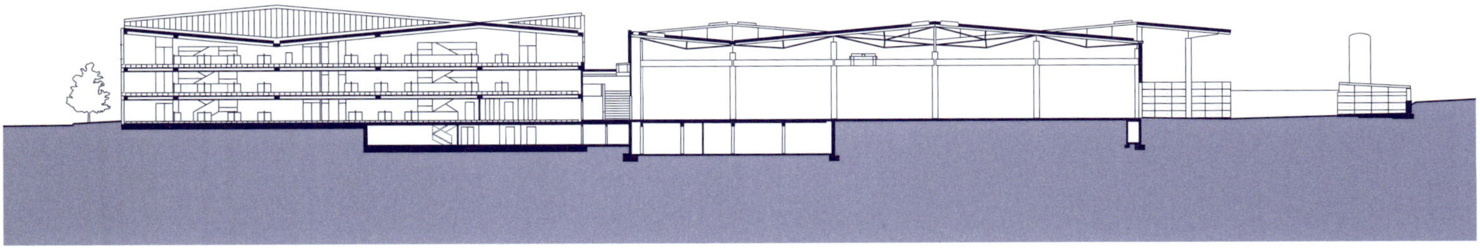

6
4

Customer and Administration Building
Ditzingen, Germany, 2003

The Customer and Administration Building for TRUMPF is located along the A81 autobahn, a marginal site due to noise and its location at the edge of the campus. The chief priorities here were to colonize a difficult site and improve communication between work teams. A spatially linked office concept connects nine split-level floors along the long section, ensuring multi-directional paths for communication and visual connectivity, which allows for groups of varying sizes and improves the work environment.

The split-level concept extends to a terraced ground floor, where three polygon volumes contain a wide-span auditorium, a reception area, and exhibition spaces. Floating above the ground floor, the two office tracts are shifted against each other both in plan and in section.

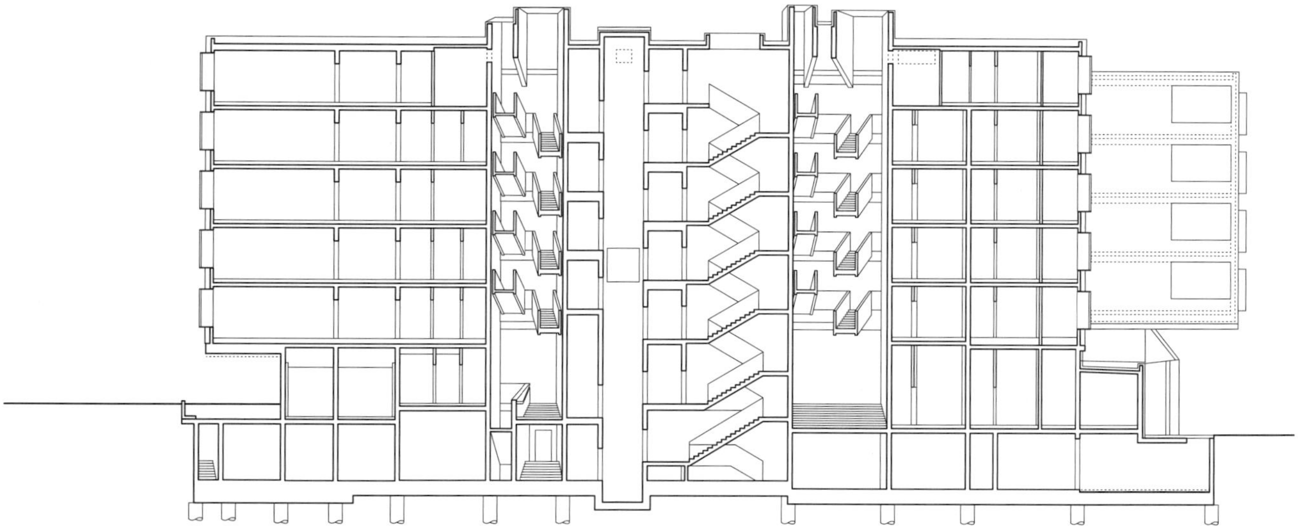

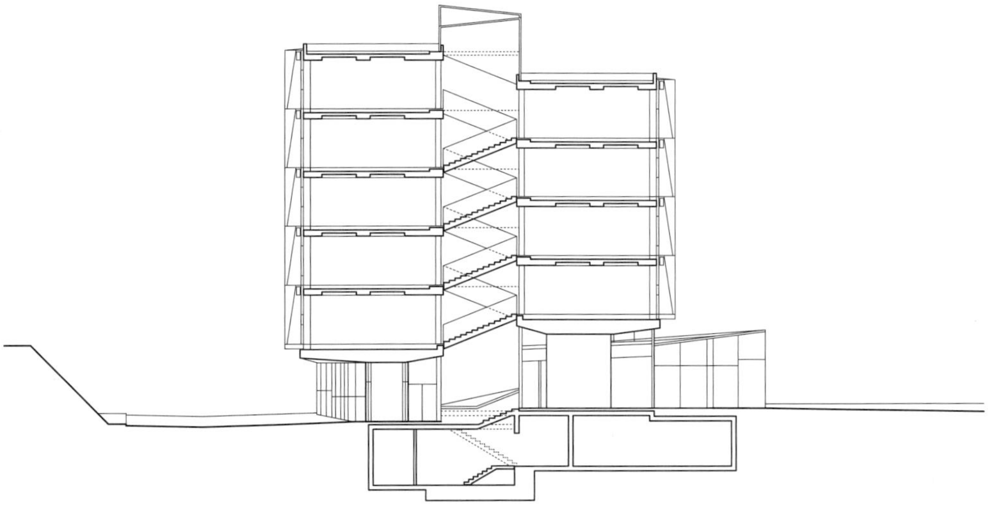

Stair-bridges span open vertical shafts connecting the half levels and are points for informal meeting and encounter. They provide visual links and become places of interaction.

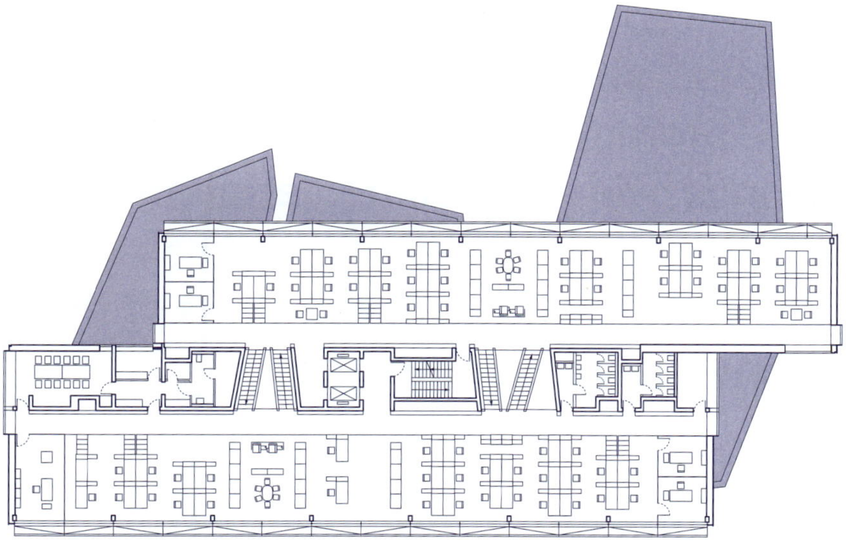

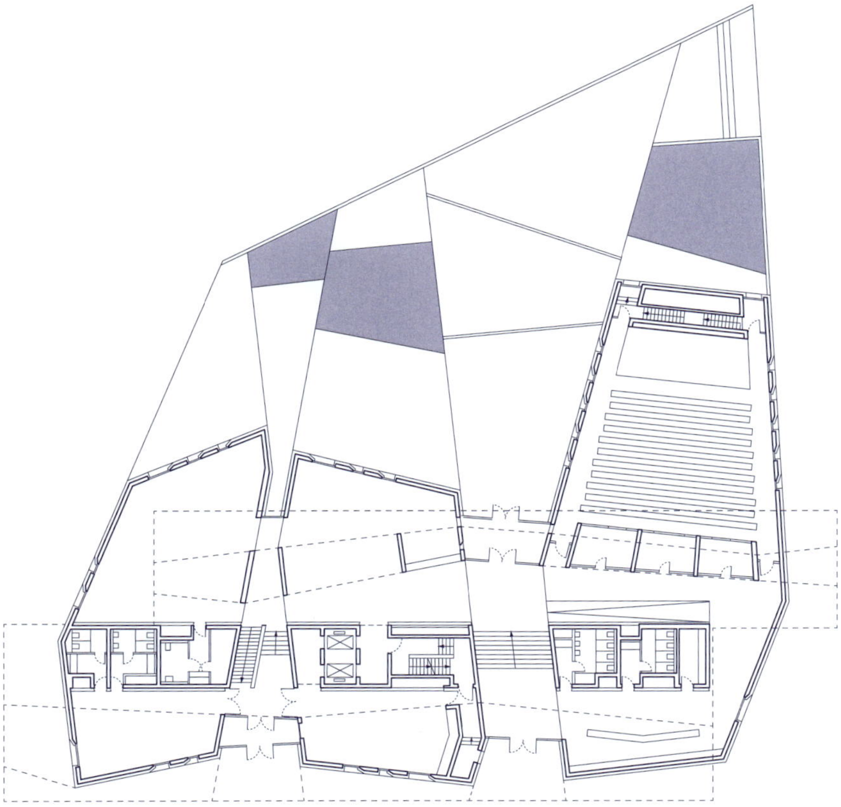

The energy concept was developed in collaboration with Transsolar. The central components of the working environment are natural light and ventilation, a passive cooling system with radiant cooling decks for summer, and an intelligent control of the extracted air with a heat gain collector for winter.

The double façade acts like a winter garden in the cold months and opens up and functions like a chimney, ventilating the building in the hot months. It creates an acoustical barrier against the traffic. In the interstitial space, which serves as a second egress space, the sun shading devices are protected from the wind and can be used at any time. The glass skin provides an acute permeability and openness, which allows the internal organization (loft-likes spaces) to be seen from outside while providing panoramic views of the agricultural landscapes surrounding the campus.

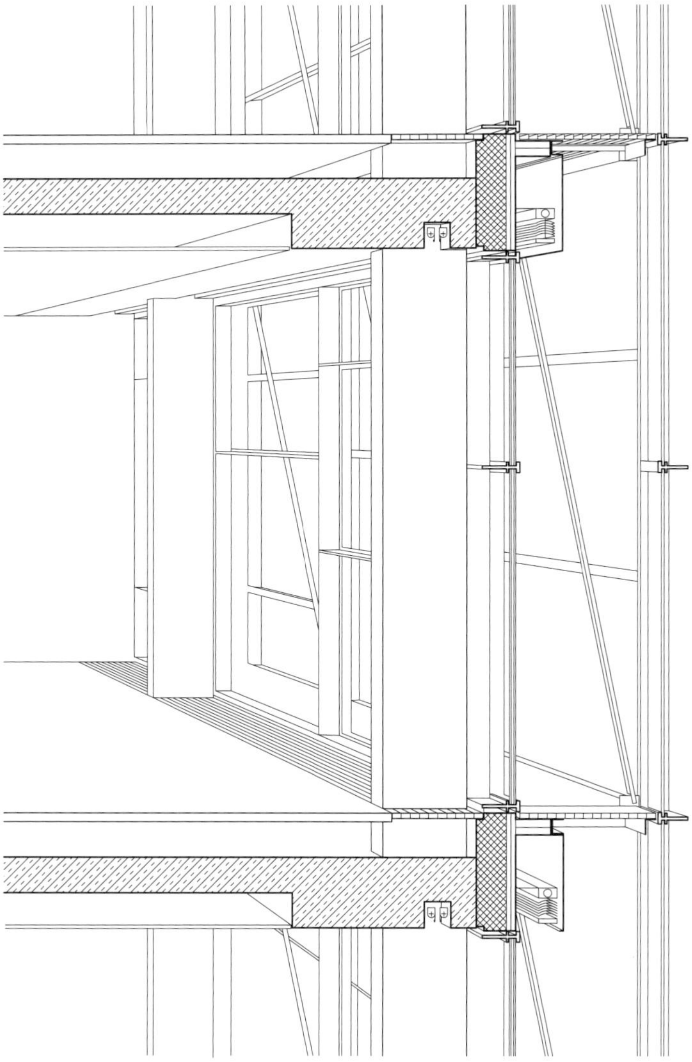

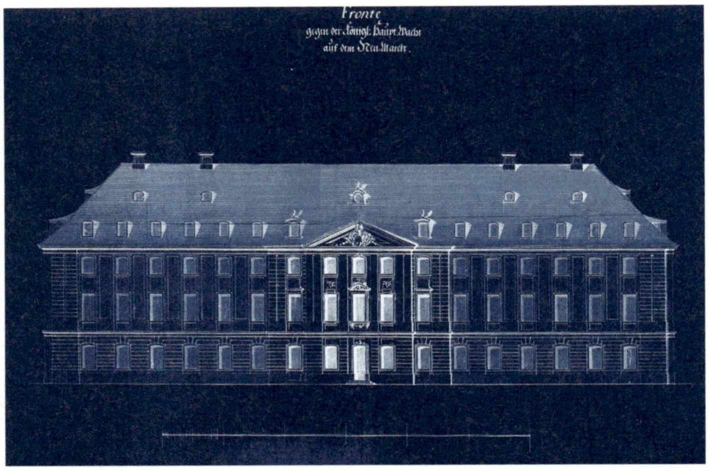
Fronte
gegen der Königl: Haupt Wacht
auf dem Neu-Marckt.

Ansicht
Der neu zuerbauenden Haupt Wacht

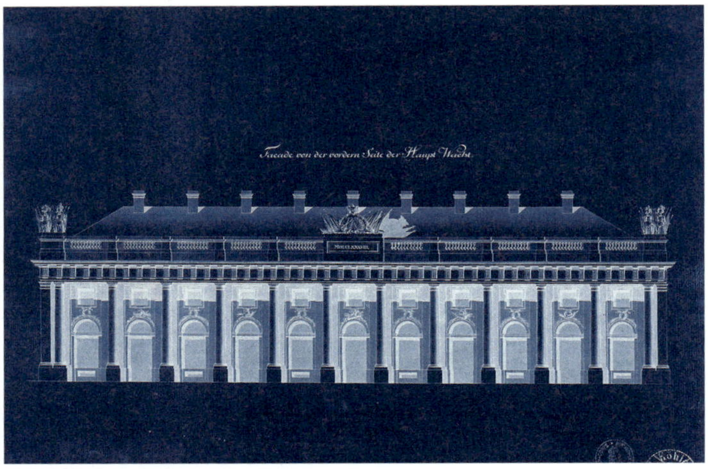
Facade von der vordern Seite der Haupt Wacht.

Fronte
gegen der Königl: Haupt Wacht
auf dem Neu-Marckt.
Ansicht
Der neu zuerbauenden Haupt Wacht
das Alte Gewandhaus in Dresden

Gewandhaus
Dresden, Germany, 2007 (competition)

This competition entry was for a sensitive historical site in war-damaged Dresden, at the Neumarkt across from the Frauenkirche. Historically a *Gewandhaus* was a trading hall for textiles. Considering at least four unbuilt designs over the last 200 years, the proposal started with a digital composite of those forms and façades as an operation to arrive at a new form sympathetic to the historical context at hand. A second strategy was to study Baroque façades and surfaces in order to make those of this project characteristic to Dresden. Utilizing digital studies, Baroque façade techniques were applied to the volume with the intention of resembling an historical typology, albeit with contemporary means.

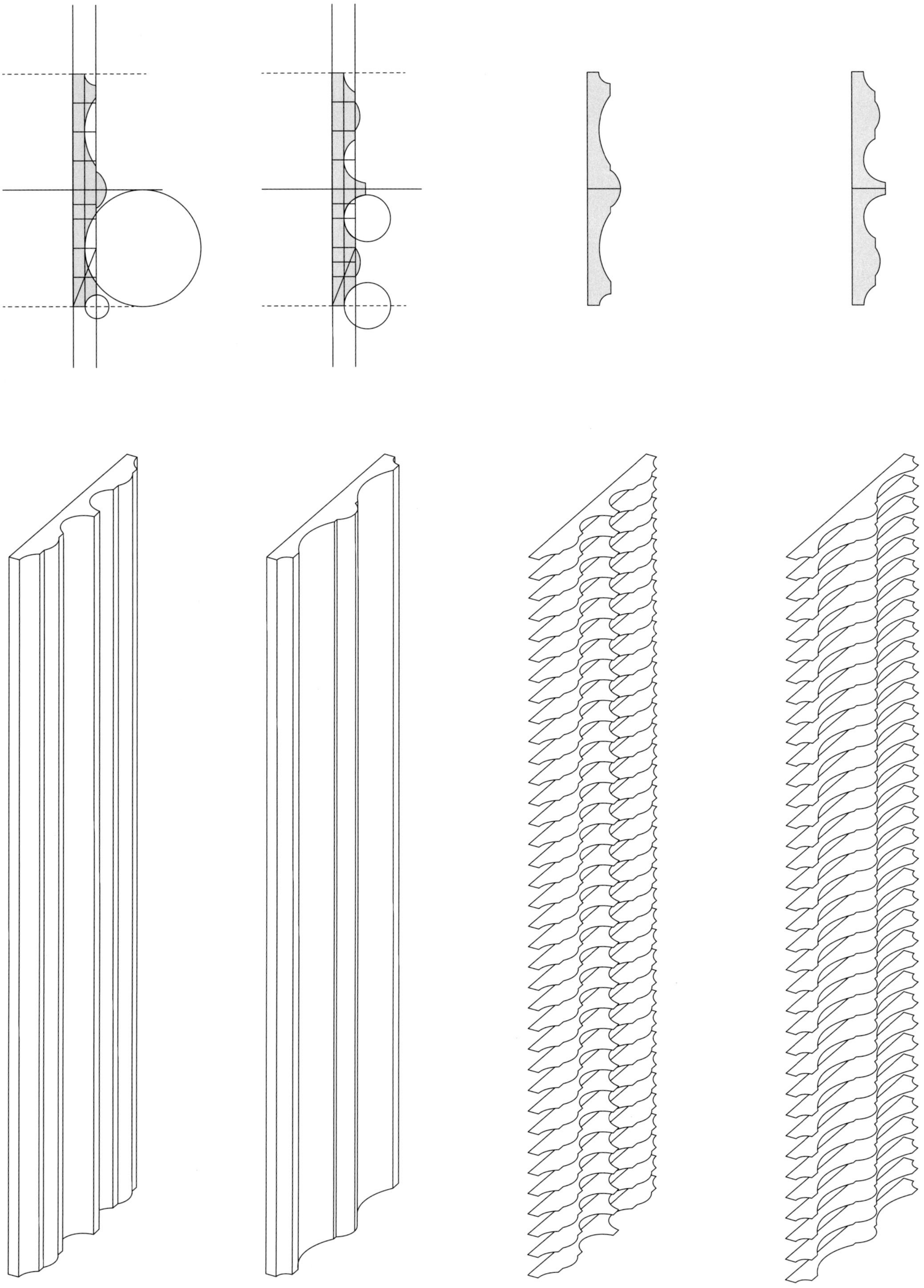

Concave and convex surfaces were used to generate "templates." These in turn led to the façade being conceived as a set of stacked, horizontal, thickened louver-like plates in stone or concrete, rending the building façade like an over-scaled lattice structure. In this way the volume is recognizable as historically contextual, while at second glance it appears "radical" in the way it is tectonically materialized. Depending on one's physical standpoint the building appears striated and opaque, or ephemeral and transparent.

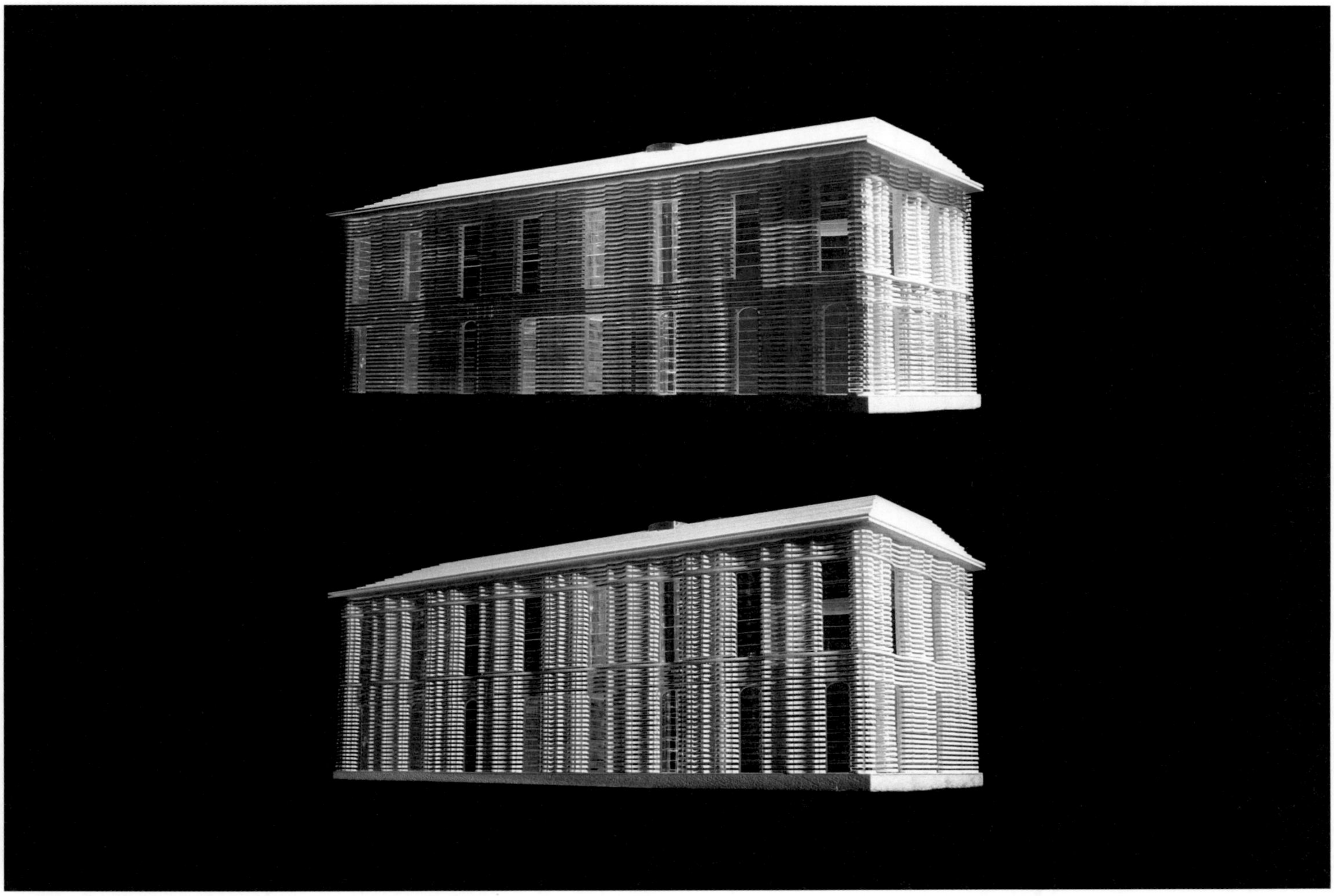

HOTEL VAUBAN
GREEN CITY HOTEL VAUBAN
GREEN CITY HOTEL VAUBAN

Stadthaus M1—Green City Hotel
Freiburg-Vauban, Germany, 2013

The Stadthaus M1 marks the gate to the Vauban quarter of Freiburg—a "green city," partially automobile free, with an emphasis on alternative and sustainable living and architecture. The construction of wood and concrete is modeled according to a "passive house" standard.

This first-prize-winning competition design consists of a separate hotel and an apartment building, unified by the continuous topography of their roofscape and façade. The taller and more public hotel is located as an entrance at the main artery of Merzhauser Strasse, while the more private apartment building is situated behind the hotel along the Vaubanallee.

The spatial gap between the two buildings forms a green "pocket park," which opens and widens toward the south, allowing for a path between the buildings and a connection to the public circulation and green-room fronting the buildings. This articulation allows for increased daylight illumination and breaks down the overall building mass on site.

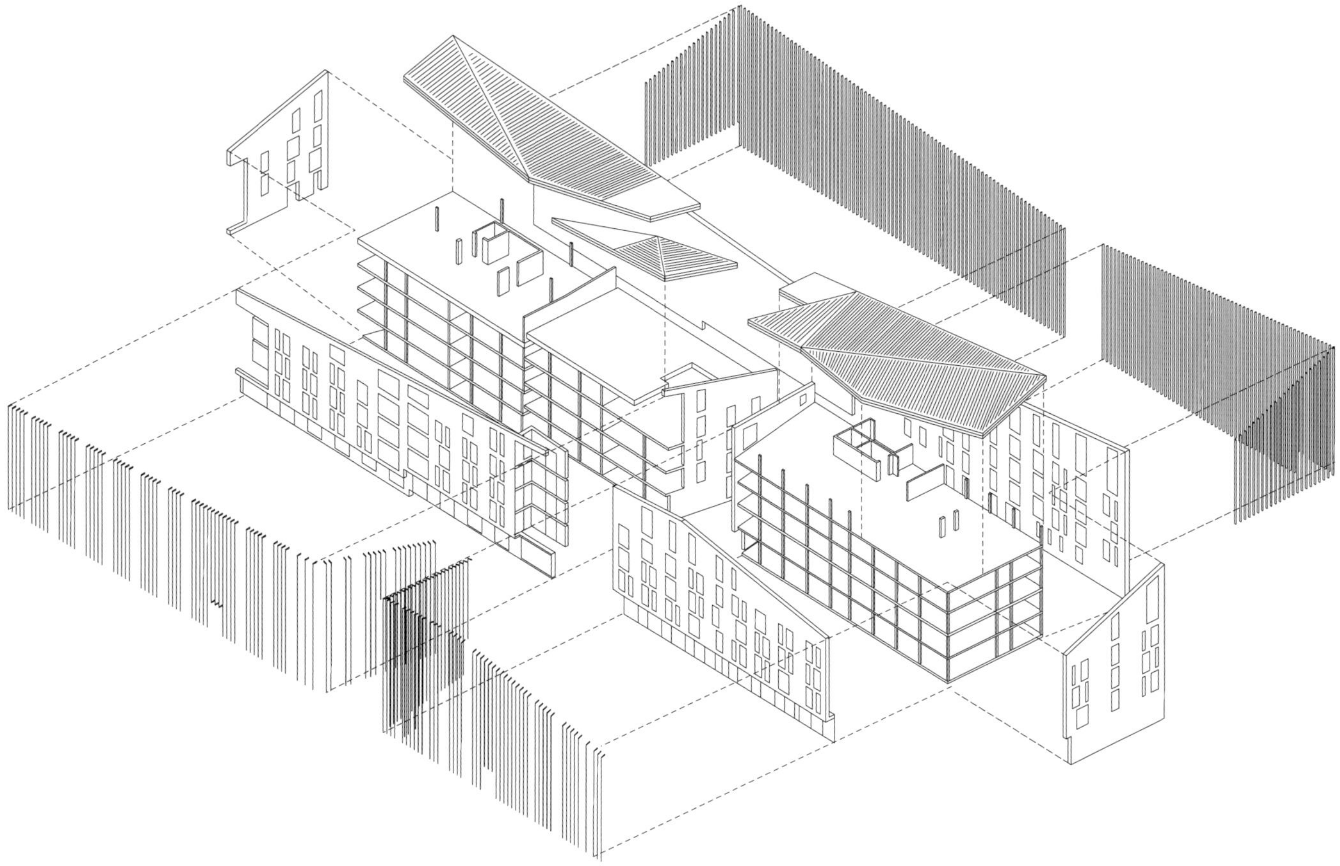

The low-tech façades save both energy and costs. They are highly insulated in wood construction and include triple insulating panel glazing with integrated retractable, louvered sunscreens. The south façades, complemented by loggias and balconies, are additionally protected by climbing plants. This layer of planting shades the interiors in the summer while allowing warming sun through in the winter. The north façades, emphasizing a vertical rhythm, are clad in vertical, cedar wood-fins, an element that further visually unifies the two independent buildings.

Paula-Modersohn-Platz

The construction of the hotel and apartment buildings is similar. Here, a passive energy standard was attained by combining a structural, concrete skeleton frame (i.e., floor slabs, cores, and columns for fire protection) with an insulated, prefabricated, wood-frame infill panel system (non-load bearing). In comparison with a conventional masonry construction this lightweight system uses a fifth less of gray energy.

Office Building and Production Hall
Hettingen, Germany, 2009 | 2013

This factory is located in Hettingen, a small village in the Swabian Alb, south of Stuttgart. Forests, rock-outcroppings, and the meandering Lauchhart trout stream on the valley floor mark the picturesque setting in which it is located. The first extension with shops and offices was completed in 2009. This addition essentially caps-off the existing factory and fronts the valley to the north, like a dam, marking a final conclusion of the village at this approach. The north façade faces a natural preserve, where no further construction is allowed.

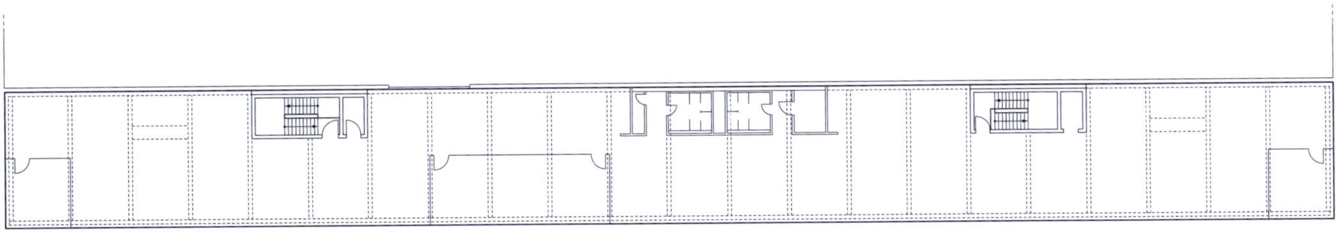

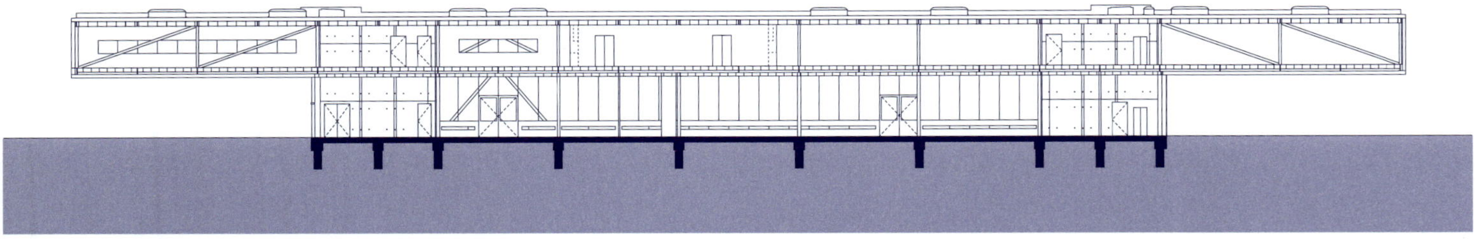

A new master plan anticipates the construction of a new production and assembly hall in four phases. The first of these phases, comprised of a new production hall, was realized in 2013, after only thirteen months of construction.

Organized as a simple, repetitive shed construction with seven bays, the production hall is bracketed by two stories of offices (to the north) and a drive-through loading bay (to the south). For the production and assembling of oversized, flatbed laser machines, a flexible and column-free space was required. The steel framework of the roof construction allows north-facing skylights within the structural depth; together with the three-meter-high strip window at ground level they provide daylight for the working areas.

The long façade facing the Lauchert Creek and Valley is articulated as a gently folded origami of corrugated metal and glass to scale the factory building to the neighboring single-family houses with pitched roofs. The office front is integrated into the shed volume but in fact has a gridded façade. The roof—as a fifth façade—is planted with local vegetation to better integrate the building into the scenic valley.

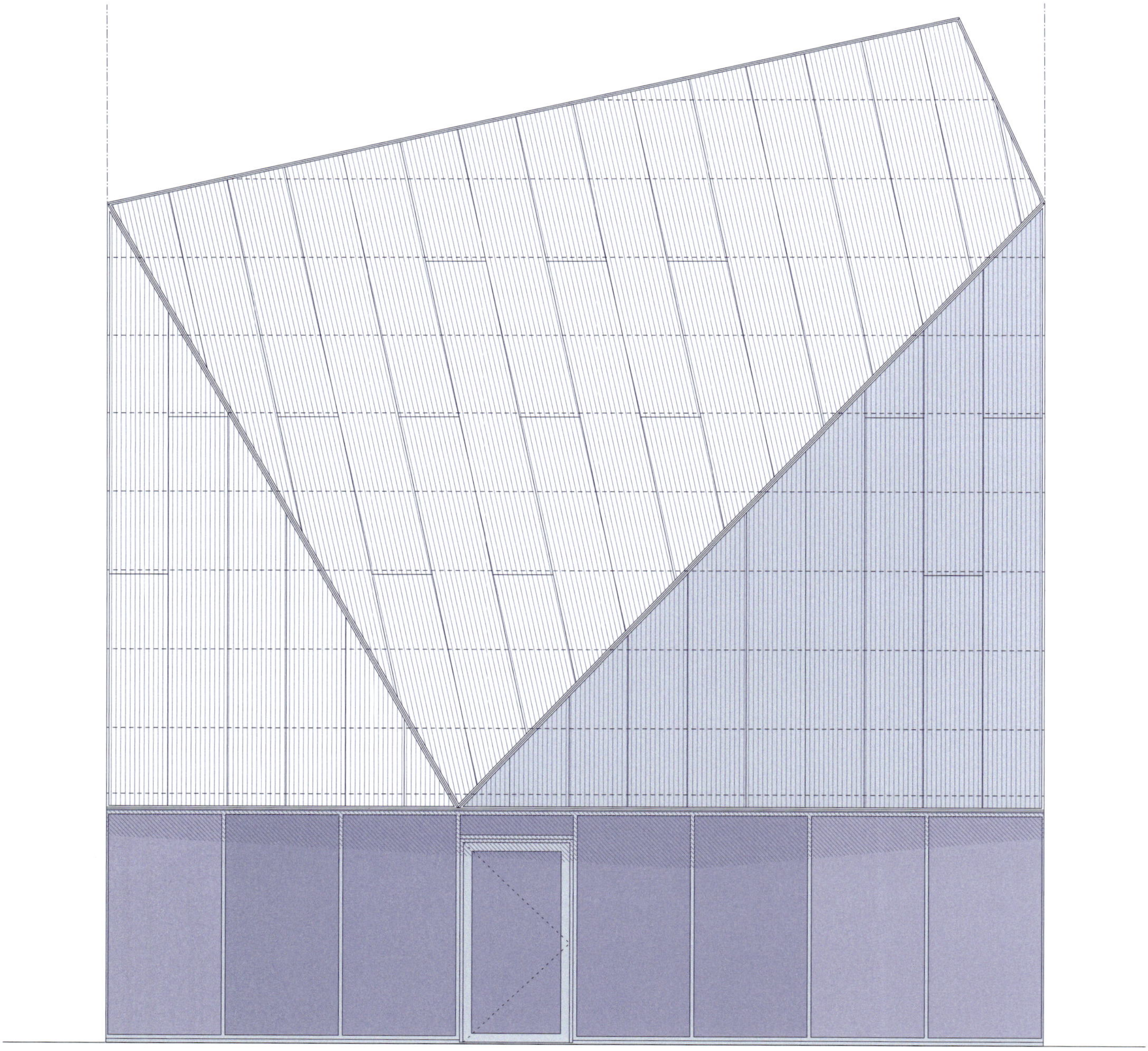

Residential High-Rise
Berlin-Alexanderplatz, Germany, 2014 (competition)

Like Alfred Döblin's 1929 novel *Berlin Alexanderplatz* this is neither the site of a historical Berlin nor a place for sentimentality. It will never be a beautiful, harmonic, unified whole or a "*Stadtkrone*." Rather it is a place that will continue to reflect the dissonance, fragmentation, and layered nuances of a truly modern pathos. This first tower in a master plan established in 1993 anticipates a future of high-rises at Berlin's Alexanderplatz that rethinks what a high-rise might mean in a city with no built historical precedents for one.

The diversely sized, stacked volumes comprising the tower, located on a trapezoid-shaped site, rotate slightly, step-by-step, in relationship to each other and in response to a multitude of views and orientations in the surrounding 360 degrees. The tower marks a logical spatial conclusion to the Karl-Marx-Allee, while also helping to define and mark Alexanderplatz spatially.

The large bulk of the tower is scaled-down to the residential neighborhood by its stacked volumes and folded façades. These simultaneously offer exterior spaces (loggias), floor-to-ceiling glazing for improved views over the city, and optimum orientations to the sun while also protecting the loggias from strong winds.

Both transparent and reflective, the tower of glass mediates between the public urban realm and the private interior one. Glass further situates the tower in the urban context while reflecting the dynamic cacophony that characterizes Alexanderplatz.

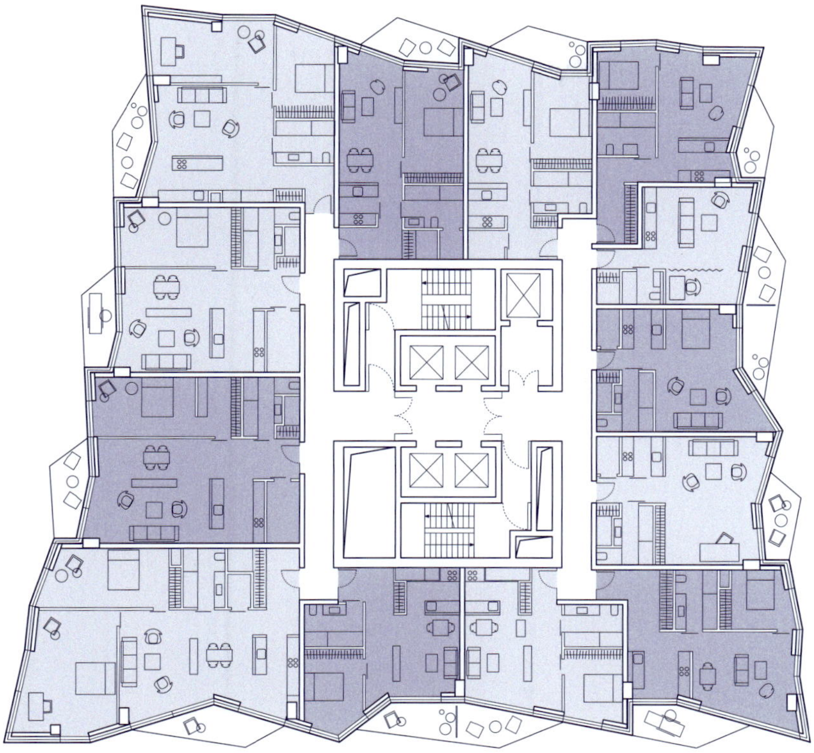

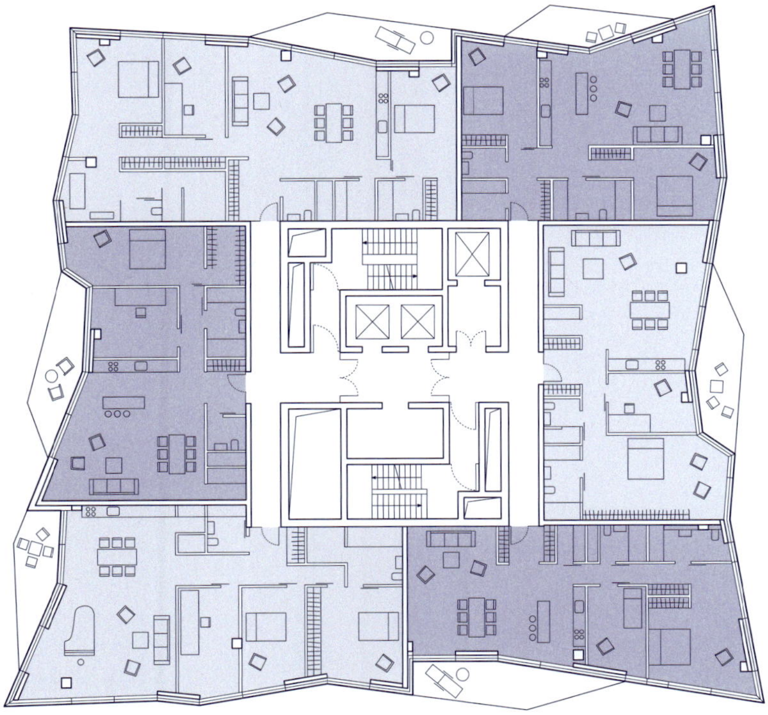

Looking Up
Sarah Whiting

Ceilings get short shrift when it comes to architecture. Even Auguste Choisy's worm's eyes, which provide fascinating and unexpected upward views, prioritize spatial and constructional information more than the ceiling per se. Ceilings are the home for all the messy stuff that eludes the architect's control: ductwork, smoke detectors, sprinklers, acoustic tiles, lighting grids, exit signs, cobwebs, and the like. Ceilings are the locus of obligation, not invention, and aside from certain well-known exceptions—the Sistine Chapel, for example—we are rarely encouraged to look up.

Floors oblige certain similar exigencies—vents, treads, thresholds, not to mention accesses and efficiencies—but the floor plan is architecture's primary tool of control. It is where definition takes place through the delineation of walls, columns, and program. Even the *plan libre* deliberately chooses how it will liberate control. Architecture's history, *grosso modo,* has been a swing between plans that *define,* delineating spaces for differentiated programs, and plans that *permit,* delineating almost nothing: the *plan libre,* universal space, loft spaces, and the like. Because the plan is the site of definition, plans are the key drawings for understanding architectural program. Ceiling designs, by contrast, are limited to reflected ceiling plans, which describe the technical and which are almost never the focus of more attention than those obligations. Roofs obtained their moment of glory with modernism, when flight enabled understanding them as the "fifth façade," but ceilings never got their due. Or maybe not until now.

Over the course of their career, Barkow Leibinger have forged a unique relationship to the ceiling: most of their projects exploit this under-appreciated surface as an experimental site for architecture, not technical obligation: their ceilings define space, provide lighting, or simply play out an architectural project of surface that would be impossible as a floor or wall, particularly in projects that are so tightly determined by their programmatic exigencies.

The majority of Barkow Leibinger's architecture so far has established a relationship to industrial production—a programmatic milieu that has prioritized a Miesian universal space of openness: sheds of production, especially for their many buildings for TRUMPF. And yet, Barkow Leibinger projects combine the universal with the defined, and they do so by exploiting the ceiling as a surface of definition within a spatial volume of total flexibility. Many of Barkow Leibinger's projects exploit the ceiling as a surface that gives character to typically anonymous shed spaces of production. This set of projects, which could be collected together as projects that create defined roofs and ceilings using structure and emphasizing geometry, includes the Laser Factory and Development Center in Ditzingen of 2000, whose folded roof strips are directly echoed inside, the bands providing relief from the vastness of the space but also providing light—trapezoidal windows—where they do not line up. Perhaps the "purest" example of the ceiling as articulated structure, however, is the simple, graceful installation *Loom-Hyperbolic* for the fourth Marrakech Biennale in 2012, where hyperbolic volumes were constructed of yarn, weaving a delicate, floating plane that articulated volumes and surface alike. Because the temporary installation did not need a weather barrier, the delicate lines of yarn were able to construct an almost ghostly surface where roof and ceiling truly are one.

While Marrakech and the Laser Factory example limit variation to a pattern that is repeated and that operates as a logic for roof and ceiling simultaneously, another Barkow Leibinger ceiling strategy pushes Ludwig Mies van der Rohe's universal space yet further from its comfort zone by using the ceiling to create discreet zones within a free plan. In the Production Assembly Hall in Neukirch of 2004, they employ more of a tartan-plaid than a checkerboard grid. Its ceiling resembles a mat-building (like Candillis, Josic, Woods and Schiedhelm's Free University Building in Berlin), but it is a compressed mat, squeezed into the tight section running only from the roof to the ceiling. This elevated grid of transparent and opaque planes illuminates the interior and articulates the hall's vast volume into sectors, but never into distinct rooms. And in the Campus Restaurant for TRUMPF in Ditzingen (2008), the strategy is pushed even further, since the roof is not a singular field but a collection of smaller triangular fields, comprised of steel plates, compressed together to form a large, almost illegible pentagon. Within each triangular field lies an irregular array of deep, polygonal, wood cells, some of which pierce the roof and operate as skylights. The larger pentagon holds the entire program as a single spatial entity. The groups of tables follow the radial logic of the triangles, whereas the food service spaces echo the polygons, but the space feels much more specific than it really is, since the geometry is complete on the ceiling and only partial on the floor. As such, the single space of the restaurant is gently differentiated without being segregated.

Barkow Leibinger's ceilings capture and convey the full complexity of the firm's geometric-structural ambitions while permitting the floor plans—and thus their buildings' programs—much looser play. In other words, these projects not only liberate the plan; they also liberate architecture itself by fostering a new site for architectural exploration. Like other contemporary practices, Barkow Leibinger also locate their architectural project in their buildings' façades, sections, and structures; this is all the more reason to remember to look up the next time you find yourself in one of their projects. It is their ceilings that elicit surprise. In an effort to describe what produces art or poetry, Gilles Deleuze and Felix Guattari turned to D.H. Lawrence, who once wrote: "people are constantly putting up an umbrella that shelters them and on the underside of which they draw a firmament and write their conventions and opinions. But poets, artists, make a slit in the umbrella, they tear open the firmament itself, to let in a bit of free and windy chaos and to frame in a sudden light a vision that appears through the rent . . ."[1] The *plan libre* may well be the known site of architectural liberation, but how absolutely liberating to find freedom in the firmament as well.

1 Gilles Deleuze and Félix Guattari, *What is Philosophy?*, trans. Hugh Tomlinson and Graham Burchell (New York, 1994), pp. 203–04.

Ultrastructure: Biological structure and especially fine structure (as of a cell) not visible through an ordinary microscope.
—Merriam-Webster Collegiate Dictionary

This work area is characterized by geometric organizational or structural systems that are assertive and primary, and that define the spaces these constructs generate. It emphasizes projects that are expressed significantly through their interiority as well as how those spaces are generated by such structures.

Most of the examples embody ideas of cellular organizational principles that are differentiated or aggregate structures resembling natural formations such as leaves, sponges, a branch, or simply the gathering or stacking of a material. An addition of similar elements characterizes this approach. Both asymmetrical and symmetrical organizational strategies further resemble natural systems. Structure here is given a kind of material thickness that can be used to form space but also to control light or generate a depth that can be occupied as programmable space itself.

Digital fabrication techniques and workflows play a key role here, facilitating the realization of complex and varied construction elements. These techniques are able to assume the multiple scales of components within a building, including structural systems, façades, built-ins, tiles, and precast concrete, allowing the architect to reimagine the possibility of a contemporary Gesamtkunstwerk unique to each project. This is one of the building areas that have profited the most from our fabrication research, superseding the standard building catalogue. Digital technologies are favorable for solving geometric tasks involving either repetitive or variable components. Patterning is a two-dimensional technique that helps organize geometry into three-dimensional structural systems. New software capabilities, such as scripting, help optimize and establish efficiencies in terms of material use and structural loading. Digital fabrication is not an exclusive priority; rather, it is often combined with analogue and handcrafted building as a composite design approach.

Within this work area, buildings like the TRUMPF Campus Restaurant and Gatehouse have been opportunities to pioneer techniques for creating unique sets of fabricated elements occurring at different scales and in varied materials for an individual building. This is an approach that re-empowers architects to most effectively determine and control both the production and the tectonic architectural possibilities themselves.

Campus Restaurant
Ditzingen, Germany, 2008

This pavilion provides a new, central cafeteria and event space for TRUMPF's industrial campus and headquarters. It is the new social center for the company's blue and white-collar workers alike. The building is conceived as a freestanding pavilion, enhancing its role visibly on the campus as the event space it is intended to be. The pavilion, with seating for ca. 700, enables the company's employees to lunch at three time slots in the large central space, with reserve seating in a mezzanine, which opens onto a roofed-over outdoor terrace. When programmed for events, the space functions as an auditorium with seating for 800.

The canopy roof of the pavilion hovers over a large excavation, positioning the main level of the space at four meters below grade. This height is determined by the tunnel level of the campus, an infrastructure system that connects all the buildings on the campus. This results in forming an amphitheater-like space: the main level extends beyond the glass façades, which are then framed by berms planted with wild flowers and connecting to the park and landscape at grade. Through this sectional manipulation the overall height of the pavilion on the campus is lowered and the true, nine-meter height of the central space is revealed only from the interior. The mezzanine level, arrived at by means of two large, precast concrete stairways, compresses the spatial experience of the roof by pushing up to a three-meter clear height.

TRUMPF

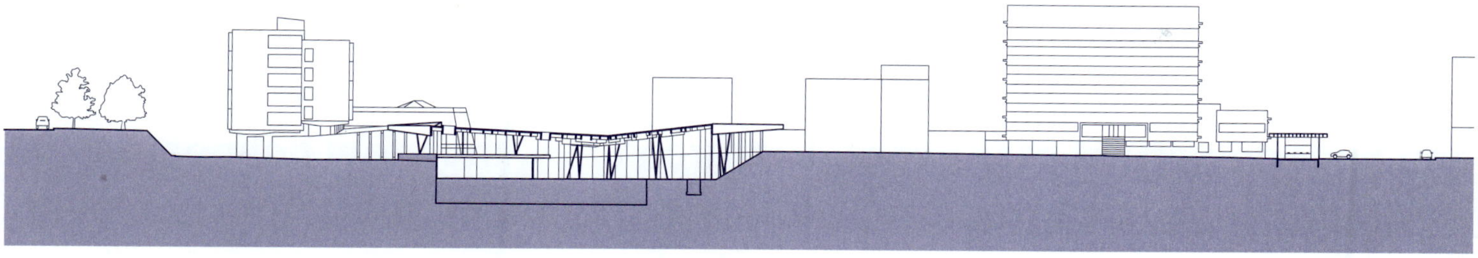

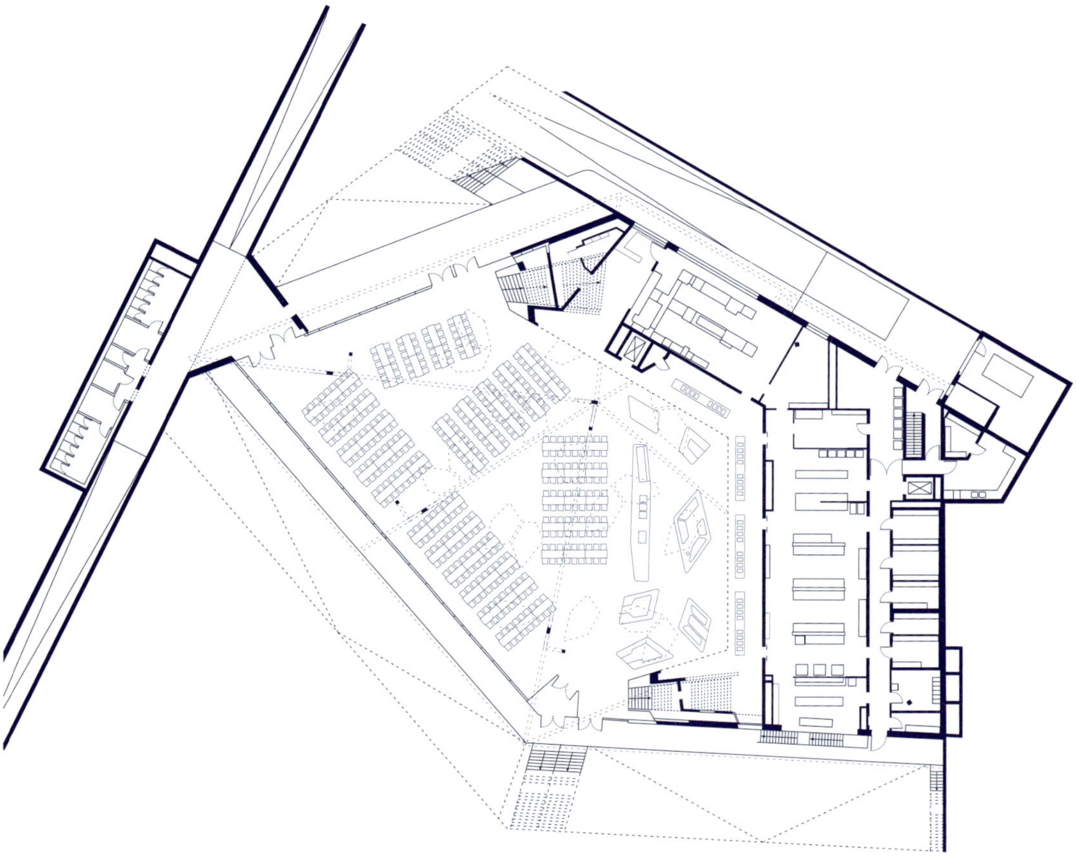

The roof structure was developed with the structural engineer Werner Sobek. The intention was to create a polygonal, leaf-like canopy that achieves long spans over groups of columns. This structure combines a steel frame and columns with a glue-laminated, wood-cell infill. The steel frame consists of nine triangular fields, which are placed on nine column groups. The columns are intentionally located away from the beam perimeters and intersections to enhance the cantilevering and hovering effect of the roof. Hierarchically, the steel delineates a primary, vein-like structure, while the Glulam construction achieves a cellular web-like infill completing the leaf analogy. The wood cells are functionally "coded" and constructed either as skylights with solar-glass, perforated wood acoustic planking (tying the roof diaphragm together), or artificial lighting cells modified by an aluminum honey-combed deflector.

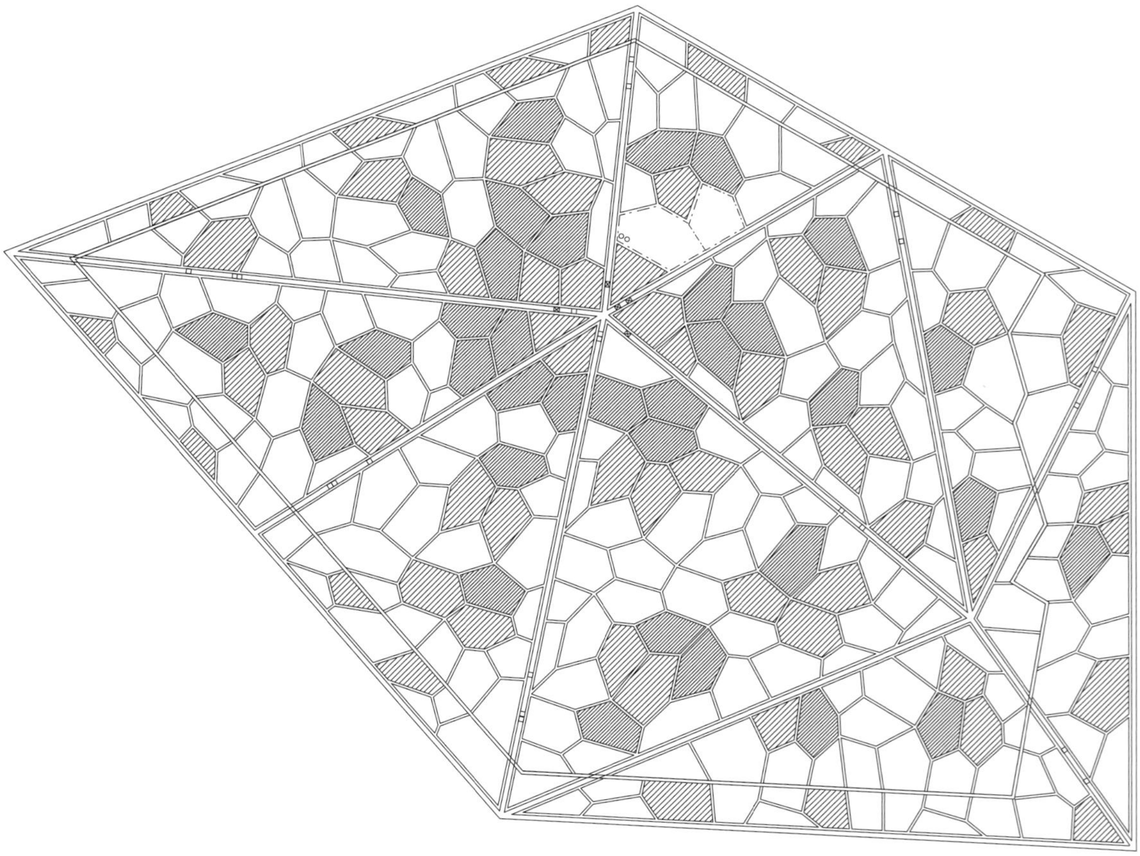

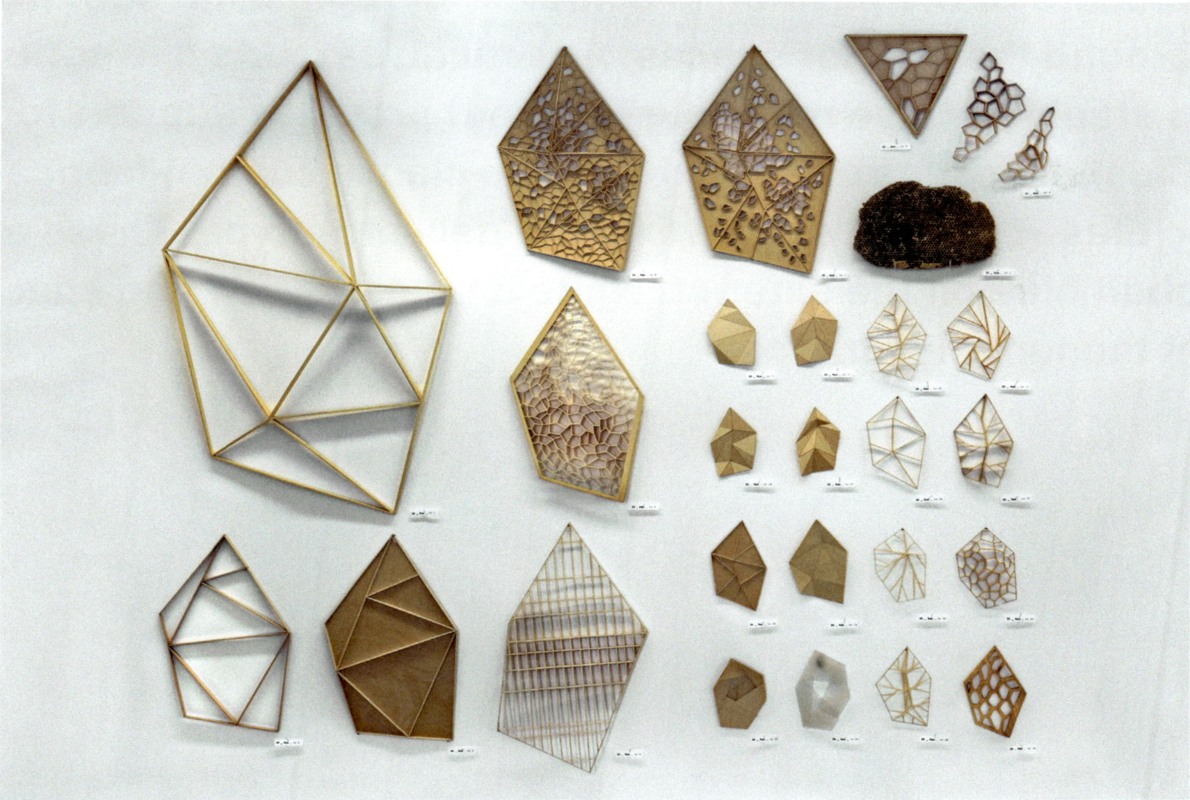

In order to economically achieve this highly complex structure CNC routing and sawing was employed to accommodate the more than 300 unique honeycomb joints. The cells are constructed of ten-centimeter Glulam of fast-growth pine in heights varying from ninety to one hundred fifty centimeters.

The enclosure of the pavilion is achieved by a glass façade, which wraps around the interior spaces. A vertical, barcode-like series of tapered steel fins (also mass-customized) provides support for solar glass. Closed façades on the exterior are clad in custom-fabricated ceramic tiles—concave or convex—as a new prototype. These are colored cobalt blue on the exterior, white on the interior, and speckled green at the tunnel entrance.

„Trumpf“
in – konkav 27 Stüc
in – konvex 26 Stü

Gatehouse
Ditzingen, Germany, 2007

The gatehouse embodies a long-standing ambition between architect and client: to use TRUMPF's high-tech, digital laser cutting tools to fabricate a unique and freestanding building. It is a building that demonstrates the client's technology in an iconographic fashion by creating a very muscular structure (a large, twenty-meter cantilevered roof) that can "show-off" the capabilities of their technology as an introduction to their campus headquarters.

In this example laser cutting no longer "accessorizes" the architecture, as in earlier projects, but contributes to essential construction areas. At the outset of the project, the earlier work of Jean Prouvé was recalled, who, with his factory in Maxéville, France, was able to construct prototypical works of architecture in which sheet metal contributed to the generation of entire building components, including furniture, structure, and glazing systems. Understanding this, the goal of the present project was to construct the building substantially of laser-cut and welded sheet metal enclosed by a glass curtain wall.

The primary organizational strategy was to cover a reception area, desk, toilet core, and support spaces with a thirty-two-by-eleven-meter stainless steel and steel roof. The roof cantilevers from four columns (two in tension, two in compression).

This roof provides a shelter for visitors and frames an axial view of the factory campus. The fifty-centimeter-deep roof was constructed with Werner Sobek's calculations as a honeycombed box-beam of three-millimeter stainless and milled steel. The triangle perforations of the bottom webbing as well as the vertical beam-webbing vary in density in order to reduce the weight at the extent of the roof cantilever. Through its varying geometry the roof illustrates mathematically the calculations following the structural loading diagrams. A series of laser-cut, 1:50 scale models was produced, interpreting the loading diagram, to arrive at the final constructed variation. This was achieved with digital cutting (mass customization), allowing each individual component to be unique.

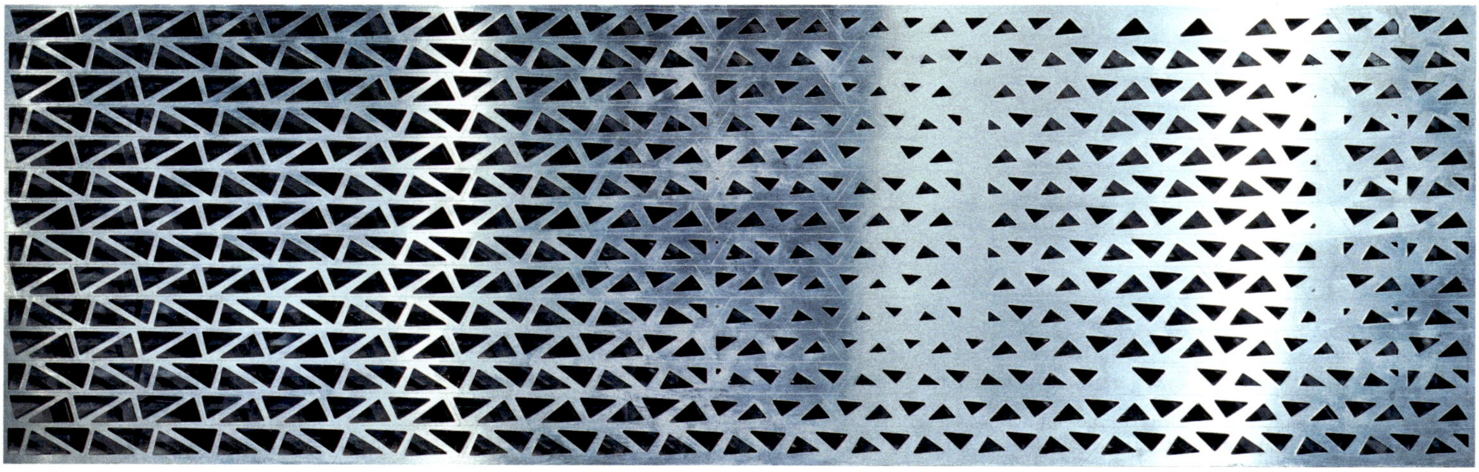

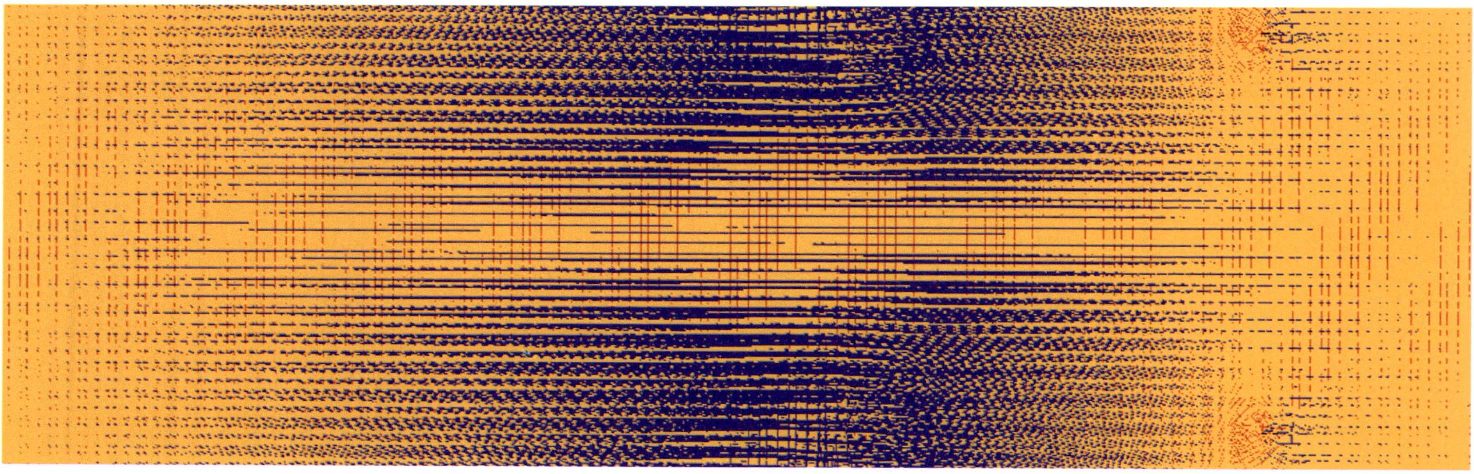

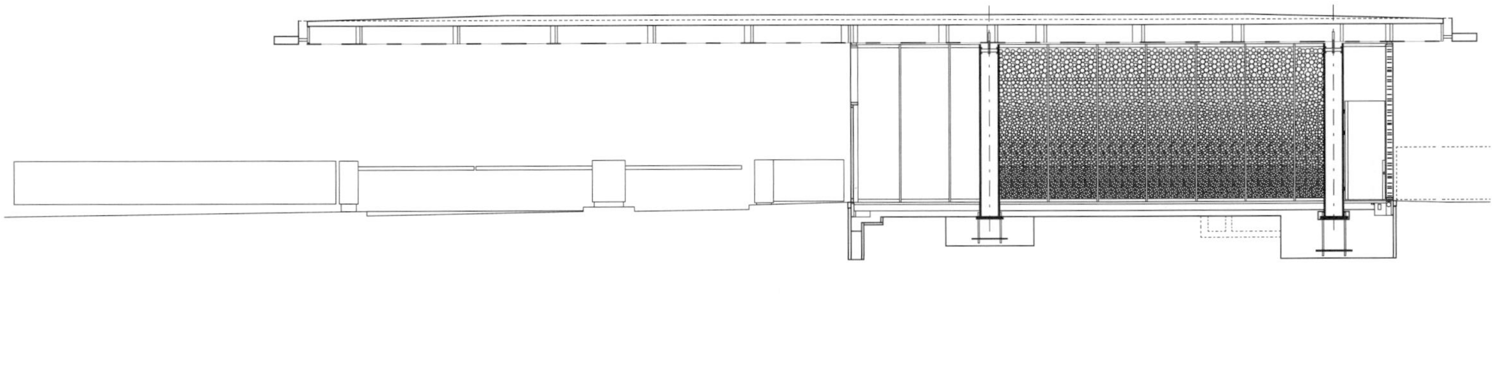

The roof is constructed of a series of 204 seventy-by-three-hundred-centimeter cassettes, fastened together to form a continuous stiff plane. These components arrived on-site as a pre-fabricated series of thirty-two-meter roof strips bolted together, which were then raised as a unified roof, placed over the columns, and fastened to pin-joints.

The underside of the roof is additionally accentuated by illuminating the coffers with LED lighting, thus further “lightening” the structure. The backlighting of the façades, by means of the opaque white Plexiglas-clad cores, ensures that the gatehouse functions as an entrance lantern at night.

The glass façades of the pavilion are a double façade consisting of two layers of iso-glass on the exterior and a single layer on the interior, improving the climatic performance of this non-load-bearing curtain wall. Between these two layers is an ornamental screen of gradating (in diameter) Plexiglas tubes, which provide sun shading. Contrasting with the digitally fabricated roof these screens are handmade by a craftsman based on a digitally drawn array of designs.

2D:3D Installation
Berlin, Germany, 2014

This installation at the BDA (German Association of Architects) Galerie in the Charlottenburg district of Berlin inaugurated a series of exhibitions focusing on two and three-dimensionality in architecture. Covering the wall surfaces of the small gallery space with wallpaper, the façade of the storefront gallery frames what Leon Battista Alberti described as a "*fenestra aperta*" (open window). In this configuration the gallery space becomes a projection as well as an extension of the streetscape within the historical, middle-class residential neighborhood.

Playing with the conceptual directive of 2-D/3-D, the wallpaper on one side of the gallery has a two-dimensional pattern: an organic looping structure that repeats and mirrors itself and is both ornamental and geometrically structural in its architectural implication. On the same axis as the street front façade at the back of the gallery is a wallpaper "portrait" of this system in black and white, but now projected in a one-point perspective, thus optically extending the perspective of the gallery itself.

Suspended from the historical Jugendstil-decorated ceiling is a new ceiling, comprised of plywood veneer loops patterned on the drawings but with a ten-centimeter depth and positioned at a 240-centimeter clear height (door height) above the floor.

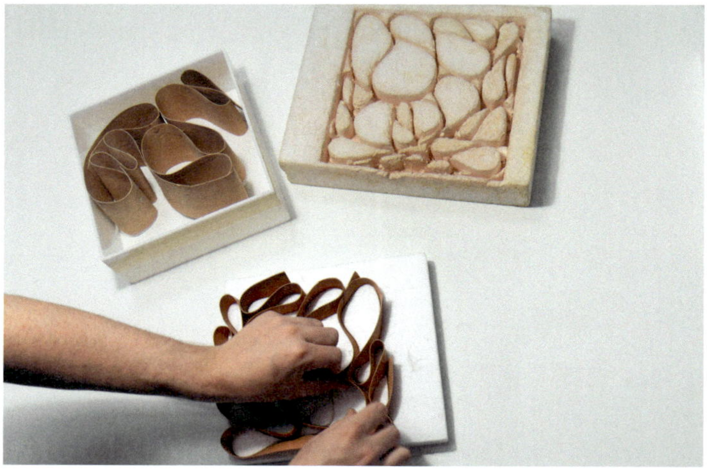

Bund Deutscher Architekten
Landesverband Berlin

Earlier studies with loop structures had been made to explore the capacities and potential of such kinds of cellular systems on a larger scale—such as a roof structure above a large, nearly column-free exhibition space with the loops as an integrated heating and cooling system.

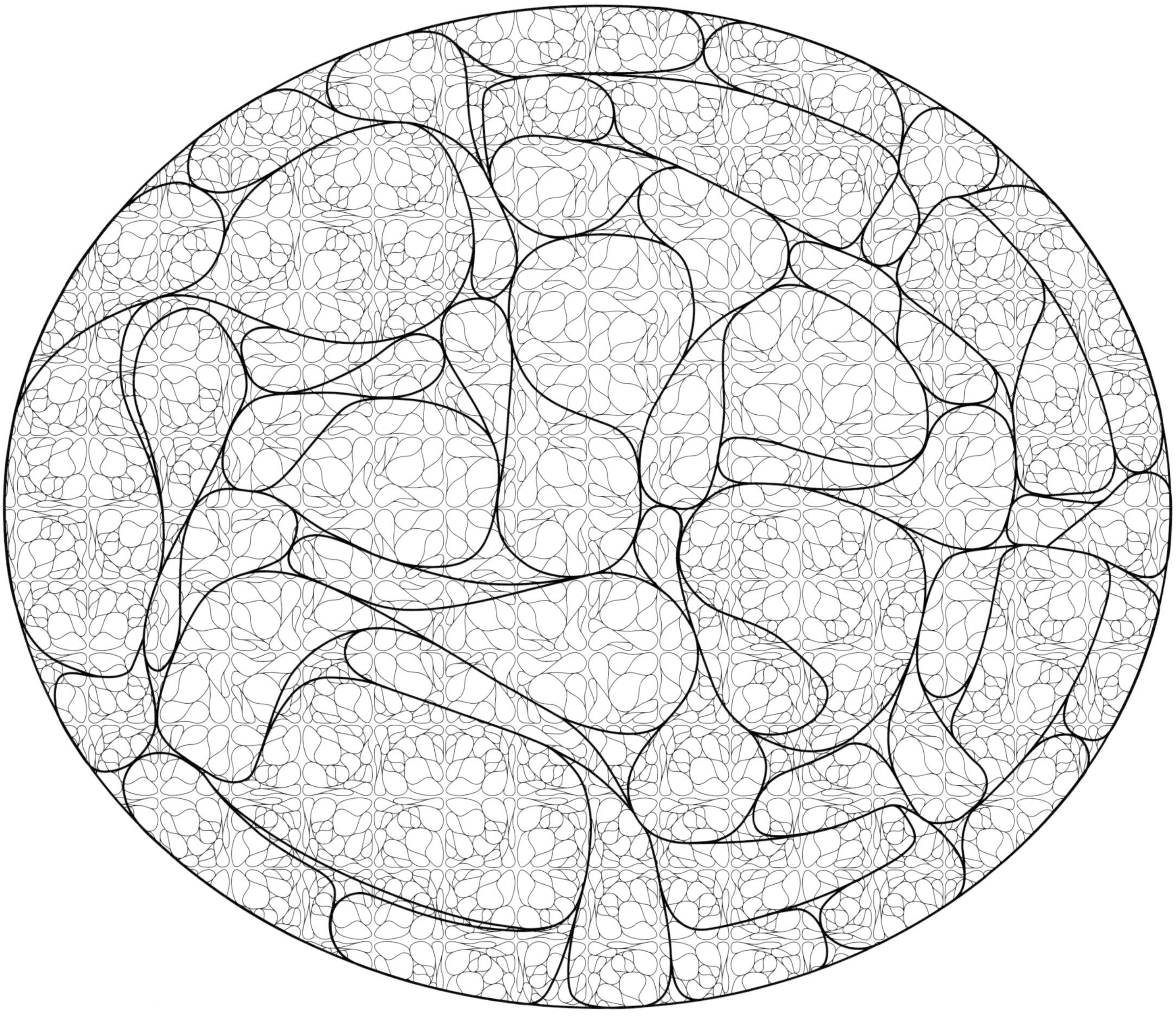

Catenary Infill Project
Berlin, Germany, 2010

This prototype is intended as a live-work concept for typical Berlin infill sites (*Baulücken*), those empty sites "generated" by bombing during the World War II. Physics tells us that a "catenary curve" is a formed when a chain is supported at each end and is acted on only by its own weight, naturally creating a parabolic arch. This creates an idealized arch capable of producing an array of structural possibilities.

This logic is applied to achieve maximum spatial continuity with little interruption and minimal structure for a low-rise, live-work building. By hanging a chain of tube-like volumes between the two party walls, the natural force of gravity pulls them downward, thus applying tension to the two walls and assuming structural stability. Programmatically, the box-chain volumes are residential, bridging an open, column-free space below for studio (work) areas. Construction is comprised of timber frames clad in plywood sheathing. A series of small stairs negotiate height differences (split-levels) within the overall topographical interior. In a step-like manner the catenary logic generates small splits at the scale of the rooms. Conceptually the prototype is a series of tube bundles spanning any site containing occupiable space while generating workspaces between them.

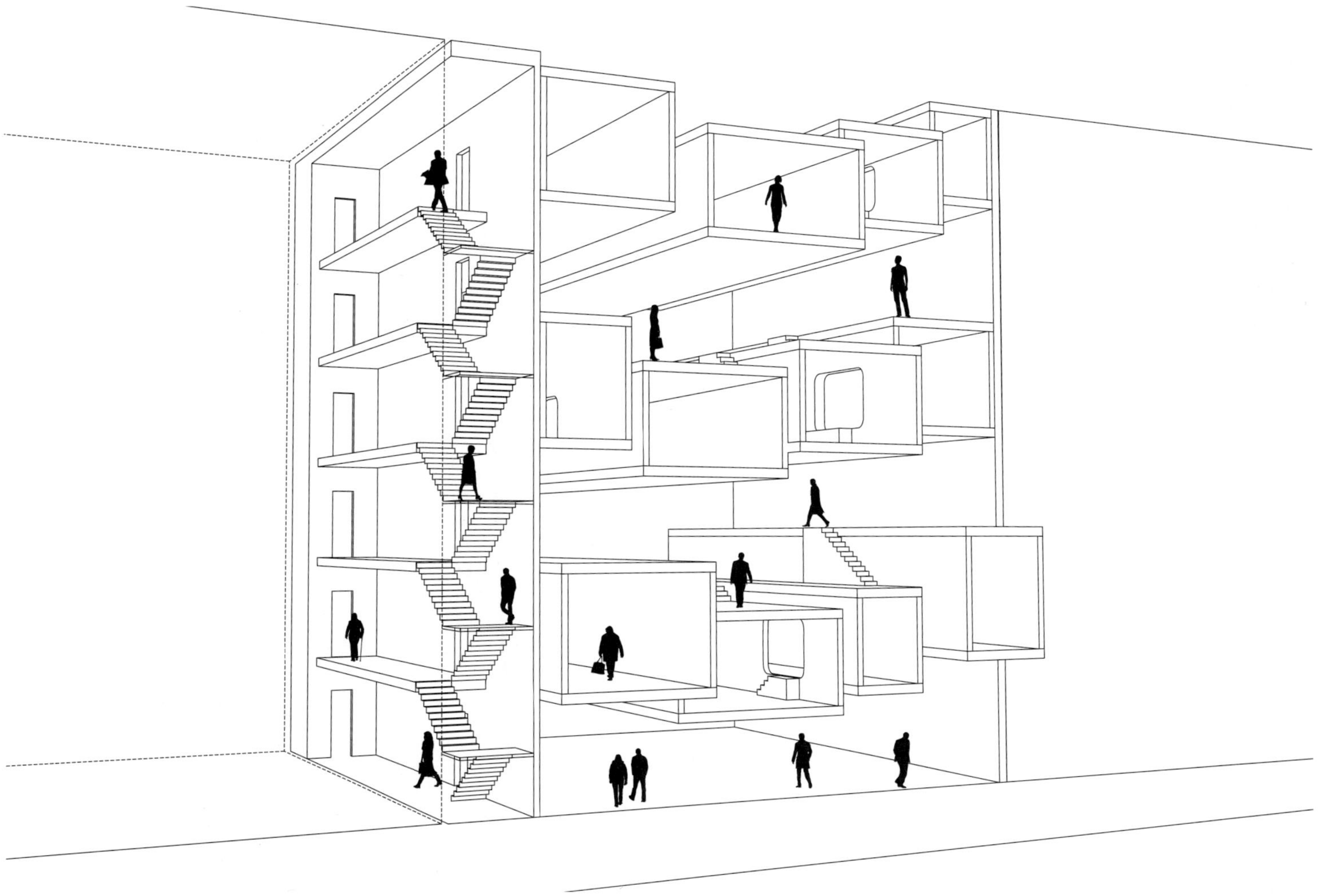

Fellow's Pavilion: American Academy
Berlin-Wannsee, Germany, 2015

Recalling earlier practice prototypes, such as the *Loom-Hyperbolic* installation at the 2012 Marrakech Biennale, and a history of twentieth-century pavilions by way of modernism Barkow Leibinger conceived a lightweight glass and steel structure for the garden of the villa of the academy. Central to enclosing a space for seven study carrels and a small kitchen is a roof of steel beams that forms a double-curved surface that appears to float over the lower spaces. The pavilion roof form is a result of "ruled geometry," with offset straight lines rotating to produce four hyperbolic paraboloids, a form that is both abstract and similar (if only in elevation) to the gabled roof forms of the historical villa. The abstractness and distinctness of the pavilion is further enhanced by its floating above the green lawn of the garden and its primarily white color. LED lighting, located at the top of the carrel walls, further emphasizes this effect at night, illuminating the "ceiling" and lightening it visually.

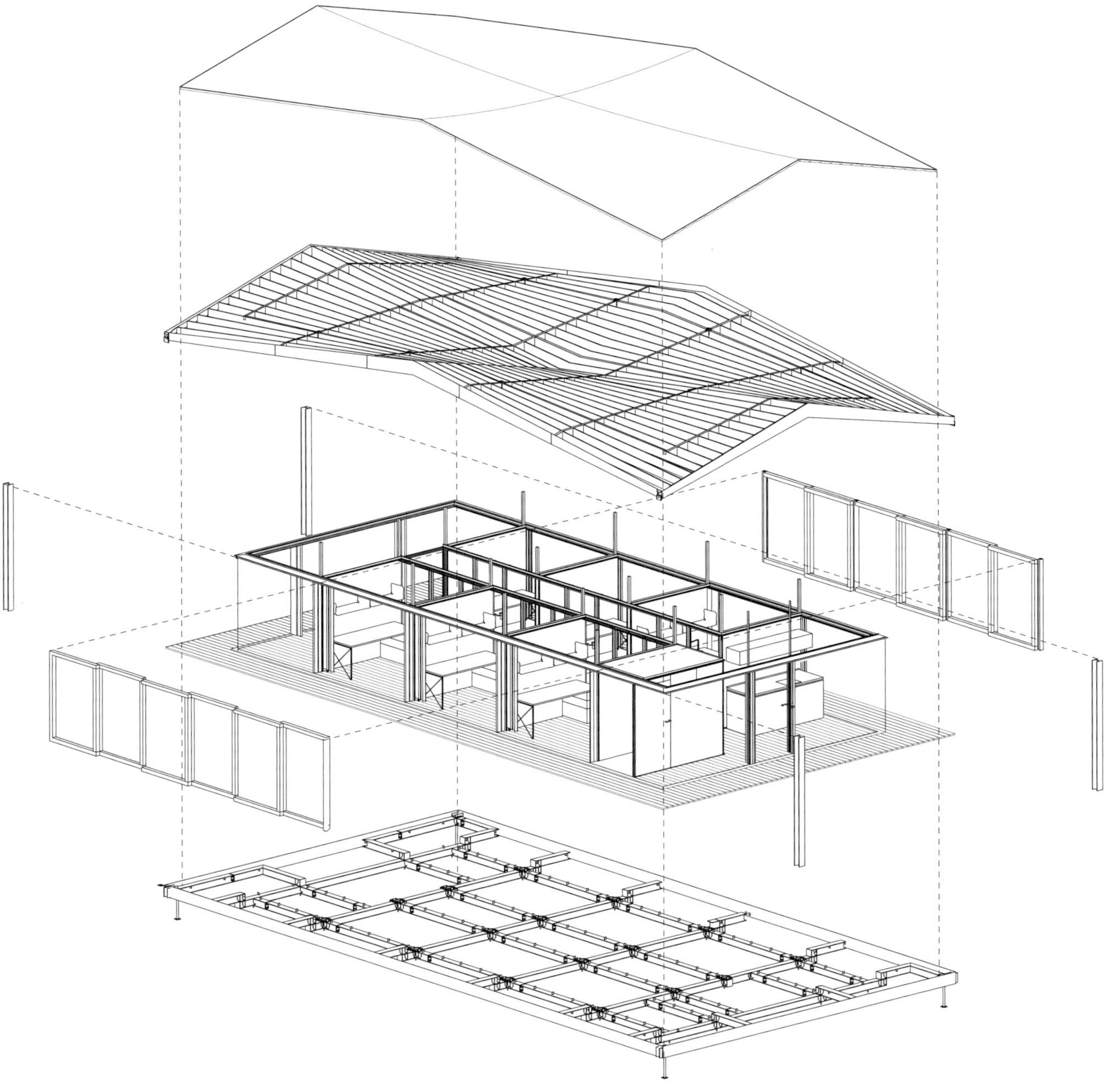

TRUMPF Pavilions
Grüsch, Switzerland, 2001 | 2004 | 2013

The three pavilions for TRUMPF Switzerland were built between 2001 and 2013 in Grüsch, in the Swiss canton of Graubünden, based on a long-term master plan. They were developed in collaboration with the engineer Jürg Conzett (Chur). The first and the second pavilions were built following the construction principle that the supporting structure should not be regarded as separate from the function of the building. Key to this thinking is the idea of structural depth as programmable space. Like a house of cards, the structure consists solely of plates and planes, without internal columns or lintels.

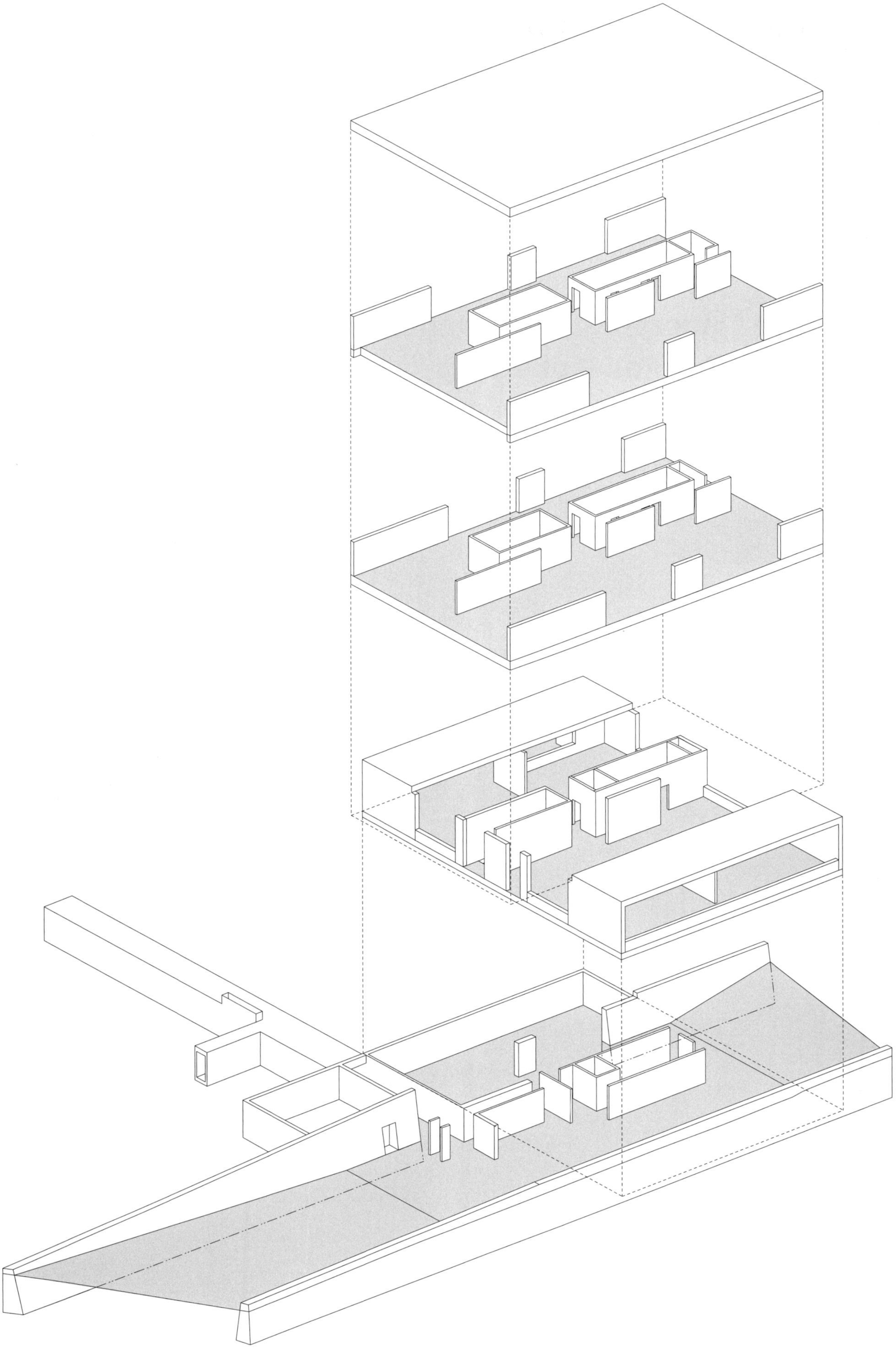

In Pavilion I, for Start-up Offices, the concrete wall plates are stacked on top of each other and connected to the ceiling planes directly above and below. This wall-and-ceiling system works like a self-supporting monocoque, facilitating large spans and flexibility in the division of internal space. The ground-floor building volume spans a ramped incline enclosed by two retaining walls. Placed above the ground-floor space at a right angle is a two-story volume, which in turn cantilevers at both ends. This system of stacked and rotating volumes produces terraces and covered areas.

While Pavilion I incorporates workshops, offices, conference rooms, and a cafeteria, Pavilion II operates like a separate, small factory on a site of similar size, containing rooms for research, development, production, and sales.

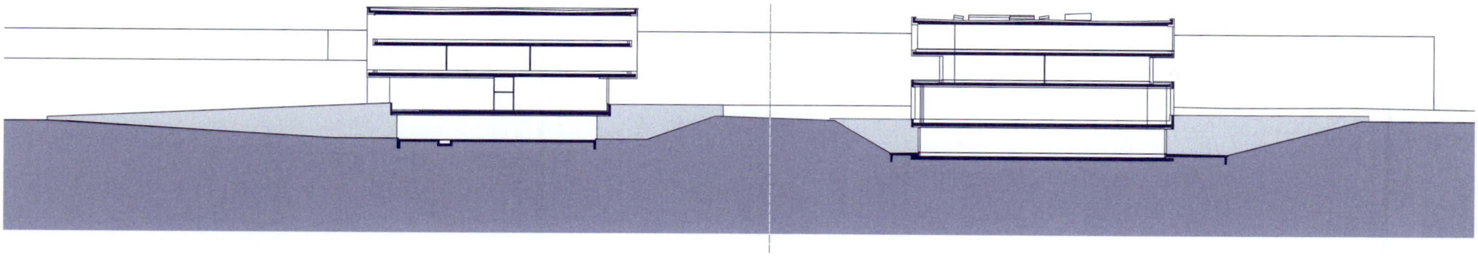

Unlike the first two buildings the third pavilion is a low-lying, freestanding, temple-like structure situated on a low concrete base. Like the two existing pavilions the new one is offset from the others to ensure views and open orientations from and to the spectacular valley. The siting of the building is emphasized by its placement in a grass-and-wildflower meadow on three sides, with the main entrance and service entrance facing the rear campus.

The flat roof is constructed by laying glu-laminated timber beams perpendicularly on top of each other, emphasizing the craft and logic of wood construction.

The massing and wood construction speaks of the alpine and agricultural/industrial context in which the building is situated. The roof construction cantilevers beyond the glass façades, aligned flush with the concrete base, creating a covered (from snow and rain) exterior walkway around the four sides of the building. In this way Pavilion III is very much a tectonic structure of additive and repetitive timber elements that convey the weight and substance of this sustainable material.

The timber roof and façade, in turn, rest on concrete columns and base. The (natural and stained) wood is complemented by galvanized-steel folding service doors and beam caps to prevent excessive weathering of the wood beams. On the east and the west sides the posts are doubled, so that they can "embrace" the purlins. The total construction time was less than one year; once the concrete columns were situated, the entire wooden structure of the roof could be completed within two weeks.

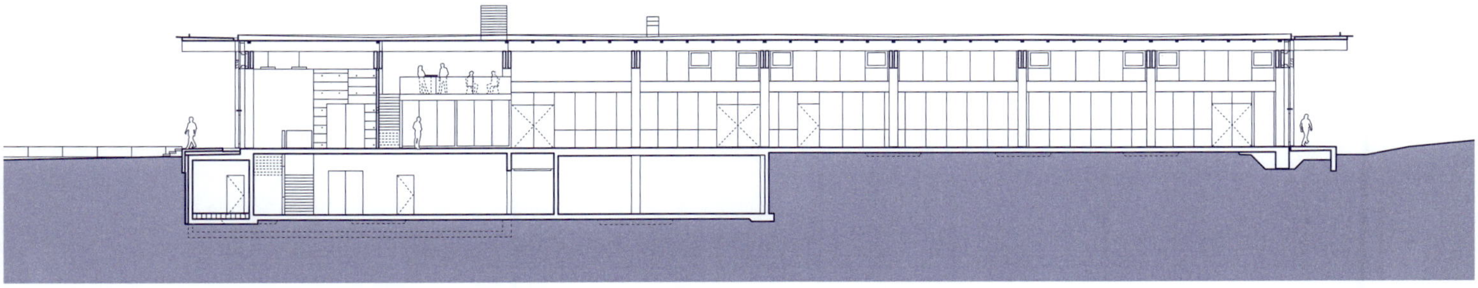

HAWE Factory
Kaufbeuren, Germany, 2014

This large, 50,000-square-meter factory in Bavaria facing the Alps is organized around a pinwheel plan surrounding a central, open-air courtyard garden for the company's 500 employees. The four large production spaces are roofed over by north-facing shed skylights that resolve across and down the façades as a triangulated patterns of transparent glass or translucent channel glass.

Extremely economical, the factory utilizes prefabricated concrete columns and beams (perforated, recalling the earlier work of Angelo Mangiarotti), allowing for rapid construction and low costs. Columns and beams are joined flush with a finger joint. The building massing is broken down into the distinct four halls, courtyard, and side yards in order to better scale the building to the landscape, views, and rural context.

Recalling as well the green factory (incremental growth along the highway with a strong relationship to the outdoors and countryside), the building scales down into smaller parts that can be added to over time, to better integrate it into the surroundings.

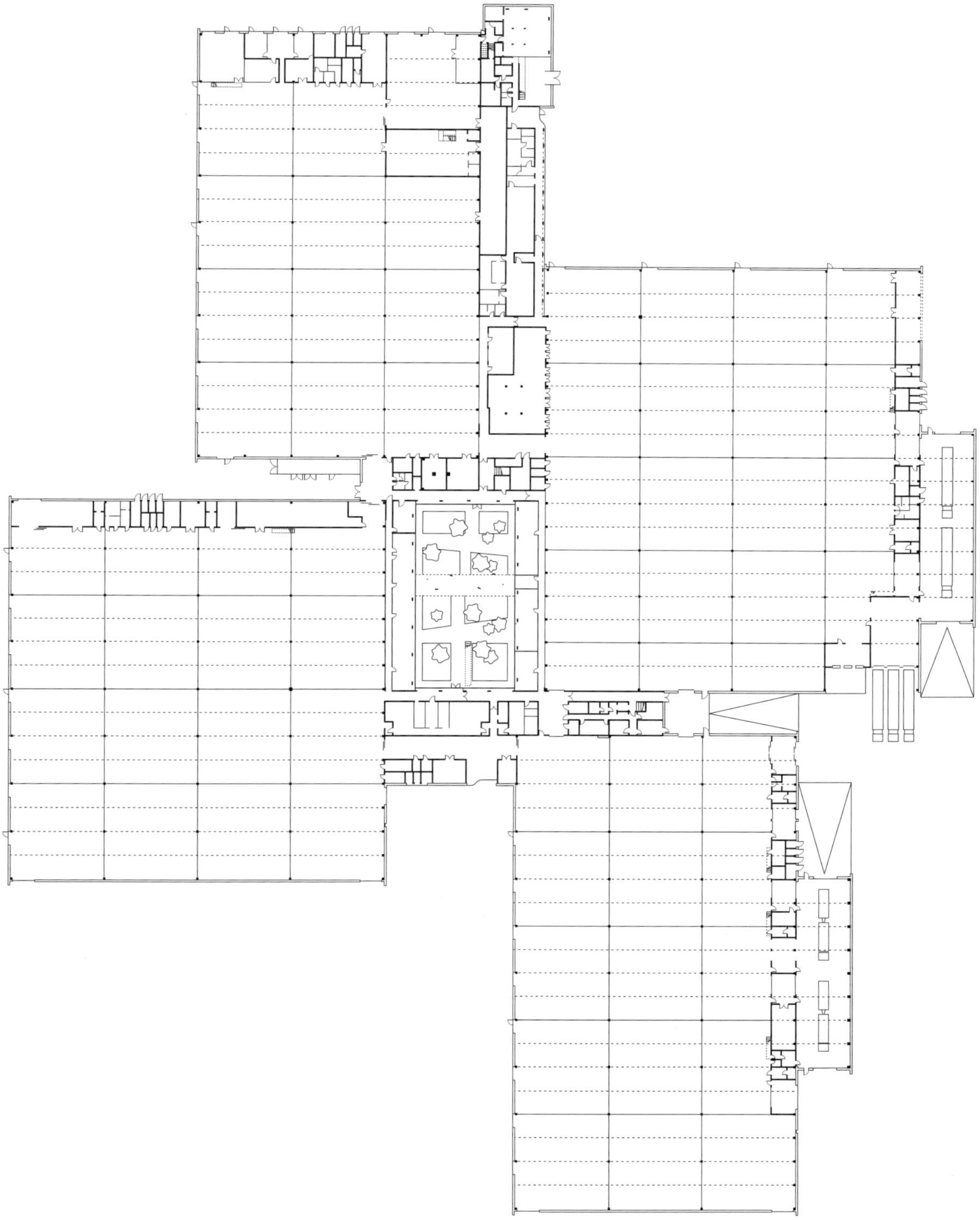

Smart Material House / Urban Living
Hamburg, Germany, 2010 / Berlin, Germany, 2014 (competition)

The Smart Material House (SMH) provides prototypical, flexible live-work housing. Infra-lightweight concrete is used as a multi-tasking construction element, which is self-insulated as it uses recycled foamed glass as an internal aggregate one-third the weight of conventional concrete. Offset by the combined use of wood construction, with its negative carbon impact, this building is able to approach a zero carbon material effect. The sculptural forms of the components provide a structurally self-supporting element, which spatializes internally and externally in dynamic fashion, shaping interior rooms and exterior loggias.

SMLXL

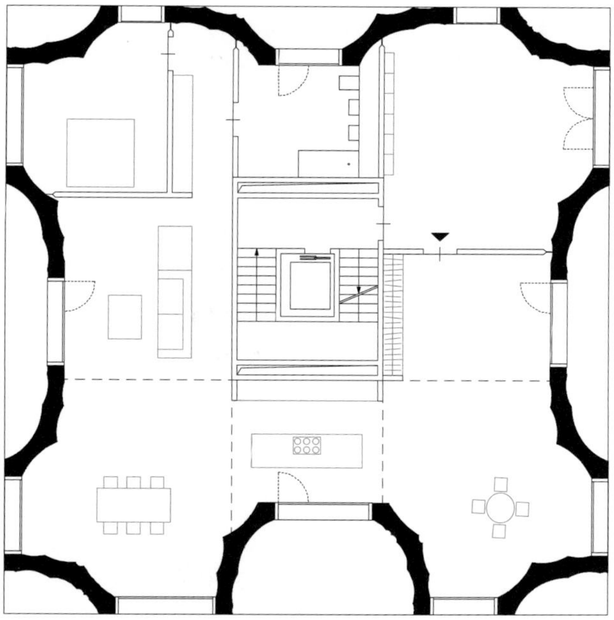

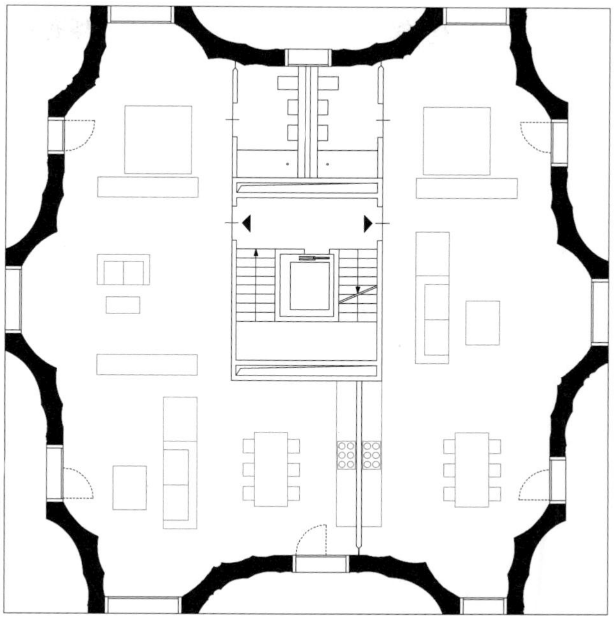

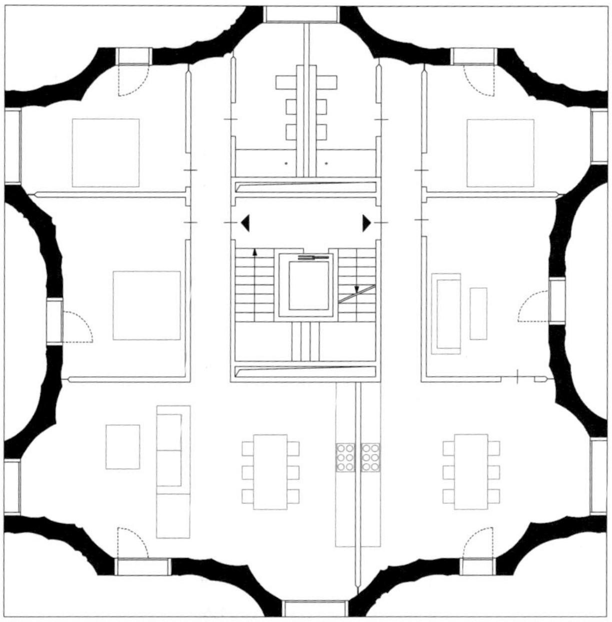

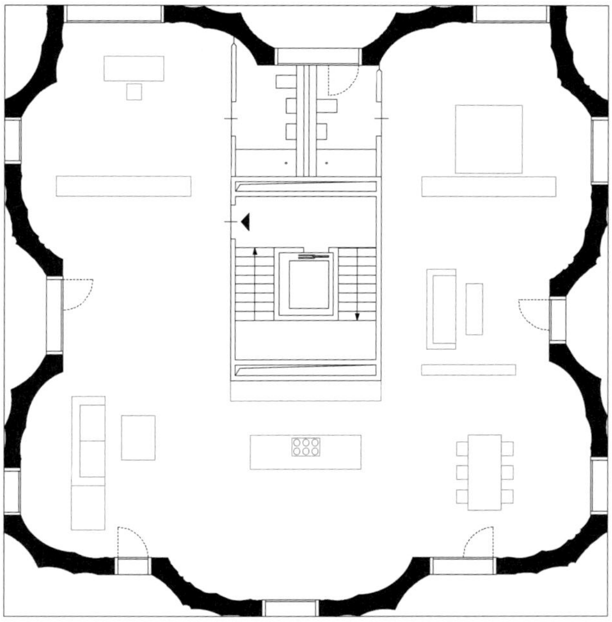

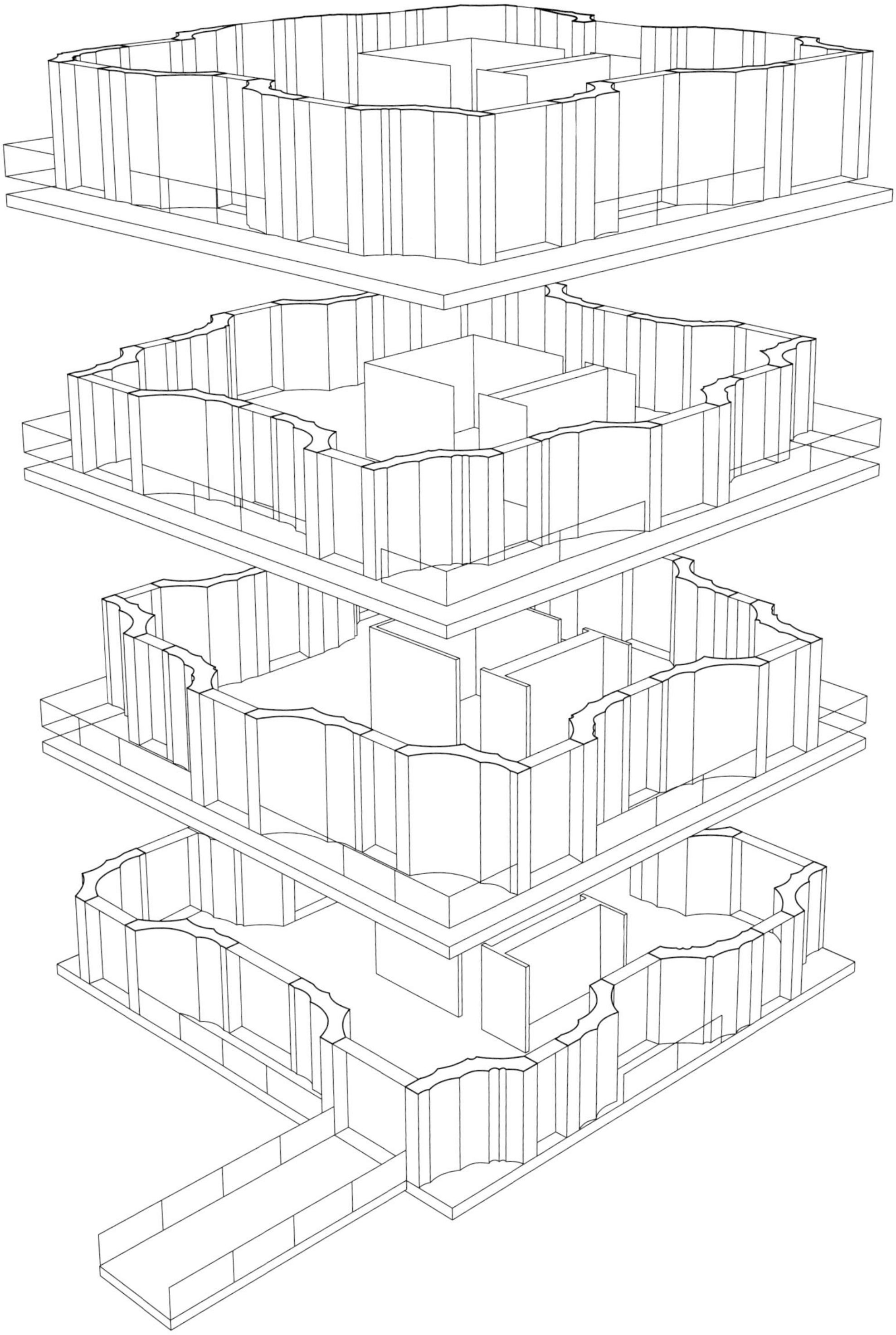

The concrete wall elements overlap and stagger as they stack on top of each other, generating a highly articulated, plastically modeled exterior. Wall-depth wood window frames with triple-insulated glass inserts complete the enclosure. Prize moneys from the European Holcim awards in 2011 enabled the construction of a 1:1 prototype, which in turn led to a Global Holcim Innovation prize in 2012.

U
Schillingstraße

park inn

A second initiative for this technical solution, the 2013 competition "Urban Living," called for affordable housing as prototypical point-towers along the Karl-Marx-Allee in Berlin. Construction here reconsiders the history of postwar *Plattenbau* (precast concrete) construction for mass social housing.

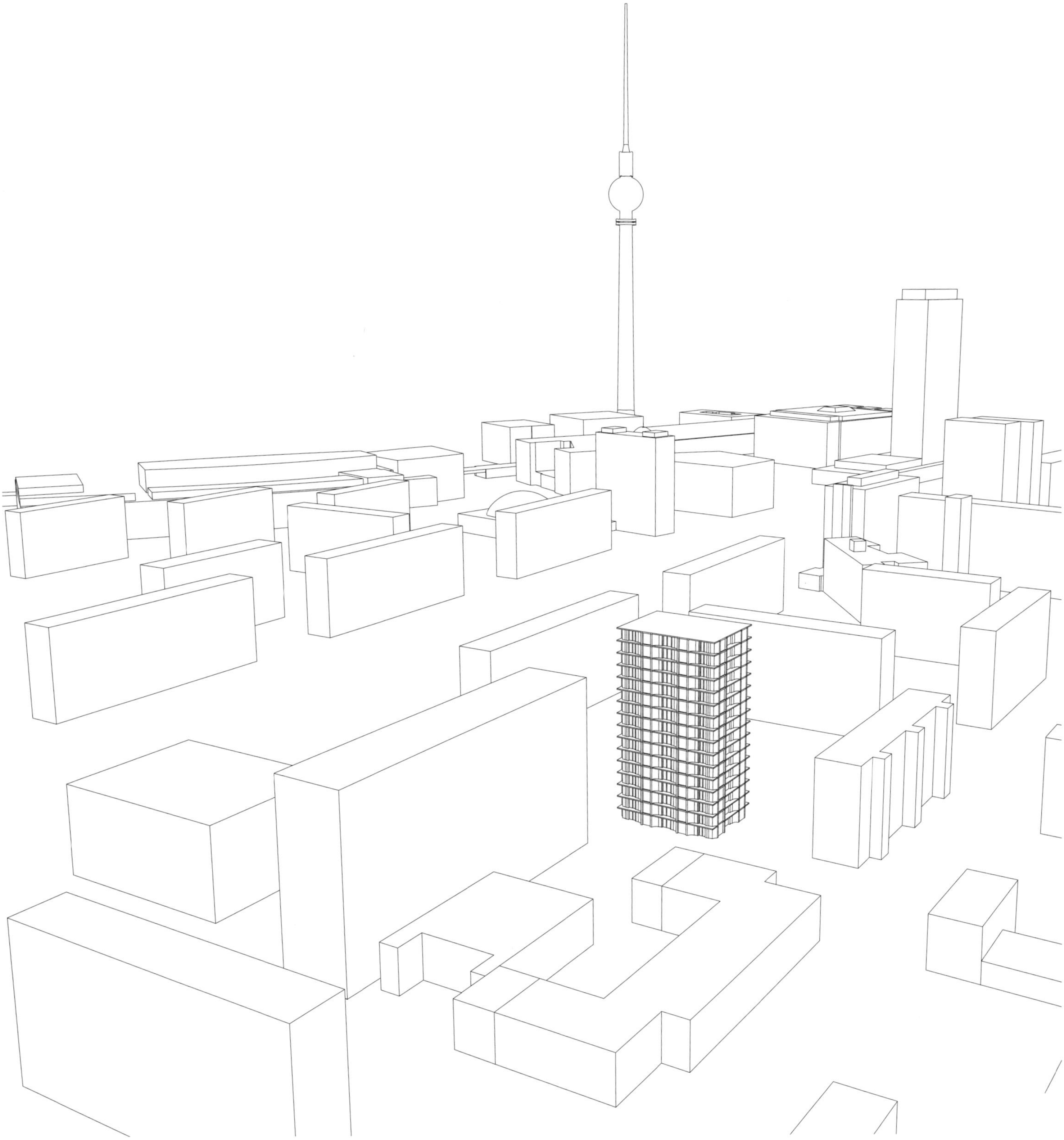

The proposal is flexible urbanistically, adding density where it can be placed within a multitude of *Plattenbau* neighborhood locations without blocking light and air while providing perimeter balconies, light, ventilation, and views for the structures' inhabitants. Apartments can easily be configured as open, loft living or in more traditional room layouts.

The construction concept—as with the Smart Material House—is being developed with Mike Schlaich. It embeds steel rods (vertical structural columns) into precast, intra-lightweight panels attached to concrete floor slabs. The low-density, infra-lightweight concrete (now non-load-bearing) has a much greater insulation value than the earlier Smart Material scheme for Hamburg. It not only lends fire protection to the steel rods but, by encasing them, also stiffens and thus prevents them from buckling. The wall panels, limited to one type, are stacked in-line, increasing the speed of construction and reducing costs.

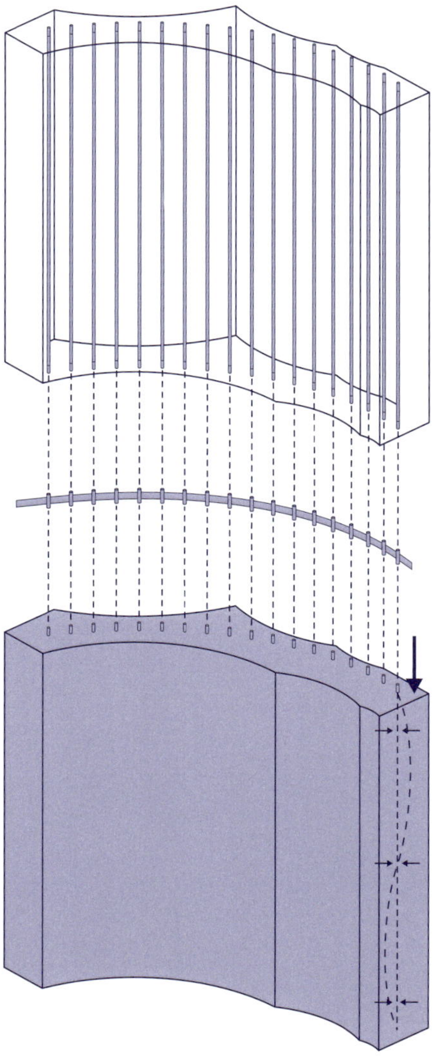

The Architecture Thinking of Barkow Leibinger
Brett Steele

> *Painting has nothing to do with thinking, because painting thinking is painting.*[1]
> —Gerhard Richter

I. Architecture's Episodic Reality

The serial structure of an architect's career is its most defining feature; it is architecture's way of thinking. Any architect's body of work is episodic: it unfolds iteratively, one project at a time; one project after another, over and over, during the many years constituting an architectural lifetime. Understood this way architecture thinking really is its doing. The architecture of Frank Barkow and Regine Leibinger recognizes and brilliantly leverages this fact in ways that are surprising, stunning, and original today.

Any architectural career is compiled by traversing a disjointed, dispersed, and random series of commissions. Architects have been aware of this fact since at least the time a young Roman named Vitruvius compiled into a single folio an uneven record and irregular collection of houses, bridges, aqueducts, column capitals, decorative elements, military machines, and other one-offs, out of which "Vitruvian" architecture was pronounced. "The random sequence of commissions on which each architect depends is the opposite of an agenda," wrote Rem Koolhaas in the introduction to *Content*, a 2004 monograph of his work. Koolhaas goes on from this mere observation to channel a familiar kind of millennial anxiety among architects, saying that "architecture is too slow . . . to address the world today."[2] From this standpoint it is a small leap from uncertainty to the outright dismissal of architecture's disciplinary necessity: "Architecture is a fuzzy amalgamation of ancient knowledge and contemporary practice, an awkward way to look at the world, and an inadequate medium to operate on it."[3]

By contrast, Barkow Leibinger's recent Smart Material House (SMH) asks us to think otherwise. It is a project that reveals the ways in which architecture thinking, when pursued in even its most constrained, traditional, and disciplinary sense (as work upon a single, bounded project, structure, or proposal), is anything but inadequate, most especially, in operating on, and not only looking at, some of the biggest challenges of our world. In the case of the SMH, this includes work on (among other things) no less daunting, topical, or even urgent an idea than that of the world's dwindling natural resources, which this building seeks to address in more ways than at first appear.

The SMH began its life in response to a straightforward, even unremarkable design competition for a building whose primary purpose (at least as imagined by its promoters) was simply to achieve a more energy efficient and affordable multi-story, multi-family dwelling for the *International Building Exhibition Hamburg* (2010), to address the ways that such structures normally consume huge, unacceptable amounts of energy. The original competition requirements defined most generalized cost parameters, site requirements, possible users or inhabitants, construction and other basic considerations. The project was constrained by little more than everyday definitions of a building's cost, performance, and build-ability (and, of course, the imagination of those considering these qualities).

Barkow Leibinger developed a project that even in its early stages went well beyond being a one-off design intended to "lower" energy costs in the building's projected future performance. Where this project is especially inventive is in the ways in which energy demands are assessed in relationship to its entire culture; not only vis-à-vis its future operation, but also in terms of the making, manufacturing, assembling, and delivering of the building's two primary construction systems. The project accomplishes these goals in several compelling ways. The use of infra-light, precast concrete vertical panels (so wide they can literally "stand" by themselves on the floors on which they are placed) is one of many smart advances. The energy demands related to the transportation and delivery of these elements, for example, are massively reduced owing to the panels' material advances alone (not to mention their considerable thermal performance, due to their consisting of porous, self-insulated elements). Even more remarkably, since the elements are self-standing and self-supporting, the considerable (always unseen) energy costs of fastening and assembling the building are also significantly reduced (as the main structural supports and scaffolding are entirely eliminated) further still.

I could go on and on here, summarizing an explanation the architects themselves have already provided about the depth of energy awareness and intelligence built into their beautiful prototype. But the topic of this essay is, you could say, another form of energy conservation entirely; the kind that allows us to see how the SMH draws upon the energy in architectural ideas, agendas, and interests of other (prior) projects. This, in the terms of the SMH, is the truly sustainable architecture of culture: that whereby the discipline of architecture sustains itself, over time, through the intelligence and ability of architects to appropriate, work upon, and advance prior forms of architecture thinking as their own.

How the SMH does this is unexpected and surprising. Barkow Leibinger look to the thinking of modern architecture's most iconic of all prototypes, Le Corbusier's Maison Dom-ino, and turn this century-old icon nearly inside out. Along the way Barkow Leibinger's SMH becomes an entirely new kind of prototype for its century. It is one that, knowingly, has been achieved by deliberately looking back to the very origins of modern architectural prototypes. Accordingly, the SMH is deliberately constrained by Barkow Leibinger in *its* forms of thought, becoming a disciplinary prototype, an architecture very much "about" architecture. It is that project that reveals to us the ways in which a genuinely narrow, disciplinary project in architecture today endures, remains vital, and can even—most surprising of all—now embrace those projects in modern architecture's past, like Dom-ino, that originally sought to break decisively with architectural history.

Barkow Leibinger rethink many of Dom-ino's most defining qualities, from the structure's foundations up. And Dom-ino is of course a project that is foundational in another sense entirely, having long circulated as the single most famous image (of an unbuilt project, no less) throughout the twentieth century; it is a project whose presence helped found the very identity of architecture. For many architects a project like Dom-ino feels, a century after its origin, somewhat tired, even irrelevant in the early twenty-first century. The SMH, on the other hand, disagrees with that sense of historicism, deflecting key parts of Dom-ino and making them malleable, while fundamentally rejecting others of its most defining qualities—not least of which is its early modern dependence upon inflexible repetition. Dom-ino's rigid, Euclidian lattice, its identical columns, its unrelenting isolation of vertical movement, and its uniform concrete slabs are all upgraded in ways that make the original nearly unrecognizable. They are nonetheless still present in the SMH's insistence that we see the organization of a universally applicable, superstructural frame, one whose principles and features are formed by close attention to the limits of contemporary constructional possibilities. While considerably manipulating material and compositional features to the point of their near disappearance, SMH nonetheless reinforces the original's fateful, universalizing impulses of modern architecture, achieved here in truly new and profound, even moving, ways.

The SMH renders its constituent elements with new form and purpose, achieved by integrating entirely new, advanced building materials, fabrication methods, and appearance. In the place of Le Corbusier's skeletal steel and concrete elements, Barkow Leibinger loosens the grip on its grid (allowing for subtle forms of a non-repetitive alignment and placement of its vertical elements, especially). The project softens Dom-ino's dependence upon pure repetition and varies the spacing and placement of the three superstructural systems comprising the whole (they are the same three systems in Dom-ino: vertical support, horizontal inhabitation, and contained vertical circulation). The longish, clam-shaped, vertical concrete support panels do not need to sit exactly on top of one another (requiring only enough overlap with those above and below to allow forces to be passed through each floor successively). The stair system can as well move to different parts of the plan, unlike Le Corbusier's insistence that this element always sit in the same party-wall or end-wall location. And the monolithic, massive slabs of the SMH are no longer concrete, having become—incredibly—solid engineered timber. The result is that each of these three key elements in the system add up in entirely new, fundamental and didactic ways. The effect is startling.

What was in Dom-ino a system of regular vertical elements, uniformly integrated with a series of stacked and identical, monolithic horizontal slabs, becomes in the SMH a combinatory system (within limits) capable of being rearranged and generating a world of differentiated units within an overall non-repetitive envelope containing subtly shifting, unique spaces and plan arrangements. This surprising outcome is the result of how two very different, even competing material systems interact, in ways that completely reject the presumed material uniformity of steel and concrete that was both the premonition of Le Corbusier's Dom-ino and its afterlife, in the form of still-common design and building assumptions today. As already mentioned, the first of these material systems is the lightweight, clam-shaped, concrete vertical panel/support (taking the place of Dom-ino's undifferentiated, non-directional columns). The second is a massive, entirely solid and heavy, timber floor plate made as a single, engineered component. The effect of these two disparate elements, and their chosen material realms, is surprising and stunning; not only as a new kind of universalizing architectural system, but also for the ways it makes us instantly see and comprehend Dom-ino (and a select few other like-minded experiments like it) very differently.

This is especially the case with the SMH's distinctive, thickened and curved, lightweight concrete shells, strange elements that operate as both columns and partitions. These single-story-high, lightweight concrete panels are modular, regular, and modern in purpose, and (thanks especially to their vertical fluting) tactile, almost Corinthian in appearance. They are prefabricated at a factory off-site, in a controlled environment that allows for extensive testing, holistic and integrated manufacture, and easy transport. Once delivered to the building site the system, without fittings, allows for speedy erection. Made by pouring concrete into vertical, milled formwork arranged on the factory floor, and fed by controllable, robotic machinery, these elements are grabbed and stood up (remaining standing without additional support) to turn into the fully finished vertical elements that are in the house, where they also operate as high-performance thermal, structural, and spatial components. Lightweight, insulating concrete aggregates (clay or foam glass) and cement are combined together and, along with other building systems (heating or cooling conduit), are embedded directly into the panels, as are the self-contained structural reinforcements. The result is an integrated building material/system hybrid that is of considerable logic, energy demand, responsiveness, and cost efficiency. This is especially evident when we contrast this preformed, precise system with the sloppy, freewheeling, and unpredictable ways that concrete/steel frames are typically formed, poured, and built on site today.

These vertical panels serve as internal support and spatial subdivision, and are deployed as the building's external enclosure as well. As mentioned above, these vertical panels stand directly upon the solid timber slabs dividing each floor of the building. This remarkable inversion of modern building materials—the placing of big, relatively heavy, concrete elements atop and supported by a wooden floor (itself pre-made as an element of engineered wooden timber) is ingenious; the project reverses an entire century's habit of establishing first a monolithic concrete "frame" as the requisite support within which wood and other "finish" materials are added to render an architectural object. In the SMH that logic, like so many others of Le Corbusier's Dom-ino, is so effectively inverted or revised that we can see it, as a project, as a very different kind of platform for living than that about which its author wrote a century ago. For Barkow Leibinger, projects are treated as the platforms they always potentially remain; the superstructure for future, like-minded projects. Mason Dom-ino can now be seen to be a platform.

II. The Project as Platform

Barkow Leibinger organize their studio in ways that seek to deliberately curate their many kinds of research. This includes not only their research into new building materials and fabrication technologies, but also the modern genealogy of projects and prototypes engaged in that very same undertaking. This side of the Barkow Leibinger's studio has been the subject of separate publications, exhibitions, and installations, and therefore is not our immediate focus in this essay.[4] The studio tests, charts, and studies the free flow of ideas and architectural thinking available not only within their own growing archive but also throughout the legacy of modern architectural experimentation that gave rise (and reason) to former examples. In this way the architecture thinking of Barkow Leibinger is a knowingly bounded one; it is a world of inquiry where any concept of a building's material, structure, fabrication, form, or even its performance is anything but abstract. For them, concepts like these are only ever observable: they are qualities and not just limitations or possibilities revealed through the close examination of prior episodes and projects, both their own and others.[5]

I have written elsewhere on Barkow Leibinger's elegant, faceted, glass TRUTEC Building (completed in the Digital Media City, in Seoul, Korea, in 2006). In the context of this essay, TRUTEC can be cited as another example of how the firm's architects systematically discipline their pursuit and production of knowledge. Despite its nearly opposite overall appearance, form, construction materials, geographical location, and brief, in comparison to the SMH, TRUTEC nonetheless establishes a relationship between itself and another iconic modernist project, Mies van der Rohe's Friedrichstrasse skyscraper of 1921. At TRUTEC this relationship is the means for directing its expertise and command of incredibly advanced, highly controllable digital Korean robotics and cutting systems, which the project uses to manufacture and assemble a delirious, iterative yet non-repetitive, rippled glass exterior that does to Mies's tower what the SMH does to Dom-ino, conceived in 1914.

I detour briefly here, however, with the brief description of the TRUTEC Building for a different reason: to show how Barkow Leibinger always operate in close, conscious relationship to other projects. It is precisely the many outright oppositions between TRUTEC and the SMH—in the willful differences the architects promote, especially in terms of appearances, but also in the realms of assembly, geography, inhabitation, and program—that reveal to us that something larger is going on here. Barkow Leibinger are architects that ignore entirely the kind of familiar, stylistic bias for portraying continuity within architecture thinking—the familiar kind of Richard Meier-esque attempts to make appearances within an oeuvre uniform, consistent, and recognizable from one project to the next. By contrast Barkow Leibinger, by nesting each of these two recent projects in relation to an earlier (now, century old even!) structure, stress forms of continuity that are entirely disciplinary. It is an unexpected project, in an era when many proclaim that architecture must expand beyond its known disciplinary borders if it is to remain relevant in a world of global uncertainties.

III. Knowledge within an Expanded Architectural Field

Rem Koolhaas's observation, mentioned at the outset of this essay, regarding architecture's limited capacity to intervene in a larger, more complex world leads him to a Houdini-like attempt at escaping architecture's limits: "Architecture needs to be liberated," he writes, "from the obligation to construct . . . in order to become a way of thinking about anything . . . everything."[6] Ours is an era when nearly every possible cultural, commercial, or intellectual pursuit is being packaged up (in everything from *Wired* magazine to contemporary cultural studies curricula, graduate design studios, and countless Silicon Valley business plans) in a world of increasingly blurred boundaries. At a time when interdisciplinary cultural studies, like the promiscuities of most research universities, make the very idea of a distinct, stable, purposeful "discipline" almost unthinkable, the architecture thinking of Barkow Leibinger offers a rare demonstration of its enduring possibility. Their thinking is at odds with a more generalized architectural expansionism that has as perhaps its most striking features those of the architectural profession's accelerating globalization.

A 2014 compendium illustrates the globally expansionist tendency well. In his editorial introduction to *Forensis: The Architecture of Public Truth* (a book whose authors claim seeks to "aestheticize global conflict," whatever that might mean) Eyal Weizman asserts that architecture thinking is (to the extent there still is such a thing) more like a point of view than a way of working or a body of experience. It is, in his view, more like a "tool": an "approach" for looking at *other* things or events in the world. Undoubtedly architecture can be used this way; but the question remains, for architecture, why? Most importantly, what does this shift in mentality afford architecture, as a means for thinking itself anew? Calling for a kind of architecture "concerned not only with buildings but rather with an ever-changing set of relations between people and things, mediated by spaces and structures across multiple scales"[7] presumes, of course, that it is possible to pursue the design and making of buildings in ways *without* this imagined mediation. Weizman, like Koolhaas a decade before, naturalizes architecture's disciplinary knowledge as inadequate for looking at the larger world: "Architecture had a modest start: it was inspired by the unassuming work of building surveyors."[8] The goal here, simply, is to expand the possible domain of architecture thinking, so that architecture's doing is no longer essential. It has somehow become merely a way of seeing.

This architectural expansionism is found in the very title of another recent article, this one first published by Anthony Vidler in 2004, titled "Architecture in an Expanded Field." The essay notes that after "several decades of self-imposed autonomy" architecture has been recently "woken up"; not so much by new ideas in architecture as by "new formal and programmatic inspiration in a host of disciplines and technologies, from landscape design to digital animation."[9] While Vidler registers rumblings about a possible recovery of "the discipline," his and this present essay's attention is clearly elsewhere: on these other social, material, or even environmental conditions that he understands as existing "outside" architecture and considers important enough that architects need to move beyond a mere awareness to a mastery of them.[10]

Architects have long struggled to articulate and convey the nature and limits of reason for their forms of knowledge, their ways of thinking, which they and other like-minded audiences continue to treat as architecture. Two millennia after Vitruvius first struggled to give this thinking a form and name in his *Ten Books,* Le Corbusier revisited this impulse in modern form, in his *Towards a New Architecture.*[11] In this summary account Le Corbusier pursues with unflinching attention architecture's most basic material properties as the means to locate (even his modern, revolutionary) architecture: "mass and surface are the elements by which architecture manifests itself."[12] How these are to be configured in a modern world is for Barkow Leibinger, as it was for Le Corbusier before them, exactly what matters most. In an early act of modern rebellion and architectural premonition about the growing influence and impact of outside forms of knowledge on modern knowledge, Le Corbusier observes elsewhere in *Towards a New Architecture* that "the American engineers overwhelm with their calculations our expiring architecture."[13] A century on from Le Corbusier's wry concern and his means of using building engineering as a way to buttress his larger interest in creating his Maison Dom-ino—that is, as a weapon for eradicating architecture's own history and past—Barkow Leibinger invert Dom-ino's formula in a surprising, paradoxical, and unexpected twist. By directing their own thinking toward the resurrection of this increasingly historical project, they take recourse in the ultimate revenge available to any truly disciplinary pursuit: its ability to make historical even the most revolutionary impulses of modern architecture itself. The work and thinking of Frank Barkow and Regine Leibinger remind us that the most stable and enduring building material of all is that of the relationships any project constructs between itself and those predating it. In a time like ours, dominated as it is by a boundless faith in what only ever seems to be an increasingly unknowable future, architecture's serial reality—the inevitability that every project will ultimately be succeeded by another—could yet prove to be its most durable fact. Just maybe, the seriality of architecture thinking is proving more valuable than ever.

1 Gerhard Richter, "Notes, 1962," in *Gerhard Richter: Text, Writings, Interviews and Letters. 1961–2007,* ed. Gerhard Richter, Dietmar Elger, and Hans Ulrich Obrist (London, 2009), p. 15.

2 Rem Koolhaas, "Contents," in *Content* (Cologne, 2004), p. 20.

3 Ibid.

4 See a statement by the architects on the role of sustained research within the office, in "An Atlas of Fabrication," in *Barkow Leibinger: An Atlas of Fabrication,* ed. Frank Barkow and Regine Leibinger (London, 2009).

5 Brett Steele, "Atlas-Tectonics," in *Barkow Leibinger: Bricoleur Bricolage,* ed. Frank Barkow and Brett Steele (London, 2013), pp. 1–2. Conceived as an atlas of design research interests at Barkow Leibinger, and a collection of works modeled upon one of the most influential art projects/publications of our era (Gerhard Richter's *Atlas,* beg. mid-1960s), this monograph suggests the ready explanation of why I chose the epigram I did to open this present essay a year later.

6 Ibid., p. 20.

7 Eyal Weizman, introduction to *Forensis: The Architecture of Public Truth,* ed. Forensic Architecture (Berlin, 2014), p. 13.

8 Weizman goes on to use such a vantage for his own self-declared purpose documented in his catalogue, which by one account seeks only to record "a material geology of contemporary conflict," which, in Weizman's account, is someone made possible by deploying the ways architects think to uncover this "geology." Ibid., pp. 13–14.

9 Anthony Vidler, "Architecture's Expanded Field: Finding Inspiration in Jellyfish and Geopolitics," in *Artforum* 42, no. 8 (April 2004), p. 142.

10 Ibid., p. 143.

11 Le Corbusier, *Towards a New Architecture,* English introduction by Frederick Etchells (London, 1931), pp. 21–31.

12 Ibid., p. 26.

13 Ibid., p. 31.

The idea of existing substance (architectural, infrastructural, urban landscape, or material) as a valuable currency continues to gain momentum in a time when a term like "sustainability" has taken on many meanings. What architect Sverre Fehn once called "a dance around dead things" refers to how museums interact with content, historical objects, art, and its many forms. It is a term, however, that could also be applied to how architects interact with what is usually referred to as "existing." "Makeover" is not an idea of restoration as a historically accurate and dutiful return to an original condition (think Villa Tugendhat by Mies van der Rohe); rather, it is the idea of a dialogue in which an existing condition is transformed, superseded, or projected beyond its purpose-built origins. Makeovers are projects that renovate, add to, change, or transform existing things.

Makeover is a strategy that encompasses observation, valuation, and exploitation, setting up a delicate dialogue between the existing and the new. Artist-architects like Gordon Matta Clark or Carlo Scarpa have revealed new architectural possibilities (spatially and syntactically) by re-mapping old buildings, radically shifting them from their original intent. An existing building here acts like a host, where an operational choreography animates them anew.

Which forces are afoot that drive decision-making when confronted with *Sanierung* (rehabilitation measures) or regeneration, be it of a building or an entire urban precinct? Functional imperatives are always at the fore, be they programmatic reorientations, phasing timelines, or technical advances, as in the goal of restoration to delay or stop a building's inevitable decay or aging. Technical restoration also speaks about how a building performs: its energy use and environmental mediation, how it conditions the elements, like sun and weather, addresses ventilation and acoustics, and supports a sense of well-being for its occupants.

Formal ambitions include spatial, density, structural, and material transformations and how they interface with existing substance and make it over again.

Makeover comes to the forefront culturally where scarcity, sustainability, (re)use value, and economic limits in our cities and industrial peripheries (no postwar tabula rasa possible) force us to revalue and reappropriate "dead things" with new vitality and urgency.

Training Center
Neukirch, Germany, 2005

A former stall on the TRUMPF Campus in Neukirch, Saxony, was renovated and significantly expanded. Architecturally it retains its historic form of a gable-roofed, agricultural building. In this sense the building mediates formally between the adjacent farm buildings off-site and the industrial buildings on-site.

The new building consists of three historical buildings, built in 1910, 1980, and 2005, like a literal timeline. This telescoping form is unified by a continuous skin of zinc shingles. Punched wooden windows are similar to those of the vernacular houses nearby. Two large, cutout terraces framed in larch complement these oversized windows.

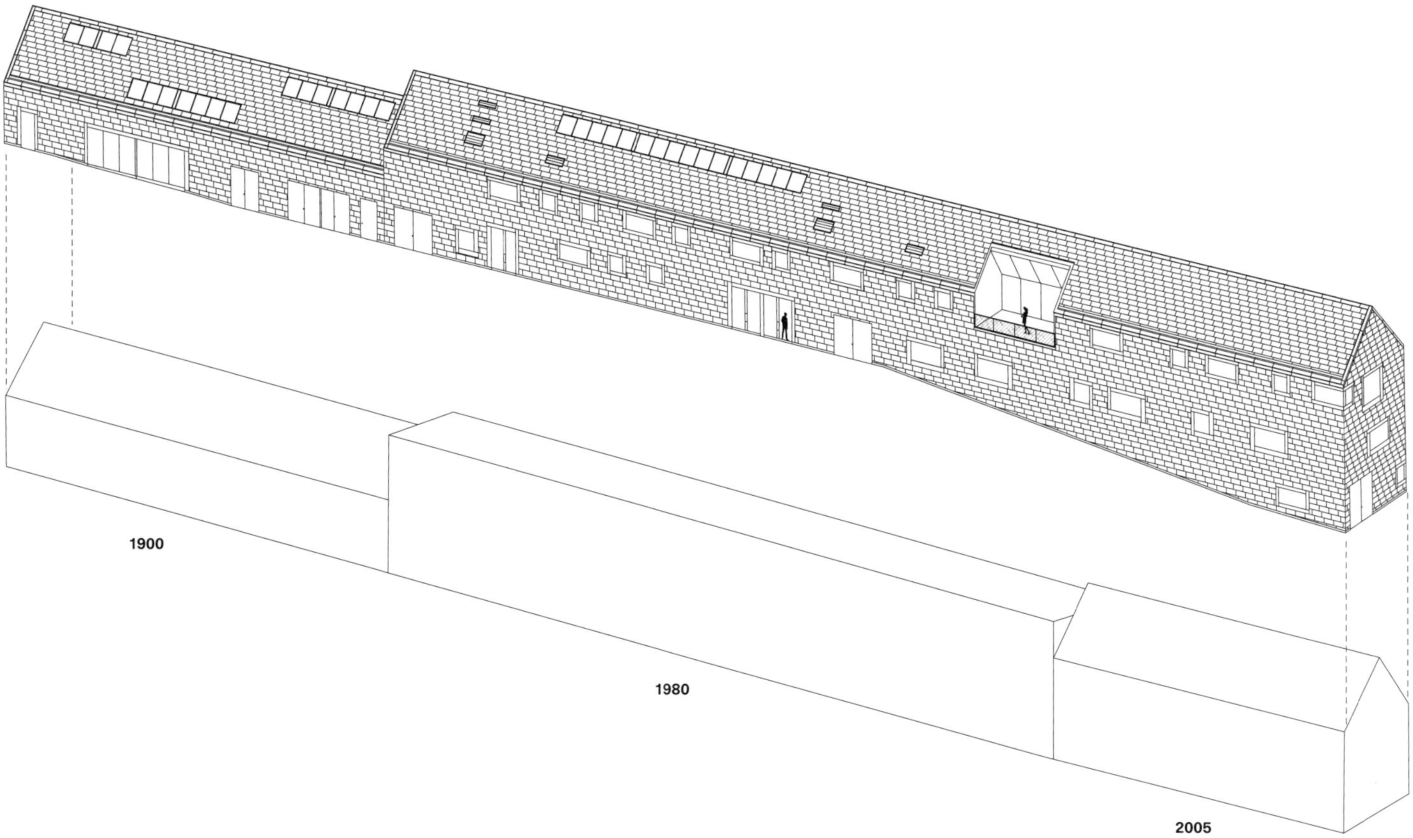

Structurally the new gable form is framed by steel-tube arches, which are spanned by hollow wooden plank-beams. Programmatically this structure houses training rooms and a loft-like cafeteria on the upper level. As a long, lineal building it forms a cohesive edge, defining the campus' west boundary while framing the terraced space between itself and the paint shop. A terraced landscape is added to the west and a small park for leisure to the north.

Service Training Center
Ditzingen, Germany, 2007

With the acquisition of an existing spice factory built in the 1970s TRUMPF was able to expand their training facilities to this 18,000-square-meter space located on their east campus in Ditzingen. This structure was reclaimed sustainably into their campus by retaining the existing production hall, bracketed by an extension of a three-story office bar to the south and the creation of a double-height entrance and exhibition hall.

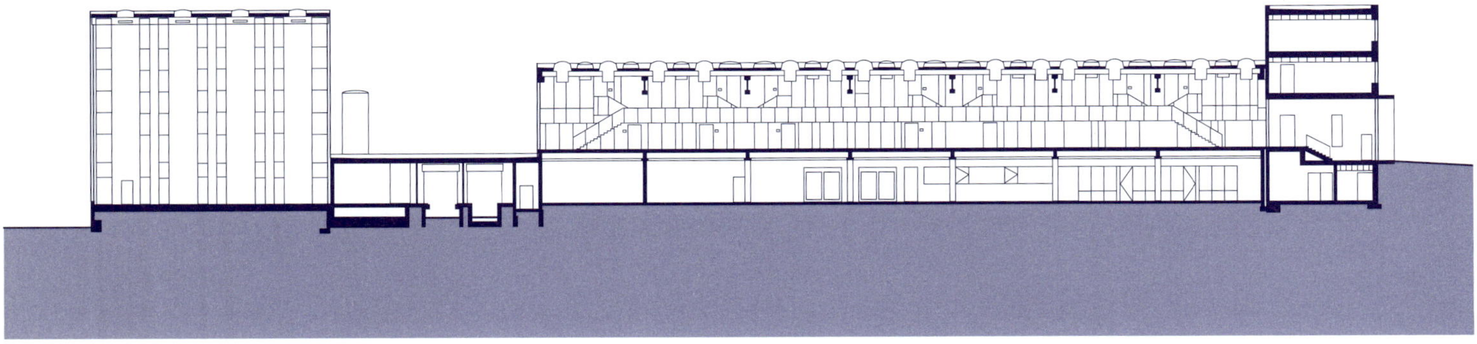

A new, double-height façade opens up the previously closed production hall to the new access road and landscape promenade, while the new, three-story office bar "bookends" to the existing high-storage volume on the north. The existing façades clad in corrugated aluminum are complemented and contrasted by a mix of anodized, brown metal panels and reflective-mirrored glass. Inside, along the new entrance lobby, warm timber surfaces and colored glass panels contrast with the exposed existing concrete roof-beams between which new classrooms weave in and out.

SMOCKSHOP BERLIN

Sprüth Magers
Berlin, Germany, 2009

This historical building, constructed in the mid-1800s and located in Berlin-Mitte, lies prominently to the south, across from the "Museum Island." A former men's club with ballroom under landmark status it has been renovated as an office building with a prominent gallery for Sprüth Magers and their offices and archives on the first, second, and basement levels.

The ensemble revolves around a central courtyard, while the double-height ballroom opens up to a garden and courtyard to the north. This space now serves as an immense, north-lit, seven-meter-high gallery flanked by smaller galleries on two levels. An inserted concrete corridor with new steel stair links the spaces together.

The front-of-house, facing the street, gained two new levels, added in the attic, while retaining the historical volume and façade articulation. The entrance at the side reconstitutes the historical entrance and passage leading directly to the former ballroom in the back. This space has been reopened to its original size and dimensions, is flexible in its use, and has been hung with the work of the artists Andreas Gursky, Cindy Sherman, and Fischli/Weiss. In kind, the additional spaces are used flexibly for open or cellular office purposes. A third use of a storefront shop for art film and DVDs opens to the street.

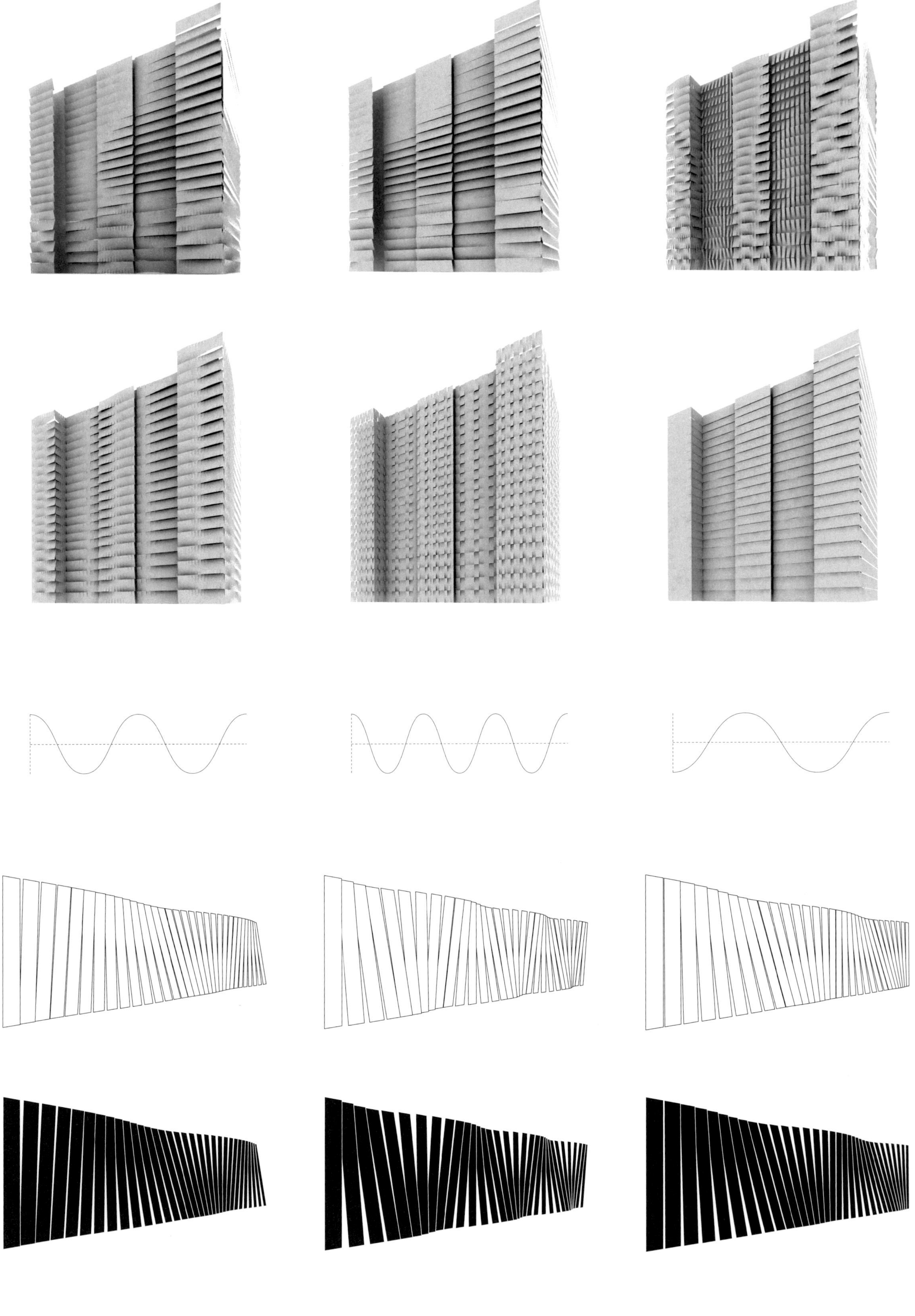

Charité
Berlin, Germany, 2012 (competition)

A façade competition for the Charité Hospital in Berlin has been a research opportunity to propose a new façade over the existing building, which dates back to the former East Germany, in order to improve its sustainable performance and aesthetic appearance. This "skin-job" solution is a very simple and economic grid of reflective glazing panels, which are either spandrel elements over opaque insulation or a transparent acoustical shield placed over a conventional, operable room window. By variably tilting the glass in the assembly frame up or down an enormous range of visual surface effects can be achieved, mimicking DNA patterns at the scale of the entire building. In this way the monumental, singular volume of the hospital within the Berlin skyline is transformed into an enigmatic, ever-changing form and image.

Berliner Currywurst
Imbiss
Berliner Currywurst
Imbiss
Kaffeespezialitäten

CHARITÉ
Express Schönefeld

NO
STOPPING
Cambridge Trust
Company

Smith Campus Center
Harvard University, Cambridge, Massachusetts, USA, 2013
(competition)

This request for proposal asked for a new campus center at, and a façade restoration of Josep Lluís Sert's Holyoke Center in Cambridge, Massachusetts. By creating a glazed-in atrium at Holyoke's Massachusetts Avenue address, a number of ideas and solutions were offered. A large urban room serves as Harvard's front door. This glazed-in space can be occupied in all weather. The new glass façade and roof construction of the Living Room generates a legible dialogue between new and old, transparent and ephemeral, physical and material. Such a structure has the additional benefit of providing a sustainable, environmental, seasonal "buffer." By reinstalling Mark Rothko's *Harvard Murals* (commissioned by the university in 1962) to their former and site-specific location the building becomes a cultural and artistic magnet and attraction. This can anchor additional programs at the roof level for galleries for Harvard students as well as visiting artists, and a café and lounge overlooking Harvard Yard.

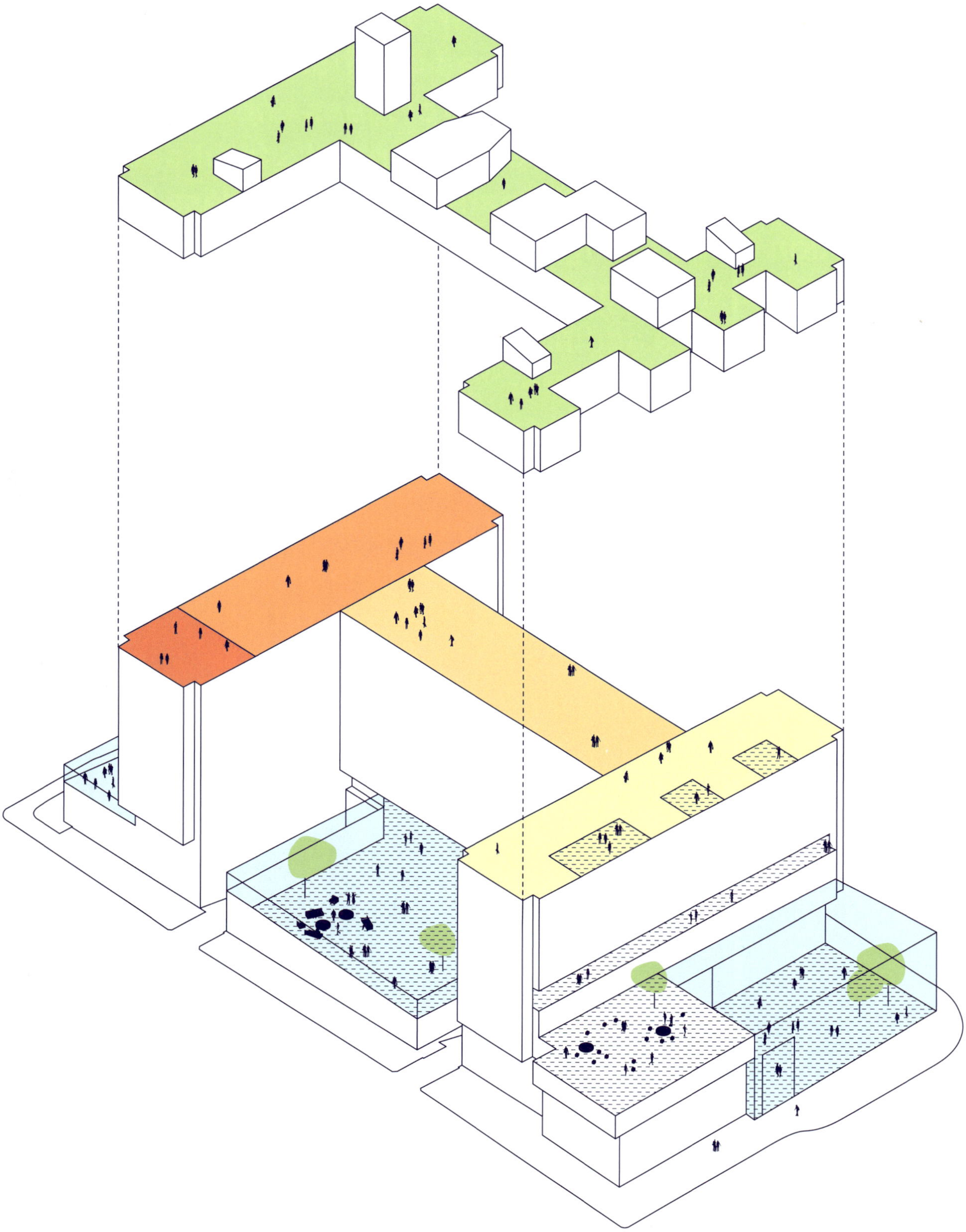

ICC-Kolonie
Berlin, Germany, 2014

The ICC (International Congress Center), a colossal, mega-structure that opened in 1979 in Berlin-West as part of the Berlin trade-fair center, is now obsolete and empty of use. A fascinating urban artifact at the scale of infrastructure, the ICC is located between the autobahn and garden allotment dwellings. As initiated by the *Berlin Morgenpost* (daily newspaper) a call for ideas sought new concepts for the structure's adaptive reuse.

Given the need for affordable housing in Berlin's current market, the ICC-Kolonie proposal has developed an idea for reconfiguring the vast interior of the ICC with stacked live-work modules that frame a central atrium garden. The operable roof attached to the existing truss construction enables a biotope climate in cold weather that can open to the sun and air in warm weather. The vertically stacked dwellings form a kind of topographical city with orientations toward the central green garden or from the exterior façades out toward the city. In this way a sheltered, quiet interior coexists with the exterior of the building, without undergoing dramatic alterations to its form or volume.

Mühle Grüsch
Switzerland, 2014 (design study)

The former mill building is a landmark in the picturesque Swiss alpine village of Grüsch. It consists of a thirty-two-meter-tall silo and a lower, four-story loft building, begun as an ensemble in the late 1930s. No longer in use the buildings are to be renovated for housing and a combined boarding house and exhibition space in the loft building.

LIETHA + CIE AG GRÜSCH
MÜHLEN LIETHA AG

A central strategy for the silo building is to retain the thin concrete exterior shell and to brace it with a new concrete skeleton frame to act as a corset to strengthen the tower once the interior grain shafts are removed. The interior is organized around a new structural and circulation core. A series of cascading platforms spiral upward and around the core, defining living spaces that are flexible: they can expand or contract up or down the spiral as needed. The apartments themselves are articulated as split level and oriented sectionally, with views both down toward the valley and up toward the mountains. Each unit has an exterior loggia, which is carved out of the tower mass, with larger units organized at the top of the tower with rooftop terraces.

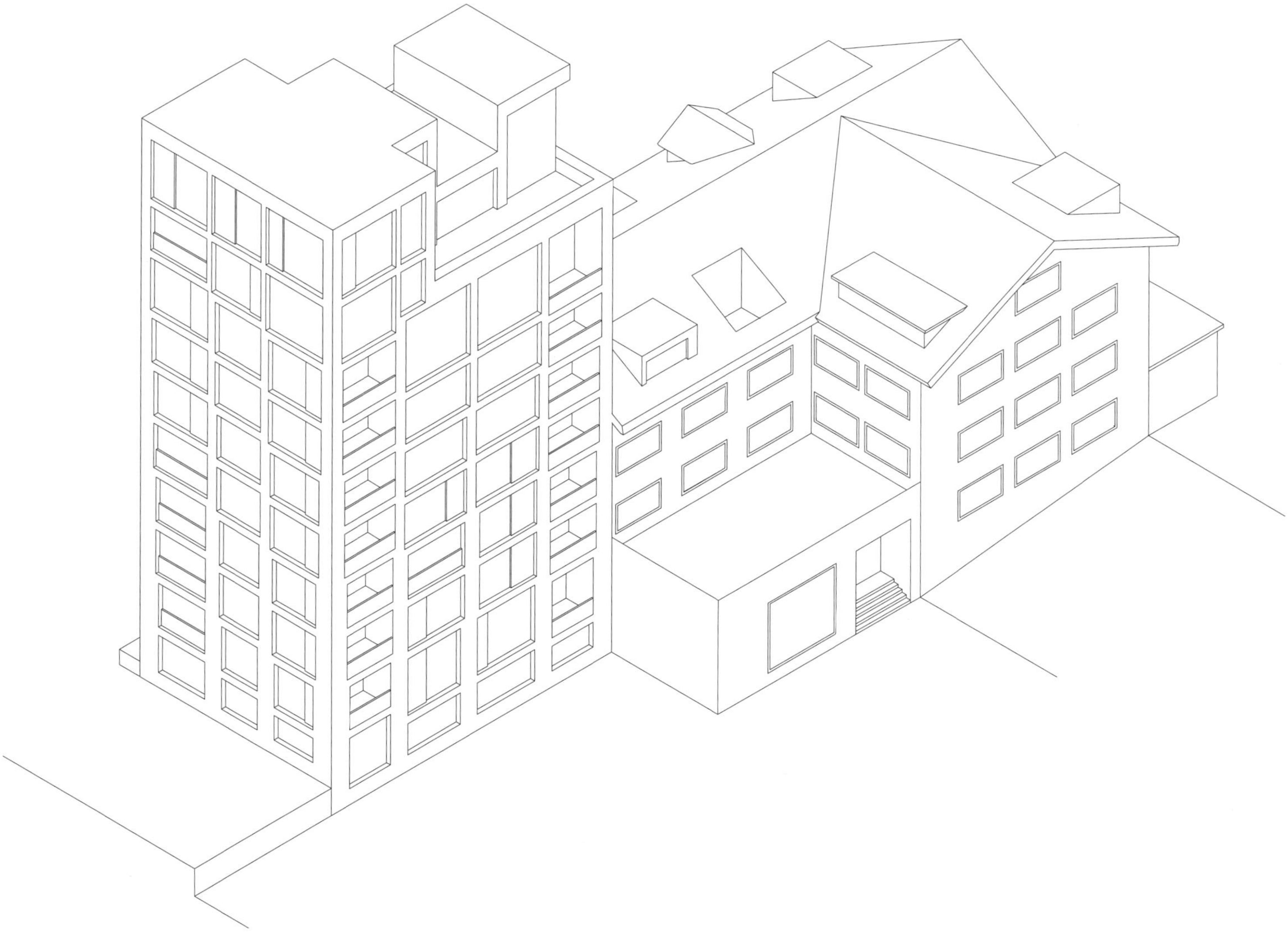

As the client, Hans-Luzi Züst, is a mechanical engineer the lower building will be used as a competence center for energy. The lower building is organized on existing floor plates but replaces the exterior with precast, self-insulted concrete panels with a decorative floral pattern. The tower defined by the corset framework is clad in wood, photovoltaic panels, or glass.

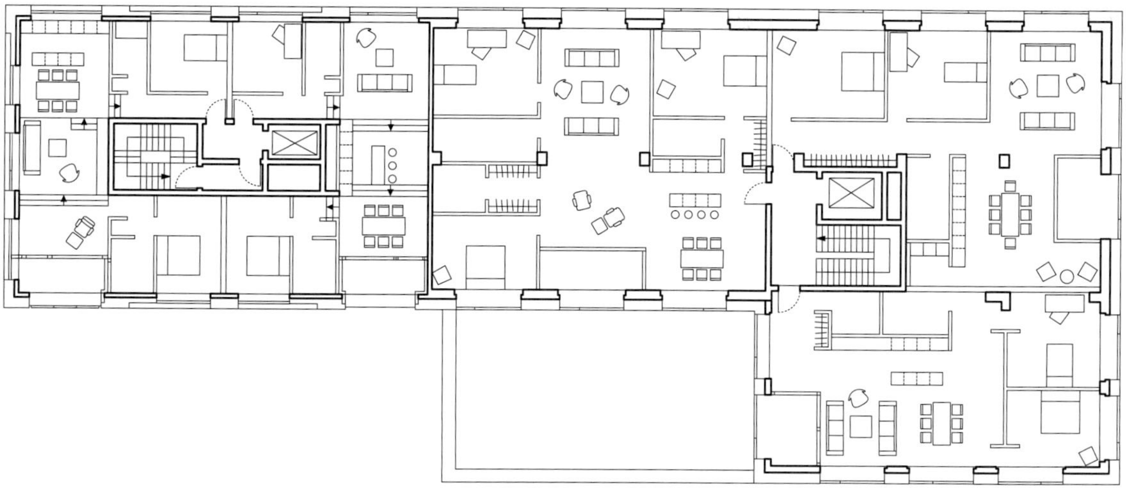

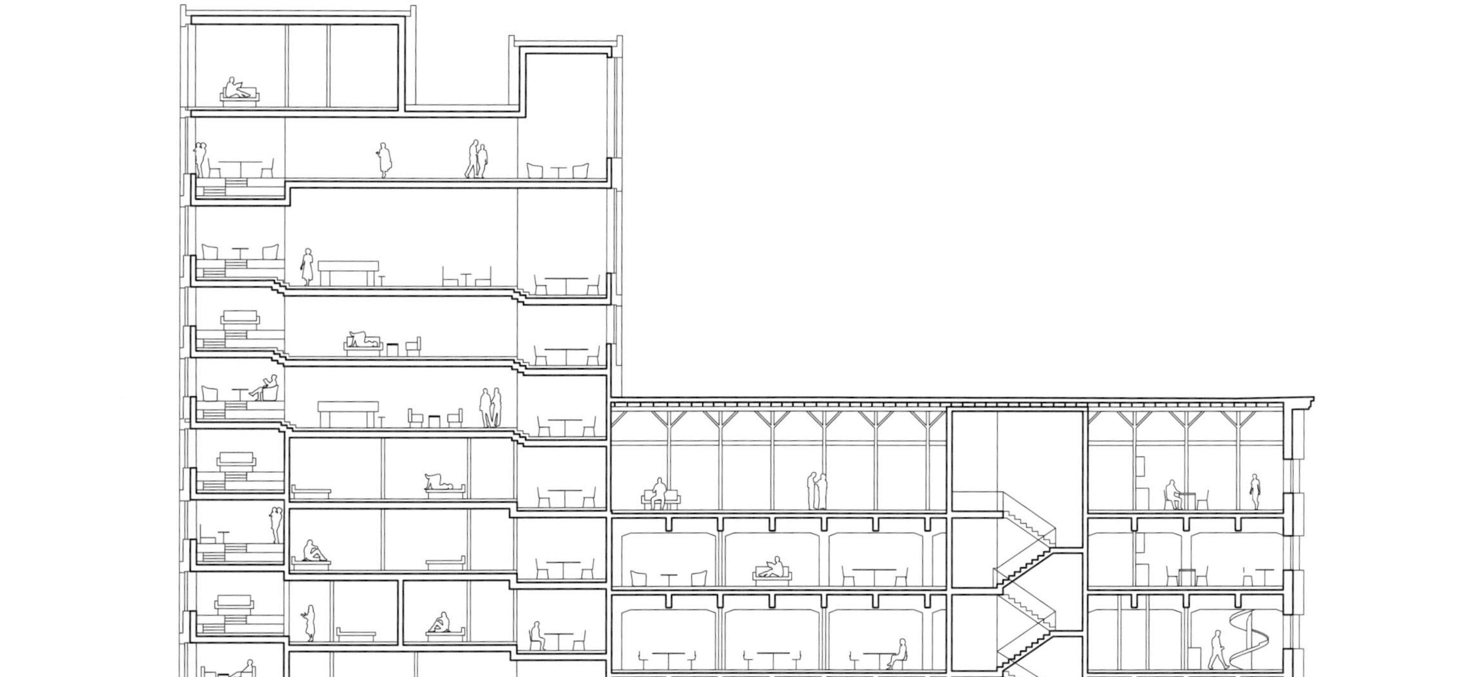

Over the years Barkow Leibinger's different projects within the TRUMPF Campus in Ditzingen near Stuttgart have been documented—typically with an emphasis on finished individual buildings—by a number of renowned international photographers. Undeniably beautiful, these images most often present the buildings as solitary objects, highlighting their formal qualities, while nonetheless largely ignoring their broader contextual relationships or how they are used on a daily basis and by different groups of people.

As the campus has been completed to a large degree and lived in for some time, beginning in the nineteen-seventies, Iwan Baan was asked to revisit the project photographically for this publication, to depict it in a more inclusive way (showing buildings in context with each other) and as populated with employees (blue collar and white), visitors, and customers and how they now occupy this site and transform the buildings by activating them. His images show how architecture frames the "work space," be it for production (the factory), offices, or social space (such as the restaurant and park). This is an essential environment in the German industrial landscape and one that is, perhaps, underrepresented, illustrating how architecture contributes to production, making, and thinking about new ideas and ways of doing things. A factory is not an ideal city. It always remains an unfinished project. It is always in construction. It is always being revised. Heterogeneous planning marks a kind of soft planning, where choices for growth are based on opportunity or limits, as a kind of patchwork of spaces and uses that change over time.

The buildings are not shown as autonomous objects but are part of an evolving, differentiated industrial campus that is like a small city. This is also a view articulated by a casual observer, who reminds us that buildings and their intended uses are often resisted by those who use them and live and work in them every day. This photographic reportage is a way for us to gauge how buildings are conceived and imagined but also to better understand how they evolve over time and how they are appropriated by those who live in them day in and out.

It has been our hope to use this type of photographic documentation to show this dynamic and ever-evolving process and make it coherent. This is a much-reduced selection from an enormous number of images that embody that experience from a casual, but in the end very astute, observer.

KÜBLER
Ihr Metzger
Verwaltung

Schranke schließt
automatisch nach
jedem Fahrzeug!

WC

TRUMPF

Vertrieb
Service

TRUMPF

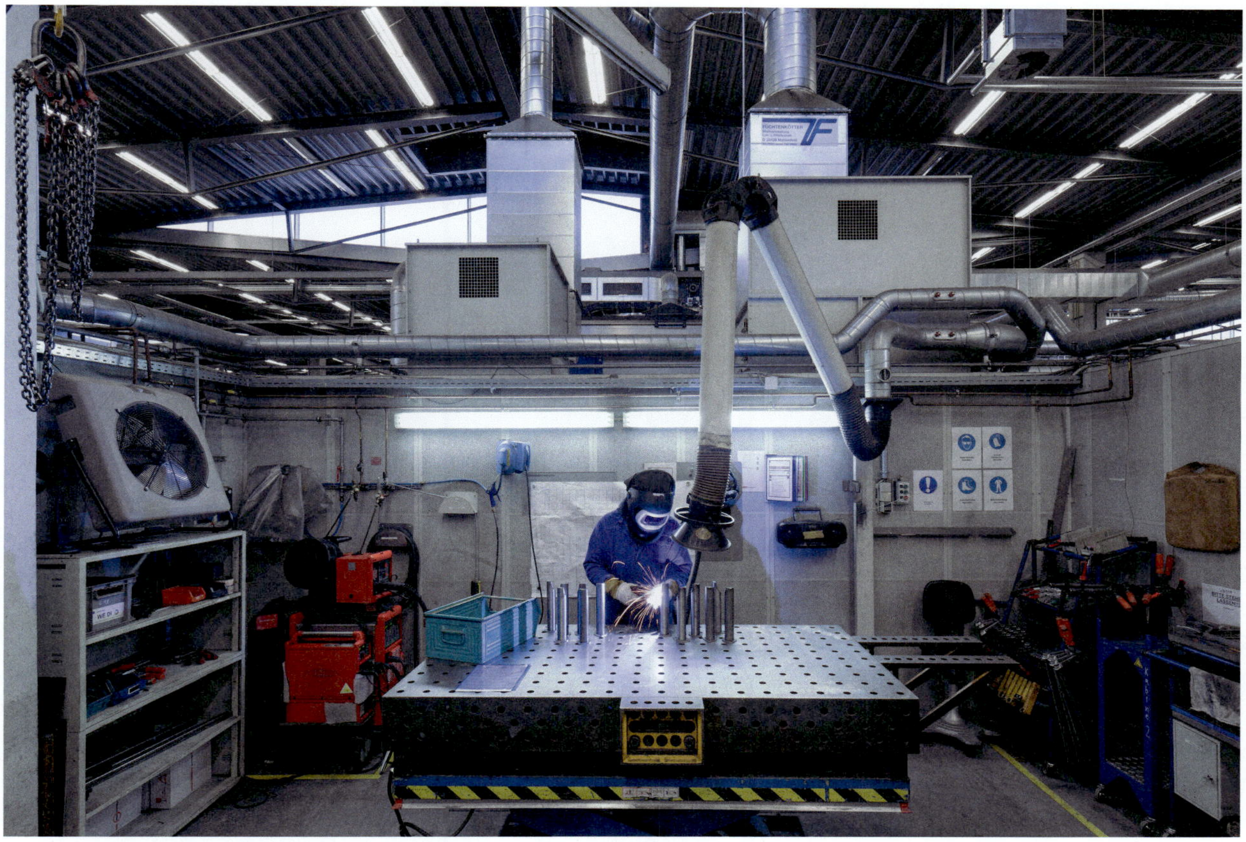

Materialwagen Kühler GB

Materialwagen Kühler GB

Site specific refers to the idea that architecture can be generated and informed by conditions, as found, where buildings are located. Site-specific *art* is created to exist in a certain place. Such art itself is indexed, bound to, or shaped by place: it does not simply exist there; it is conceived of and can be situated only at that specific site.

If renovation work (chapter 4, Makeover) points to a dialogue with an existing building, site specificity refers to a broader sense of place or context, what its limits are, and how its particular circumstances influence and shape a building embedded within them. This implies a skill-set where observation and determination go hand-in-hand with the ability to shift and select the characteristics that are latent and powerful enough to conceptualize a project.

The question then becomes: what is context and how does it inform a site-generated building? The obvious and historical meaning of contextual, a part relating to a large whole, architecturally, seems to be a syntactical one of things resembling each other, either visually or tectonically (how a thing is made). A key question for Barkow Leibinger is asking: what is the context—what are the key characteristics of a place and how can they be instrumentalized to make a project? While context here may refer to the historical identity of a place, city, street, or urban context, other, more abstract content is equally legitimate: the construction of a landscape, the geometry and scale of adjacent buildings, material context, climate, geological memory, among other things.

What makes site specificity such an enduring and compelling work area for the practice is the plain singularity of each site and the problem being responded to. This means there is the chance that each work of architecture can derive a relative autonomy in an overall portfolio of work. It marks the practice as an evolving, changing discipline, since it is driven by the specifics of time, place, and encounter. While a material tectonic endures as an operational field of interest, the response to a particular site differentiates the work, because it is dependent on the uniqueness of each situation. While not a mandate for all work, site specificity is an escape from the trap of a self-determined formalism, which is, in the words of Richard Serra, simply "site-adjusted," without any direct correspondence to place.[1]

Site specificity delineates context as a highly subjective and complex environment, yet one that is also a fruitful and compelling source for the making of architecture. The point is to register such apparent or hidden systems and to harness them toward generating a new outcome.

1 Yve-Alain Bois, "A Picturesque Stroll around Clara-Clara," *October* 29 (Summer 1984), p. 39.

Biosphere
Potsdam, Germany, 2001

The Biosphere was built in Potsdam near Frederick the Great's palace of Sanssouci, where an eclectic collection of exotic architectures makes up his palace grounds. The Bornstedter Fields, where the site is located, were used as a parade ground for the Prussian military, then later by the Nazis for military exercises. After World War II the Soviets occupied the site and crisscrossed it with a series of earthen berms to enclose and protect their barracks. This raw, defensive landscape provided the conceptual and formal basis for the present scheme.

The intention was to extend the infrastructure of the existing earth mounds to form an artificial valley running east-west, generating the form of the new pavilion. This approach allowed the overall height of the building to be reduced by cutting into the ground plane and then using the displaced earth for the construction of new berms. The excavation produced a building in proportion to the existing earth mounds and prevented it from competing with the historical monuments of the Pfingstberg and Ruinenberg.

The newly constructed berms provide an economical material for the enclosure of the pavilion. They are veneered with various materials, including plants and flowers on the southern exposures and wood logs and concrete on the north. The earthen berms are carved to allow gaps for daylighting the interior, to provide views to the adjacent park, to generate spaces for the restaurant and bar, and to house service spaces.

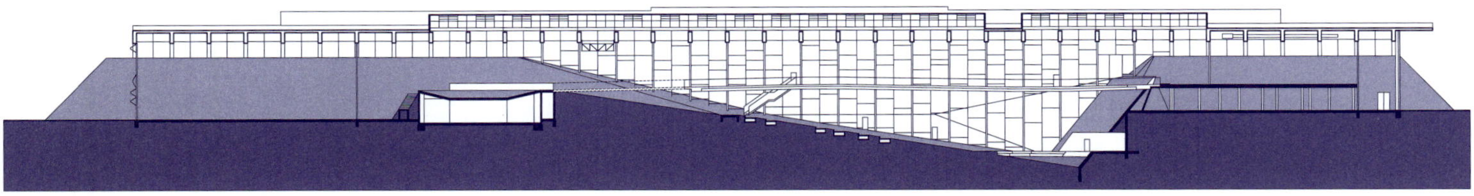

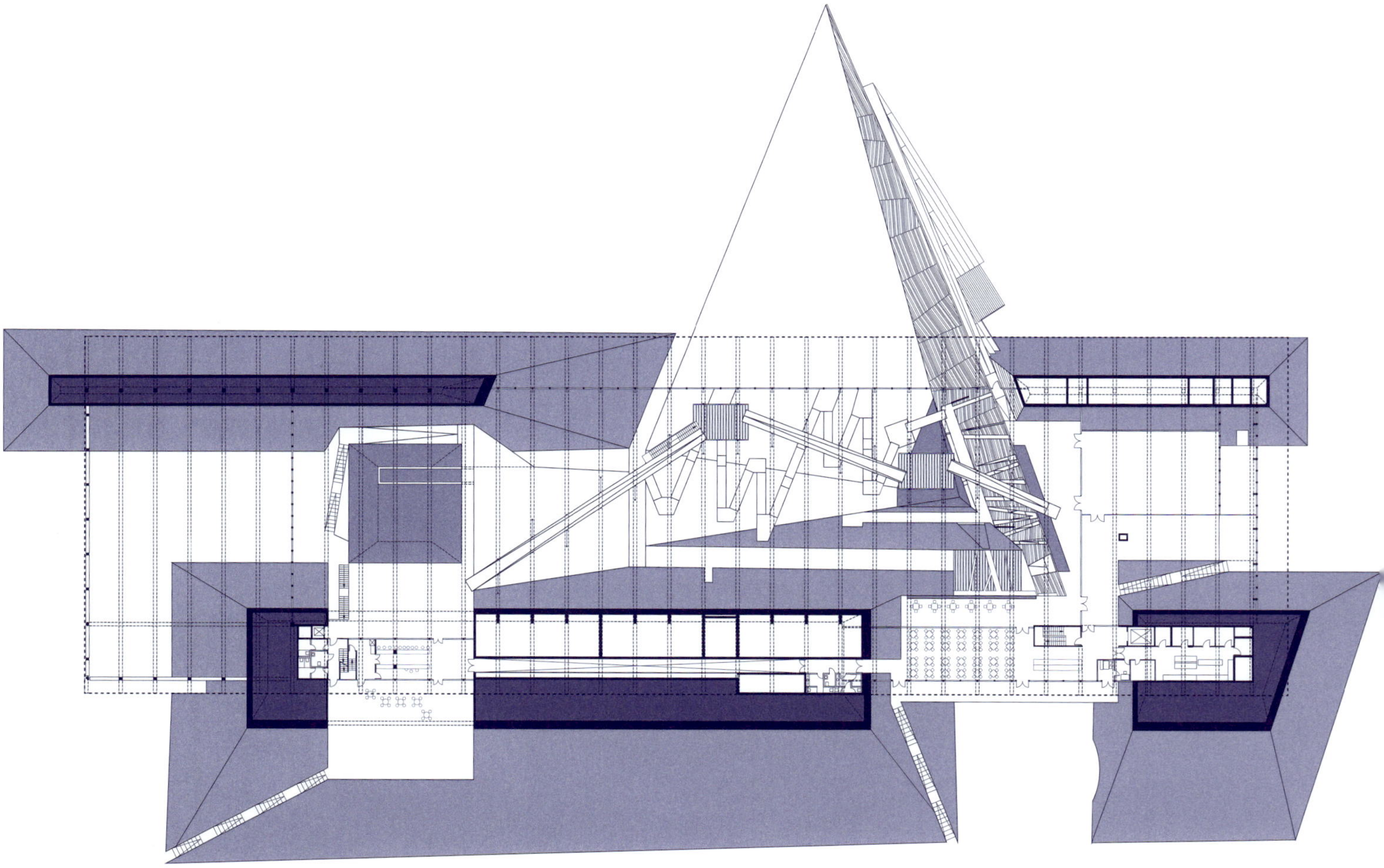

The continuous ground plane forming the berms of the pavilion gives shape to a 200-meter-long space, which is simply enclosed by a steel-and-glass curtain wall and covered by a flat roof of precast concrete beams upon which sit glass skylights. The central, enclosed, garden space is framed by two anchor points—the entrance foyer and lab level on the east end and the Orangerie on the west.

A series of paths zigzag up the slope from this space, passing under a translucent water basin and filtering light into the space below. A slate-clad wall forms a cliff that separates the foyer area from the central garden.

TRUMPF CUSTOMER AND TECHNOLOGY CENTER

Factory Campus
Farmington, Connecticut, USA, 1996–2008

The Farmington campus and master plan for TRUMPF consists of four buildings that unify the various existing buildings and are sensitively placed within the existing wetlands in a semi-rural industrial park near a regional airport. The buildings are low-scale and constructed of a lightweight steel frame infilled with an iron-spot brick, recalling both the Miesian modernism that is characteristic of the industrial park and the heritage of the New England regional architecture.

The Customer and Technology Center (1997–99) is a freestanding pavilion that responds to these landscapes, its pinwheel-like plan rotating and orienting itself toward ponds and meadows. A double-height demonstration hall featuring laser machine tools is wrapped by supporting programs, including a lobby, cafeteria, lounge, theater, and offices. The hall is ringed at the second level by a suspended catwalk for viewing, which links additional offices and conference rooms. The goal was to use exposed steel-frame construction infilled by brick or sandblasted concrete brick, thereby emphasizing material and construction principles. The project responds specifically to the context and to its particular building culture.

RUMATIC L 3030

Musée national des beaux-arts du Québec
Canada, 2010 (competition)

The Musée national des beaux-arts du Québec is an ensemble of distinctive pavilions of diverse historical identities that constitute a cultural campus in the Parc des Champs de Bataille. Rather than an “institutional monument,” a new building was proposed as “integrated cultural fabric” in the form of a matt structure comprised of a double-story exhibition and public forum that enables flexible and well-integrated spaces for experiencing art or for public discourse.

The new museum is integrated directly with the existing historical church and presbytère, anticipating their future integration programmatically into the museum; the church tower remains the landmark for the immediate site. The new pavilion references an industrial architecture with north-facing shed roofs, and, clad in brick, it also recalls the local tradition of building in brick and stone, exemplified by the angular neo-Gothic style of the church.

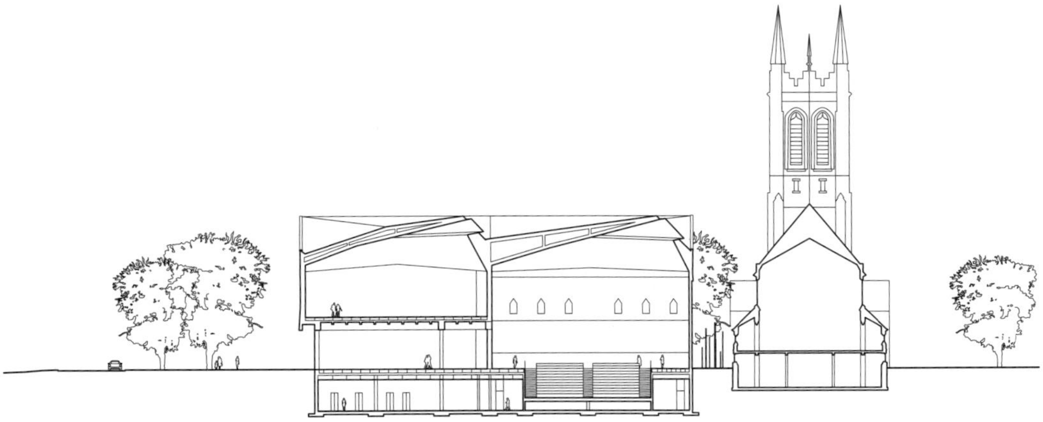

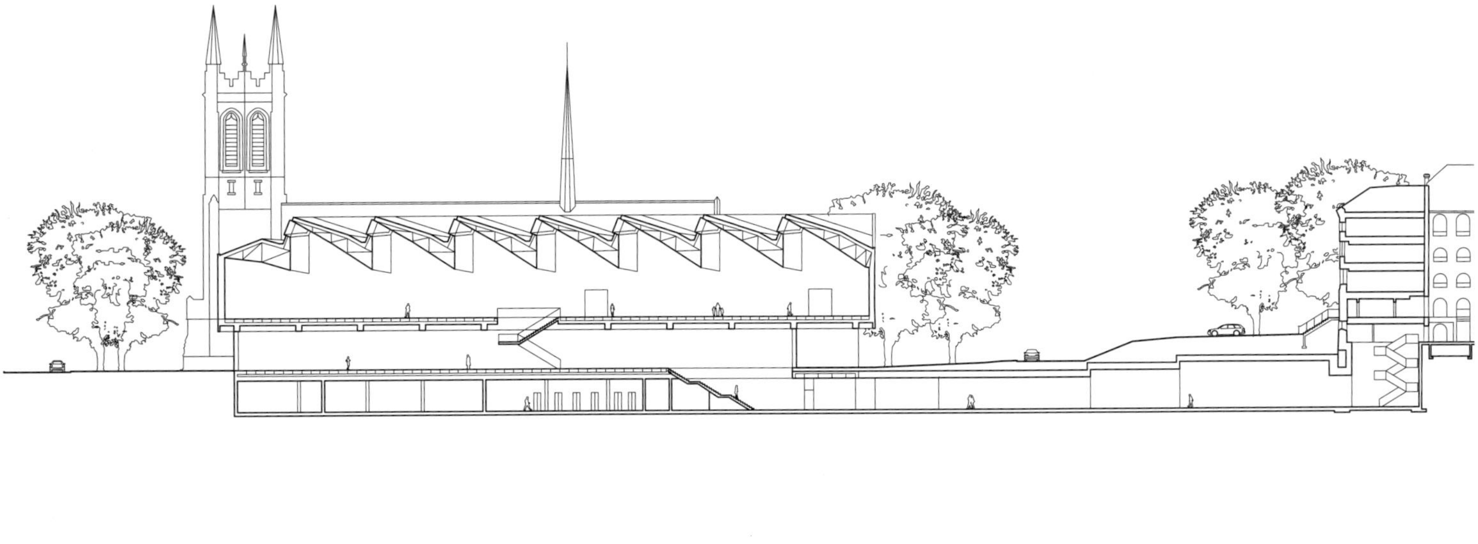

Fraunhofer Research Campus
Waischenfeld, Germany, 2014

A research center for the Fraunhofer Institute for Integrated Circuits is an innovative working environment for scientists situated in a seventeenth to nineteenth-century village in the idyllic landscape of northern Bavaria.

The design is organized as a cluster of similar-scaled buildings, resembling the formation of a small village and adapted to the topography of the surrounding landscape and scale of the village. Each of the two to three-story, gable-roofed buildings houses offices, laboratories, or dormitory rooms. The central cafeteria acts as the communicative and connective focal point between the four research buildings. The timber-webbed roof of the cafeteria, as well as the adjacent terraces, offer additional spaces for work or leisure.

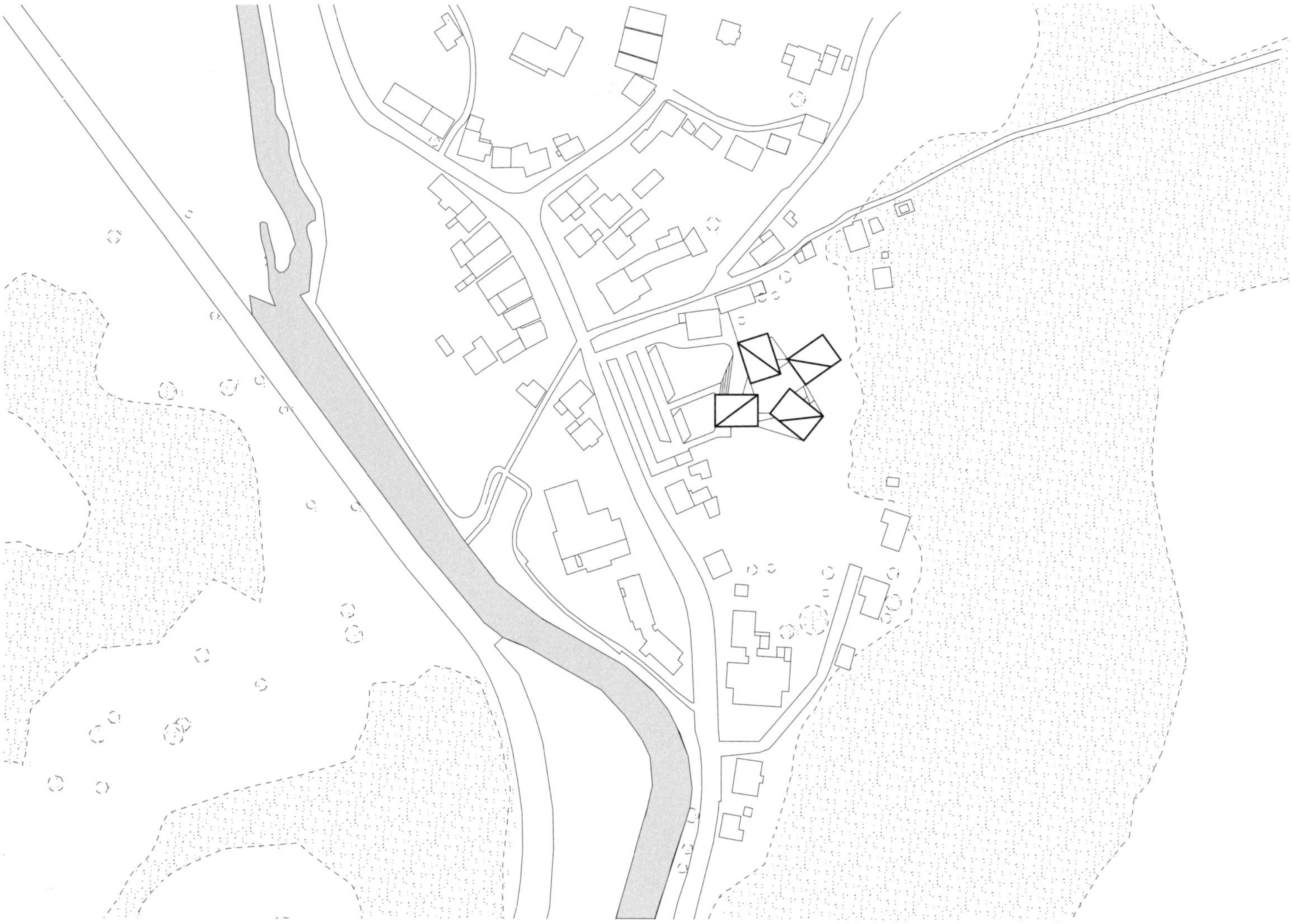

Regional timber is utilized to achieve a well-insulated, sustainable, "passive-energy house" standard. The board-and-batten wood siding is similar to the local vernacular of the nearby village, while the roofing is of standing seam copper. The oversized wood windows also speak of this tradition at the same time that they improve ventilation and offer views of the surroundings. The research institute, like an enclave, is both modern and forward-looking while also respecting the local architectural vernacular.

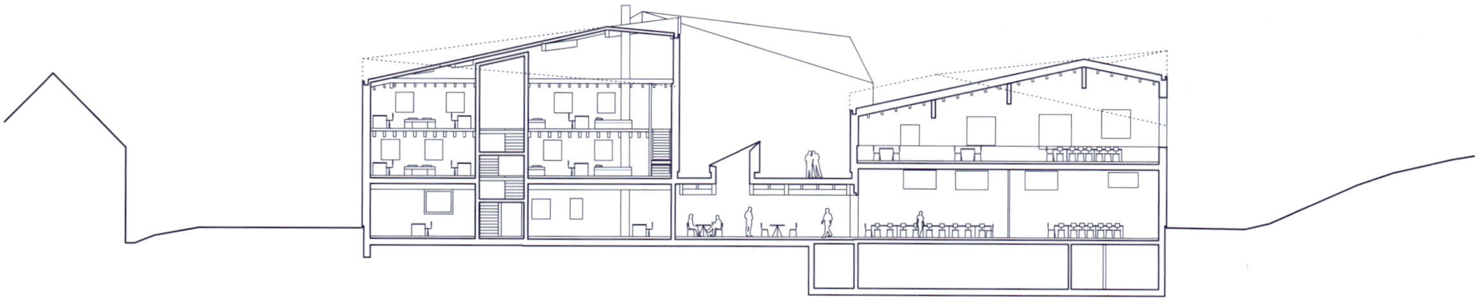

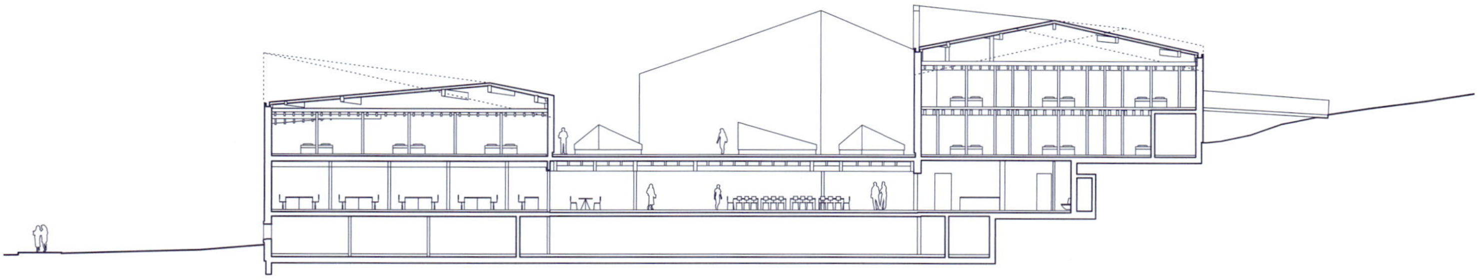

Aufbau Haus 84
Berlin, Germany, 2015

With this addition to the first “Aufbau Haus 85”—a center for contemporary artistic and creative industries—the *Baulücke* (gap) in the historical fabric is filled, thus spatially improving the urban character of the Moritzplatz in Berlin-Kreuzberg, which had remained fragmented and incomplete since its destruction in World War II.

The new infill of loft spaces and shops mediates between the first phase, completed in 2011, and the historical Elsnerhaus from 1914. The new building deploys a concrete frame that is manipulated by a split-level articulation; it emphasizes the hinge character of the head of the building, which faces the public square and is distinguished by an open arcade at the ground level and an open, large-scale loggia on the third level. The arcade projects diagonally toward the center of the traffic circle, visually and spatially connecting to the rear, open court-yard of the block.

Recalling the topology of loft buildings in Kreuzberg, the design makes reference to a particularly significant example: Max Taut's nearby office building (1933) at Oranienplatz. Programming is aimed toward the arts, a design academy, and studio spaces for artists and graphic designers.

aufbau
verlag
planet
modulor
Moritzp

Loom-Hyperbolic
Installation, Marrakech, Morocco, 2012
4th Marrakech Biennale—Higher Atlas

Marrakech is a city that offers an indigenous, madly inventive, and vivid handcraft culture, which oscillates between ad-hoc kitsch and archaic sublime. One of the local techniques is traditional Moroccan weaving on a wood-frame loom. This craft involves wool or cotton yarn, strands of which, in a (typically colored) array, are warped through a loom and woven and tied in order to produce a woven fabric surface. For the temporary installation *Loom-Hyperbolic* this traditional technique was combined with digital technology, that is, a modern form of knowledge brought to the situation.

The question was: what effects can be produced by considering geometrical form as found in the architecture of Marrakech and as constructed by using current algorithm software programming (such as Grasshopper, Rhino) to then begin speculating on how these forms might be rendered (made physical) by local craft techniques and materials?

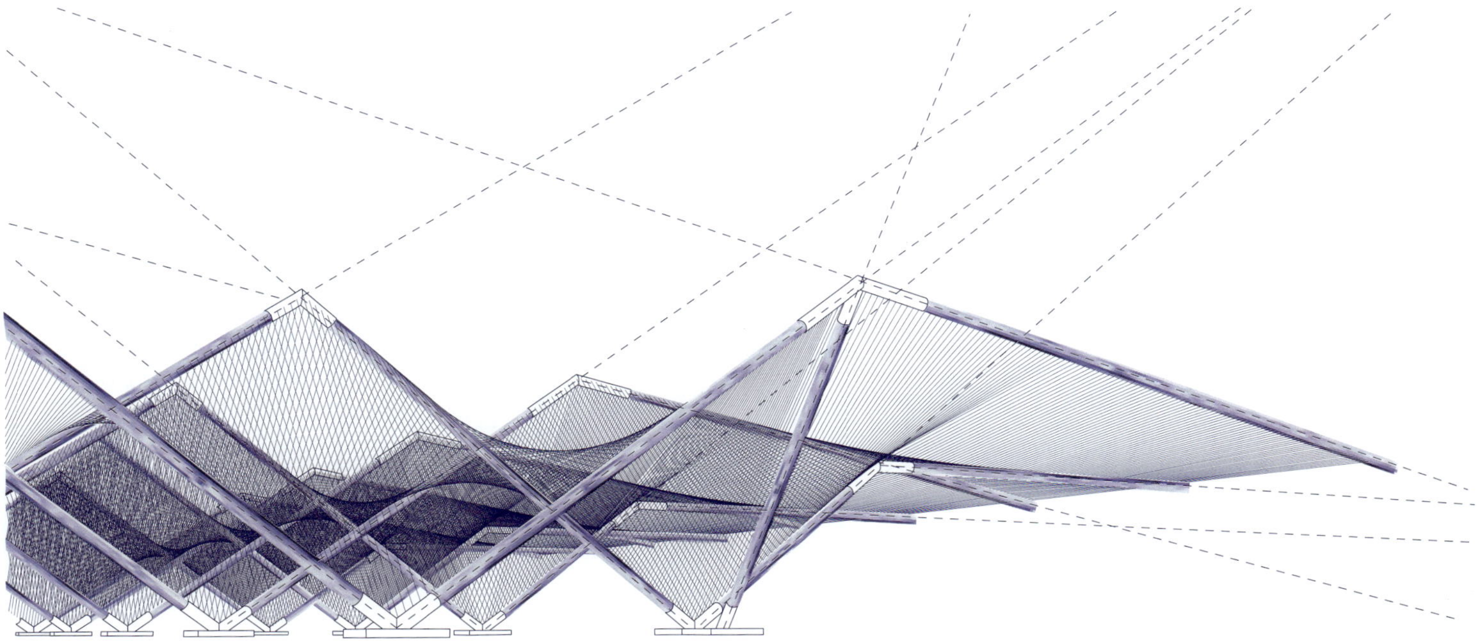

The site for the installation, the ruin near the Koutoubia Mosque, informed and located the project and established a scale for the work. In this way the piece became site-specific to this place and its corresponding restraints and opportunities. The ruin's broken-off columns established a grid of five square meters to which the installation was adjusted by halving it to a two-and-one-half-square-meter grid. In the logic of a hyperbolic surface this established a two-and-one-half-meter height, in relationship to viewers, who could walk around or through the installation as a place of public encounter.

The simple construction consisted of hand-peeled pine poles attached to steel plates and tubes (which establish and fix the geometry) and yarn pulled over the frames, which alternated and were tied off as if they were laid over a giant loom spaced closely together. The lines of the yarn generated a lineal "ruled-geometry," which formed hyperbolic surfaces.

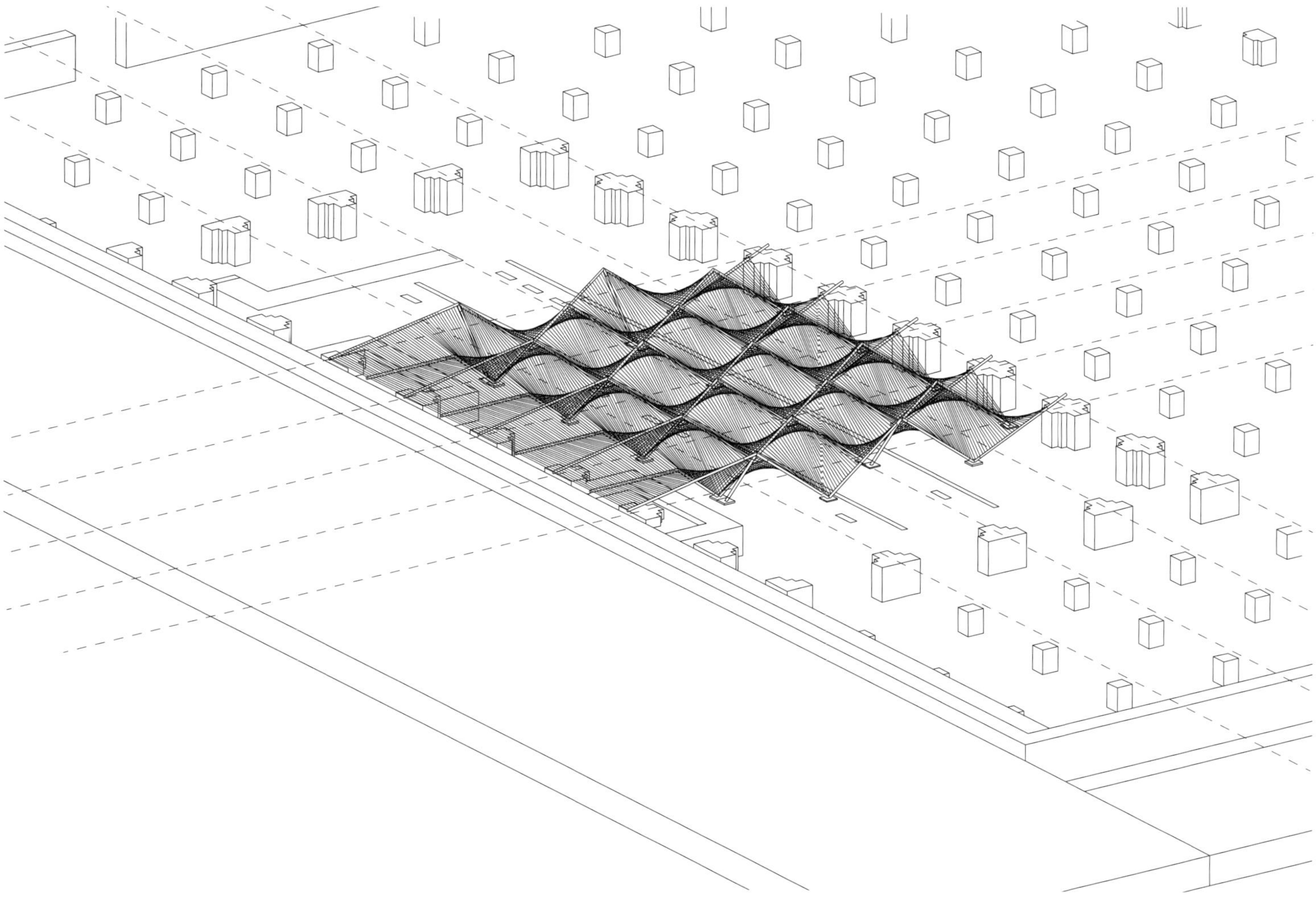

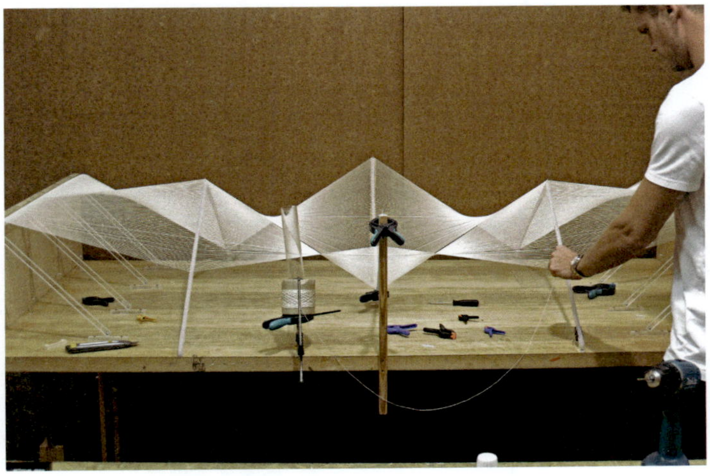

Estrel Tower
Berlin, Germany, 2014 (competition)

Complementing the existing Estrel Hotel, the largest in Germany, a new hotel tower and conference center will establish a new gateway from the Schönefeld Airport to the center of Berlin. With a height of 175 meters the tower will be the tallest high-rise in Berlin to date. Located on the Sonnenallee at the intersection of the Ship Canal, S-Bahn, and autobahn the site is a threshold between the heterogeneous industrial and residential periphery and the historical neighborhoods of Neukölln. Free from the historical constraints of the city center the project is an ensemble of elements revolving around the sloped silhouette of the tower, with its roof terrace oriented toward the city.

In response to the existing Estrel Hotel and resembling the children's game "tangram" the proposal is organized into a series of extruded triangulated volumes of different sizes and heights, thereby mediating the tower into the low-rise surrounding neighborhoods.

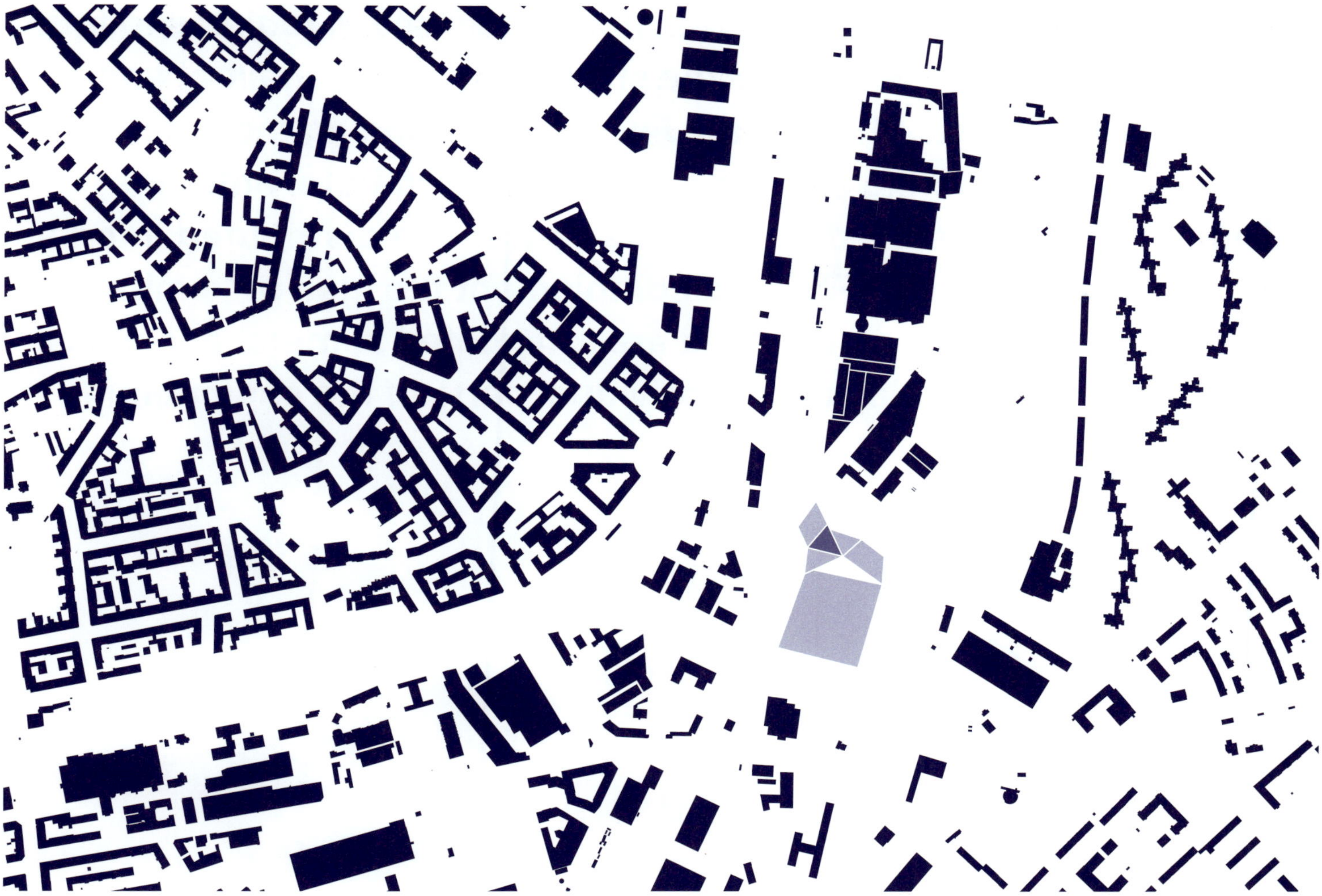

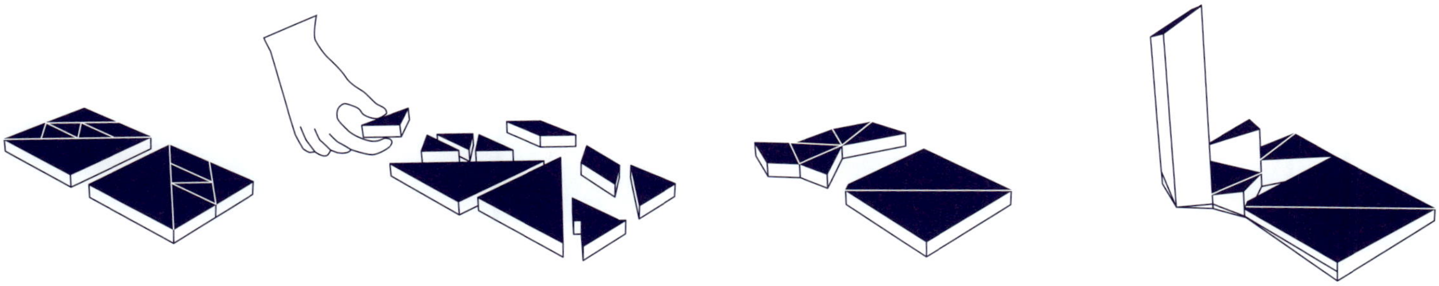

This cascading family of forms, from high to low-scale, radiates to form two strong orientations: toward the street side (Sonnenallee) and toward the waterside (Ship Canal). Functions, including the hotel, an office building, a parking structure, a glass-roofed hotel entrance atrium, and the low-scaled conference center, are distributed into the different-sized volumes. Façades complement the idea of "similar but distinct" building volumes and are articulated in metal and glass to enhance the verticality of the individual parts of the ensemble.

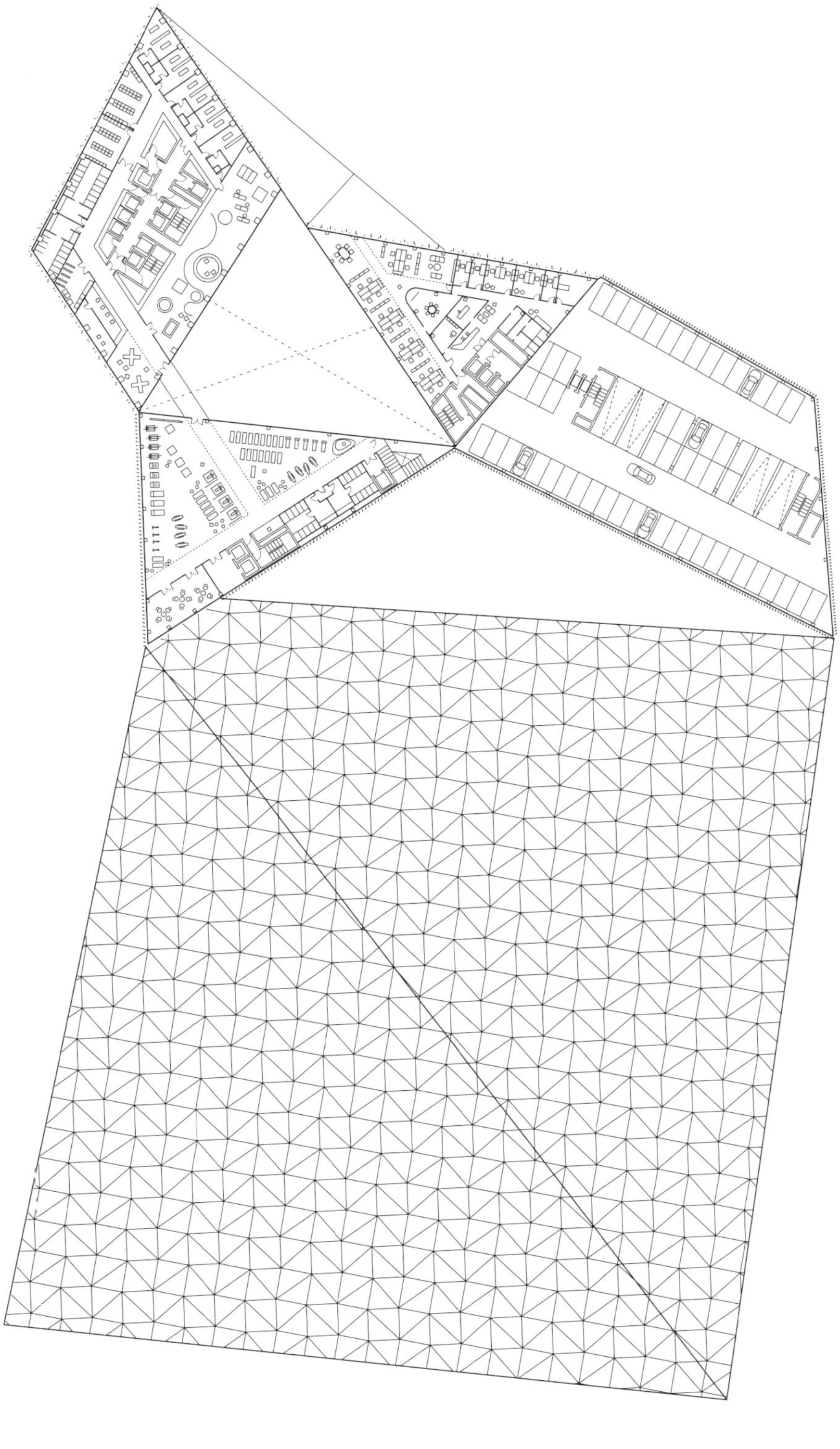

Architektur als Instrument
Hal Foster

Einer der Ursprungsmythen moderner Architektur handelt von den Reisen deutscher Architekten in nordamerikanische Städte – man denke nur an Walter Gropius in Buffalo –, wo sie erstmals die Industriebauten, wie beispielsweise Kornspeicher, tatsächlich besichtigen konnten, die sie zuvor schon als Vorbilder für funktionalistisches Bauen in Europa eingeführt hatten. Die Partnerschaft von Frank Barkow und Regine Leibinger ist eine zeitgenössische Variation dieses alten Themas internationaler Begegnung: In den späten 1980er-Jahren trafen sich der Amerikaner Barkow und die Deutsche Leibinger an der Graduate School of Design der Harvard University (deren Architekturfakultät einst Gropius leitete). In der Literatur über das Büro wird diese Begegnung als Urszene verstanden: Frank Barkow, der hochgewachsene Mann aus Montana, beeindruckt von den riesigen Infrastrukturprojekten und der großen Land-Art des amerikanischen Westens (also einerseits von den Staudämmen und andererseits von Robert Smithsons *Spiral Jetty)* lernt Regine Leibinger kennen, ihrerseits die kultivierte Tochter des Geschäftsführers von TRUMPF, dem Erfinder und Hersteller innovativer Werkzeugmaschinen und Lasersysteme in der Nähe von Stuttgart (wo ein Klassiker der europäischen Moderne angesiedelt ist: die Weißenhofsiedlung). Nach ihrem Studium an der GSD, damals unter der Leitung von Rafael Moneo, gründeten die beiden jungen Architekten 1993 in Berlin ihr Büro; zu einem Zeitpunkt, als das neue Europa zu werden begann, wofür einmal das alte Amerika gestanden hatte: ein erweiterter Horizont für anspruchsvolles Bauen.

Auch wenn sich viele Meister der Moderne mit Hingabe der Industriearchitektur widmeten, kam ihre persönliche Handschrift am deutlichsten bei Wohnhäusern zur Geltung. Heute dagegen, wo Kunst und Unterhaltung bedeutende Wirtschaftsfaktoren darstellen, werden zeitgenössische Architekten oft durch Museen berühmt. Obwohl Barkow Leibinger sowohl Wohnhäuser als auch öffentliche und kulturelle Bauten realisierten und mit dem TRUTEC Building in Seoul (2006) und dem Tour Total in Berlin (2012) zwei zeichenhafte Bürotürme geschaffen haben, sind sie doch vor allem für ihre Industriearchitektur bekannt. Dabei ist ihnen der Bedeutungs- und Motivwandel solcher Entwurfsaufgaben vollkommen bewusst. Einerseits gibt es keine zwingende räumliche Trennung mehr zwischen Fabriken und anderen

Gebäudetypen wie beispielsweise Laboratorien. Andererseits lösen sich die Grenzen zwischen Fabrikation und Forschung auf: Auch in der Produktionshalle wird experimentiert und mit Modellen oder an Computern gearbeitet. Während Barkow Leibinger also »wesentliche Aspekte« der Industriearchitektur »wiedergewinnen«, reagieren sie auf deren sich verändernde Parameter und nehmen sogar zukünftige Entwicklungen vorweg.[1] Wenn »Technologie [heute] bildlos [ist]«, wie Frank Barkow anregt, können und wollen Barkow Leibinger jener Fantasie der Entmaterialisierung, die hinter der postfordistischen Ideologie der »leichten Bauweise« steht, nicht folgen.[2] Sie betrachten Industriearchitektur als eine Abfolge von Vorgängen, bei denen sowohl alte als auch neue Technologien und Materialien zum Einsatz kommen, und überführen diese Prozesse in architektonische Formen, die »repetitiv, seriell und additiv« sind.[3]

Auch wenn sie sich als amerikanisch-deutsches Architekturbüro von der Masse abheben – in den USA ausgebildet und in Deutschland ansässig – sind Frank Barkow und Regine Leibinger dennoch Vertreter einer Generation, die manchmal als »post-kritisch« bezeichnet wird. Dieser Terminus trifft nicht wirklich den tatsächlichen Sachverhalt, da sich diese Generation nicht a priori auf eine Theorie verlässt, wie es ein Peter Eisenman häufig tat, aber auch nicht abhängig von irgendeiner Art imagistische Szenografie ist, wie dies bei Robert Venturi und Denise Scott Brown, den postmodernen Gegnern Eisenmans, der Fall war. An der GSD unter Moneo lernten Frank Barkow und Regine Leibinger, sich zwischen der Scylla und Charybdis angewandter Theorie und angewandter Leitbilder hindurch zu navigieren.[4] Und was genauso wichtig ist: Im Verlauf ihrer Entwicklung widerstanden Barkow Leibinger außerdem zwei heutigen Sirenen, die vielleicht noch verführerischer waren. Denn in vielfacher Hinsicht verwandelte sich der theoretische Formalismus, den Eisenman repräsentiert, in einen digitalen Formalismus, dessen prominenter Fürsprecher Greg Lynn ist, während sich die von Venturi und Scott Brown repräsentierte Szenografie zu den »Fetisch-Ornament[en]« einer Architektursprache im Sinne von Zahid Hadid verhärtete.[5] Während erstere Strömung die tektonische Klarheit eines Großteils der modernen Architektur aufgegeben hat, hat letztere die imagistische Oberflächlichkeit eines Großteils der postmodernen Architektur noch verschlimmert. Barkow Leibinger haben sich keiner der beiden Strömungen angeschlossen: Ihrer Ansicht nach erübrigt sich die Frage nach der Struktur keineswegs durch neue Materialien und Fertigungstechniken – ganz im

Gegenteil. Und genauso wenig halten sie die Auffassung von Architektur als skulpturalem Objekt für einen Fortschritt gegenüber der von einem Gebäude als fadenscheinigem Zeichen.

Wie mag dann ein dritter Weg aussehen, wie ihn Barkow Leibinger verfolgen? Vor zehn Jahren sprachen einige Vertreter ihrer Generation vom »neuen Pragmatismus«, während andere auf einer »Design Intelligence« bestanden, die eher »bewahrend« als »kritisch« sein sollte. Beide Ansichten verwiesen auf ein neues Bekenntnis zur Praxis: keine Aversion gegenüber Theorie oder Repräsentation per se, sondern vielmehr ein Eintreten für jenes Wissen, das der Architektur innewohnt, das sich aus Forschung, Experiment, Berechnung und Ausführung ganz natürlich ergibt. Barkow Leibinger bevorzugen dafür einen etwas anderen Begriff, den der »Design Performance«, der einerseits auf eine Architektur verweist, die höchsten Ansprüchen der Industrie (oder jedes anderen Bauherrn) genügt, aber auch auf andere Art performativ ist – im erfinderischen, ja sogar im spielerischen Sinne. Damit gehören sie zu einer Gruppe von Architekten, der es nicht darum geht, ihren ganz eigenen, typischen Stil durchzusetzen, sondern die stattdessen auf die gegebenen Bedingungen durch den Bauherrn, das Programm und den Ort eingeht und mit großer Wachsamkeit aktuelle Fortschritte in der Bautechnik und Konstruktion verfolgt, um diese ihren architektonischen Zielen dienstbar zu machen.

»Für mich muss Architektur nachvollziehbar sein, und sie muss angemessen sein«, bemerkt Regine Leibinger, »das sind die Schlüsselbegriffe für [unsere] architektonische Haltung.«[6] Diese Herangehensweise ist auch und vor allem eine ethische, wie sie es gewiss für die frühen Verfechter moderner Architektur war. Der tragende Begriff des Bekenntnisses zur Moderne war »Transparenz«, was im etymologischen Sinne »Durchschaubarkeit« bedeutet. Dieser Wert wurde über eine Analogie wirksam: Wenn Materialien, Struktur und Konstruktion eines Gebäudes nachvollziehbar gestaltet waren, so dachte man, würden andere, oft im Verborgenen gehaltene Aspekte des Lebens – gesellschaftliche Beziehungen, wirtschaftliche Vorgänge, politische Entscheidungen –, ebenso an die Oberfläche und ins Licht des demokratischen Verständnisses gebracht werden. Diese Analogie, die auch in der modernen Kunst Gültigkeit hatte (wo der gängige Begriff »Materialtreue« lautete), war nie besonders wirksam, und heutzutage wird sie von genau jenen Architekten belächelt, deren Entwürfe durch atmosphärische oder sentimentale Effekte eine

Verschleierung derselben Wirkungsbereiche begünstigen (also in Gesellschaft, Wirtschaft und Politik).[7]

Deshalb ist es so wichtig, dass Barkow Leibinger auf den Begriff der »Lesbarkeit« bestehen, den sie der »Transparenz« vorziehen. Dabei ist die Lesbarkeit, um die es ihnen geht, kaum die einer postmodernen »architecture parlante« und ebenso wenig die einer modernen strukturellen Transparenz, die scheinbare Selbstverständlichkeit eines Bauens mit Mauerwerk, Beton, Glas oder Stahl. Wenn es stimmt, dass ein Großteil der Technologie heutzutage »bildlos« ist, dann lassen Frank Barkow und Regine Leibinger sie nicht in ihrer eigenen Blackbox; sie setzen nicht nur verschiedene Konstruktionsweisen und Fertigungstechniken ein und machen Technologien auf diese Weise sichtbar, sondern passen sie auch heutigen Bedingungen an. Ein Barkow-Leibinger-Mantra lautet, dass »Tools Materialien gestalten, die Formen generieren, nicht andersherum« – womit die übliche Reihenfolge des Entwerfens umgekehrt wird.[8] Dies ist ein Bekenntnis zu der einstmals wegweisenden symbiotischen Beziehung mit TRUMPF, einem wichtigen Bauherrn, der Barkow Leibinger darauf brachte, »wie digitale Fabrikationstechnologien angewendet werden können, um Gebäude zu bauen«.[9] Aber auch durch die Zusammenarbeit mit anderen Herstellerfirmen und Ingenieuren wurden neue Materialien und Techniken in den Entwurfsprozess integriert. Auf diese Weise blicken Barkow Leibinger einerseits in die von Unternehmen wie TRUMPF vorgezeichnete Zukunft, und andererseits schauen sie gleichzeitig in eine Vergangenheit vor der modernen Architektur zurück, auf einen Materialismus der Fertigung, wie er von Gottfried Semper verfochten wurde (ihr Interesse an Oberflächen erinnert an Sempers Faszination für Textilien). Das Ergebnis ist ein unverwechselbarer »Atlas of Fabrication«, in dem Materialien und Fertigungstechniken durch die Konstruktion und den gebauten Raum auf eine Art lesbar werden, die alle Aspekte des Bauens vereint: Entwurfskonzept, Programm, Bauweise und Ort.

Ein weiteres Barkow-Leibinger-Motto lautet: Kein Stil, sondern Haltung. »Haltung stellt in unserem Fall«, so fügen sie hinzu, »den Prozess über eine vorgegebene Form«; und mit »Prozess« meinen sie spezifische Arbeitsschritte mit spezifischen Materialien, die für das jeweilige Projekt angemessen erscheinen.[10] Vor 47 Jahren entwickelte Richard Serra, unzufrieden mit der Bildwirkung einer minimalistischen Kunst, die seinem eigenen Programm der buchstäblichen Transparenz widersprach, ebenfalls eine Zusammenstellung spezifischer Vorgänge, die mit spezifischen Materialien durchgeführt werden sollten – ein Protokoll, das in seiner berühmten *Verb List* (1967/68) angelegt war: »rollen, knicken, falten…« Diese Aufgaben bestimmten seine ersten ausgereiften Arbeiten: gerollte, gefaltete, gerissene oder anders manipulierte Bleibleche; geschmolzenes Blei an einen Mauersockel gespritzt und dann in faltigen Reihen wieder abgezogen; aufeinandergestapelte Betonplatten oder aneinandergelehnte Bleiplatten, et cetera. In ihrem Ausstellungskatalog *An Atlas of Fabrication* (2009) stellen Barkow Leibinger ihre eigene »Liste von Handlungen« vor: »zweidimensionales Schneiden, Gießen, Schneiden/Stapeln, Biegen, Lochen, Schweißen/Aufblähen, dreidimensionales Schneiden (Rotieren), Antizipieren«.[11] Diese Vorgänge, manchmal einzeln ausgeführt, manchmal auch in Kombination, sind zwar technisch anspruchsvoll, meist aber für einen Betrachter leicht lesbar. Wie Serra verstehen Frank Barkow und Regine Leibinger ihre Baupraxis nicht nur als eine Sache des Experimentierens und Ausführens, sondern auch als eine der Darstellung und Offenlegung von Prozessen.

Man denke zum Beispiel an spezifische Verarbeitungsweisen durch Laserschnitt und Rotation, wie sie für die Fassade des Bürogebäudes in Seoul oder das Dach des Betriebsrestaurants von TRUMPF in Ditzingen eingesetzt wurden. Im erstgenannten Gebäude ließen Barkow Leibinger Glasscheiben in unterschiedlichen Winkeln zuschneiden und in zwei- und dreidimensionale Stahlrahmen einpassen. Den so entstandenen Grundtypus eines Fassadenmoduls drehten sie um 180 Grad, sodass »eine äußerst variations- und facettenreiche Fassade« entstand.[12] Im zweitgenannten Gebäude ließen Barkow Leibinger Brettschichtholz in unregelmäßige Zellformen schneiden und fügten diese Struktur wiederum in Stahlrahmen ein, wodurch eine »Art Gewebe« entstand. Wieder war das Ergebnis vielgestaltig und nuanciert, und zwar nicht nur im Erscheinungsbild, sondern auch in der Funktion, da die Zellen sich »als Oberlichter sowie zur Einbringung akustischer Paneele oder künstlicher Beleuchtung nutzen [lassen]«.[13] Selbst wenn die Prozesse leicht ablesbar sind, klingen darin komplexe Wirkungsweisen an: Die Fassade in Seoul erinnert an ein riesiges Kaleidoskop, während das TRUMPF-Dach Bilder eines Baldachins aus Blättern evoziert.[14] Auf diese Weise stellen Barkow Leibinger sowohl Material als auch Technik in den Dienst menschlicher Erfindungskraft und schaffen Bezüge zur Natur. Anders gesagt, genauso wie sie der Technologie nicht erlauben, in der Blackbox zu bleiben, was uns vor ein Rätsel stellt, machen sie aus ihr auch keine »zweite Natur«, die uns beherrschen könnte.

Hier zeigt sich eine weitere Verbindung zur postminimalistischen Kunst, die nicht nur den Prozess abbildet, sondern auch große Sensibilität für den Ort voraussetzt. Wie Serra verstehen auch Barkow Leibinger Werke als etwas, das in einen bestimmten Kontext eingebettet ist und unter den spezifischen räumlichen Bedingungen körperlich erfahren werden muss. Schon beim TRUMPF-Campus wird dies offenbar, noch stärker gilt es für die Potsdamer Biosphäre, deren Umgebung eine Gebäudestruktur hervorbrachte, die wiederum das Gelände definiert. Die Kritik am »Bildermachen« wird hier durch ein Engagement für das »Raumschaffen« deutlich: Gebäude sind keine Kisten, die in einen abstrakten Raum geworfen werden, sondern vielmehr Interventionen, die ein spezifisches Umgebungsfeld extrapolieren, demarkieren und aktivieren.[15] Eine der Stärken der Barkow-Leibinger-Generation liegt darin, Architektur und Landschaft einander gegenseitig bedingen zu lassen, aber Frank Barkow und Regine Leibinger wollen noch mehr: Architektur wird grundsätzlich als Instrument verstanden, um einen Ort à la Richard Serra zu ergründen, und um einen Zustand zu kartieren, »in de[m] sich Natur und Technologie« im Sinne Robert Smithsons stets im »Wandel« befinden.[16] Ähnlich wie die Postminimalisten Serra und Smithson den Minimalismus in der Kunst kritisierten, so kritisieren Frank Barkow und Regine Leibinger eine heutige »minimalistische« Architektur, die in ihrem Streben nach Atmosphäre und Affekten nicht nur dazu tendiert, Struktur und Raum zu verunklaren, sondern auch über Nutzungsanforderungen und örtliche Gegebenheiten hinwegzugehen.

Obwohl Barkow Leibinger Architektur manchmal als »technisierte Struktur« bezeichnen, stellen sie doch jede eingesetzte Bautechnik in den Dienst der architektonischen Form .[17] Auf diese Art vermeiden sie eine weitere große Gefahr zeitgenössischen Entwerfens: übertriebene Konstruierwut, die als Baukunst daher kommt, aber in der Regel mit einem architektonischen Spektakel endet (man denke an Santiago Calatrava). Häufig ist das Repertoire von Barkow Leibinger hinsichtlich der Materialwahl und Fertigungsprozesse weder neu noch besonders hoch technisiert; einiges ist nicht nur traditionell, sondern im Ursprung fast archaisch (beispielsweise die Holzverarbeitung oder bestimmte Gusstechniken).

Letztendlich sind Barkow Leibinger genauso sehr »bricoleure«, also Bastler, wie Ingenieure. Der »bricoleur«, schreibt Claude

Lévi-Strauss in seiner berühmten Definition, agiert mithilfe von »Überbleibseln von früheren Konstruktionen oder Dekonstruktionen«; er hat »jederzeit mit dem, was ihm zur Hand ist, auszukommen, d. h. mit einer stets begrenzten Auswahl an Werkzeugen und Materialien, die überdies noch heterogen sind.«[18] Durchaus sensibel für die Materialität dieser Überreste, behandelt der »bricoleur« sie doch vor allem als Zeichen, die vom Bezeichneten zum Bezeichnenden werden können und umgekehrt, oder gar als Werkzeuge »eine Gesamtheit konkreter und zugleich möglicher Beziehungen« herstellen.[19] Dasselbe trifft für Barkow Leibinger zu. Oft lassen sie sich von gefundenen Bildern und Objekten inspirieren: von der Mikrofotografie eines Blattes, dem Schnappschuss eines Holzstapels, einem übriggebliebenen Stück Luftpolsterfolie, einem alten Spielzeug wie dem Slinky (diesem Wunder an tektonischer Elastizität in Form einer zylindrischen Metallfeder), einem Bild der geschwungenen Backsteinmauern, die Thomas Jefferson für die University of Virginia entwarf, und so weiter. Manchmal machen sie sogar »Gussformen aus interessantem Zeug, das im Büro herumliegt«.[20]

Dieses Interesse beschwört einen zentralen Aspekt brutalistischer Architektur, der vor knapp sechzig Jahren von Reyner Banham folgendermaßen definiert wurde: die »Würdigung der ›vorgefundenen‹ Materialien«. Tatsächlich sind noch zwei weitere Kriterien seiner Definition von Brutalismus bedeutend für Barkow Leibinger: »formale Lesbarkeit des Plans« und »klare Zurschaustellung der Konstruktion«.[21] »Unsere Mechanismen mit dem Raum in Dialog treten zu lassen, ist die zentrale Herausforderung«, schrieben einst Alison und Peter Smithson, die wichtigsten Protagonisten des Brutalismus, und Frank Barkow und Regine Leibinger würden dem zustimmen.[22] »Der Brutalismus will sich der Massenproduktionsgesellschaft stellen«, erklärten die Smithsons, »und eine raue Poesie aus den verworren und stark wirkenden Kräften schöpfen.«[23] Barkow Leibinger aktualisieren diesen ethischen Einsatz für eine »individualisierte Massenfertigungsgesellschaft«; ihre Architektur, die sie als Prêt-à-porter bezeichnen, schöpft eine raue Poesie aus den komplexen Kräften unserer Zeit. In vielerlei Hinsicht war der Brutalismus ein Versuch, die Werte der modernen Architektur von Ludwig Mies van der Rohe und Le Corbusier nach dem Zweiten Weltkrieg vor einer »Degradierung« zur rein stilistischen »Hülle« zu retten.[24] Barkow Leibinger nehmen eine ähnliche Haltung gegenüber jener Architektur ein, die sich heute dem digitalen Formalismus und einer fetischistischen Ornamentik hingibt.

»Das Werk von Barkow Leibinger erreicht uns aus dem Inneren der Architektur«, schreibt George Wagner, und es ist wahr: Ihre Sprache ist reflexiv und aus der Praxis des Bauens selbst entwickelt.[25] Es ist eine Sprache, die flexibel auf die Zwänge des Bauprogramms und auf die Bedingungen eines Ortes reagiert, und es ist eine Sprache, die durch die Beschäftigung mit Wettbewerben und Masterplänen, durch die Entwicklung von Prototypen und deren Katalogisierung und durch Lehre und Ausstellungen weiterentwickelt wird. Es ist eine Sprache, die Architektur zum Instrument werden lässt, so komplex oder so einfach, wie es der jeweilige Fall erfordert.

Dies bringt uns zurück zur »Design Performance«, aus der ich eine letzte Schlussfolgerung ziehen möchte. Der »bricolage«, dem Basteln, wohnt immer ein Element inspirierten Handelns inne. Und wie wir von den größten deutschen Philosophen der Ästhetik wissen, ist ein solches Spiel auch für die Kunst grundlegend wichtig: Es eröffnet einen Raum für fantasievolle Antworten auf alle gestellten Fragen. Letztendlich ist es das, was die Architektur von Barkow Leibinger uns anbietet: Spielraum, Raum für Erfindungen.

1 Jan Otakar Fischer, »Über die Null-Ebene hinaus. Gespräch mit Frank Barkow und Regine Leibinger«, in: George Wagner, *Barkow Leibinger. Werkbericht 1993–2001,* Basel 2001, S. 29.

2 Ebd. Vgl. Terence Riley, *Light Construction,* New York 1995.

3 Fischer 2001 (wie Anm. 1), S. 28.

4 In dieser Hinsicht verweisen Barkow Leibinger auch auf den Einfluss von Robin Evans an der Harvard University, der trotz all seines Interesses an der Repräsentation vor allem auf die »Erfahrung« von Architektur bestand.

5 Fischer 2001 (wie Anm. 1), S. 32.

6 Ebd., S. 27.

7 Vgl. Hal Foster, *The Art-Architecture Complex,* London und New York 2011.

8 Frank Barkow und Regine Leibinger, *Barkow Leibinger. An Atlas of Fabrication,* London 2009, o. S.

9 Ebd. »Das Pförtnerhaus des TRUMPF-Geländes in Ditzingen war das erste Barkow-Leibinger-Gebäude, bei dem die TRUMPF-Technologie in die gesamte Strategie integriert wurde.«

10 Frank Barkow und Regine Leibinger, »Peripheral Vision«, in: JaeHong Lee, *Barkow Leibinger Architects,* Seoul 2007, S. 11.

11 Barkow und Leibinger 2009 (wie Anm. 8), o. S.

12 Ebd.

13 Ebd.

14 Das Dach mag aber auch an einen Baldachin aus Kristallen erinnern. Auf eine gewisse Art und Weise vollziehen Barkow Leibinger hier den aktuellen Wechsel von einem biologischen zu einem ökologischen oder sogar geologischen Paradigma in der Architektur. Vgl. Stan Allen und Marc McQuade, *Landform Building. Architecture's New Terrain,* Baden 2011.

15 Vgl. Aaron Betsky, »From Field to Form, With an Attitude«, in: Lee 2007 (wie Anm. 10), S. 16–23, hier insb. S. 16.

16 Fischer 2001 (wie Anm. 1), S. 28.

17 Auch Richard Serra, der manchmal Skulptur als »gebaute Struktur« bezeichnet, setzt das Konstruieren immer für skulpturale Zwecke ein.

18 Claude Lévi-Strauss, *Das wilde Denken,* Frankfurt am Main 1968, S. 30.

19 Ebd., S. 31.

20 Barkow und Leibinger 2009 (wie Anm. 8), o. S.

21 Reyner Banham, »The New Brutalism«, in: *The Architectural Review,* Dezember 1955, S. 354–361; Nachdruck in: *October,* 136, Frühjahr 2011, S. 23.

22 Alison und Peter Smithson, *Without Rhetoric. An Architectural Aesthetic 1955–1972,* Cambridge, Massachusetts 1974, S. 14.

23 Alison and Peter Smithson, »The New Brutalism«, in: *Architectural Design,* April 1957, S. 113; Nachdruck in: *October,* 136, Frühjahr 2011, S. 37. Siehe darin auch Hal Foster, »Savage Minds (A Note on Brutalist Bricolage)«.

24 Theo Crosby, »The New Brutalism«, in: *Architectural Design,* Januar 1955; Nachdruck in: *October,* 136, Frühjahr 2011, S. 17.

25 George Wagner, »(Tat)sächlichkeit. Die Architektur von Barkow Leibinger«, in: Wagner 2001 (wie Anm. 1), S. 15.

Fabrication / Research

Der Ausdruck »Revolutions of Choice« beschreibt die architektonische Chance, die vom Zuwachs digitaler (und analoger) Fähigkeiten und Fertigkeiten ausgeht; er bedeutet aber noch etwas Grundsätzlicheres: ein Verlangen des Architekten danach, das Wesen des architektonischen Schaffens, das unserer Vorstellungskraft entspringt, vorauszusehen und zu steuern. Aber, so könnte man fragen, wie können wir die Tools, die wir verwenden, noch besser miteinander verknüpfen, und wie beeinflussen sie das architektonische Ergebnis?

Wenn man behauptet, dass Barkow Leibinger ihre Architektur aus dem Material entwickeln, wie es in ihrem Manifest für die Architekturbiennale in Venedig von 2008 heißt, so meint dies schlicht, dass »architektonische Ideen und Materialien unauflösbar miteinander verbunden sind. Mit anderen Worten: Architektur ist physische Substanz, und die wesentliche Aufgabe der Konzeptfindung besteht darin, herauszufinden, wie mit dem jeweiligen Material umzugehen ist.«[1] Hierbei handelt es sich nicht nur um einen Aspekt der Herangehensweise, sondern um den ursprünglichen Arbeitsansatz des Büros, der sich stets weiterentwickelt. Eine entscheidende Motivation dafür, mit tatsächlichen Baumaterialien (alten wie neuen) zu arbeiten, und das vorzugsweise in einem Maßstab von 1:1, ist der Wunsch, Probleme zu umgehen, die durch repräsentative Darstellungen (Zeichnungen und Modelle) aufgeworfen werden. Renderings können zwar die Konstruktionsweise eines Gebäudes illustrieren, jedoch nicht dessen visuelle und räumliche Wirkung so simulieren, dass sie erfahrbar wird. Vielmehr bieten Modelle, Prototypen, Installationen und Eins-zu-Eins-Umsetzungen darstellerische Alternativen, die zwischen einer ersten Idee und dem tatsächlichen Gebäude vermitteln. Diese Betrachtungsweise folgt der Überzeugung, dass Ideen genauso aus den Dingen, die man tut, wie aus erdachten Konzeptualisierungen entstehen.

»Design follows technology« ist das Credo, auf dem sich jene Herangehensweise gründet. Seine Anhänger machen sich Technologien zunutze, die durch eine große Bandbreite an Experimenten, also durch klassische Trial-and-Error-Methoden, entstehen. Die Arbeitsweise ist bewusst nicht linear. Während des Entwicklungsprozesses sammeln sich Kernwissen und Fachkompetenzen an, die es dem Architekten ermöglichen, die Bauweise und damit das Wesen seiner Gebäude zu bestimmen. So wird er selbst zum Experten, der prototypische Bauteile entwickelt und so den Standardbaukatalog überflüssig macht. Ebendieser Ansatz, eine Atmosphäre experimenteller Freiheit – semiautonom von Projektanforderungen, Baufristen und Konstruktionsbedingungen –, erlaubt es dem Büro, zu florieren und sich zu entwickeln. Wahrscheinlich stehen die Chancen, alle Koordinaten eines Projekts einschließlich ästhetischer Fragen, Performance, Nachhaltigkeit und Wirtschaftlichkeit im Sinne des Architekten zu vereinen, zu keinem anderen Zeitpunkt besser als während der Forschungs- und Entwurfsphase.

1 Barkow Leibinger, »Architektur muss nicht brennen ... sie kann glühen. Ein methodologisches futuristisches Manifest«, in: *Entwurfsmuster* (Arch+, 189), Aachen 2008, S. 84 f.

Marrakesch, Seoul und Berlin. Barkow Leibinger im Kontext
Carson Chan

Kenner von Barkow Leibinger schätzen sie dafür, wie die innere Logik des Materials ihre Arbeit lenkt und durchdringt. Für Aaron Betsky werden in ihrer Architektur klassische Bauelemente »zusammengedrückt und auseinandergezogen«;[1] Anthony Vidler sieht sie als Wegbereiter eines neuen Verständnisses von Oberfläche.[2] Ihre Gebäude, so heißt es, verkörpern einen Denkprozess, der durch das Material rationalisiert ist; Barkow Leibinger kommunizieren mit Materialien und lassen aus deren physischen Eigenschaften Erzählungen entstehen, wie Schriftsteller dies mit Worten und Sätzen tun. Visuell kann man »ein Barkow-Leibinger-Gebäude nicht sofort an seiner Architektursprache erkennen«, erklärte Regine Leibinger einmal. Man könne aber »eine bestimmte Haltung an unserer Arbeit ablesen«.[3] Zwei Beispiele mögen dies bereits deutlich veranschaulichen: Zwei ihrer Pavillons im schweizerischen Grüsch (2001, 2004), im Hügelvorland zwischen Chur und Vaduz, bestehen aus Wandscheiben, die statisch als Zugglieder genutzt werden – die auf diese Weise sehr weit spannende Konstruktion ermöglicht frei bespielbare Grundrisse. Das Dach der Hauptpforte (2007) des Technologieunternehmens TRUMPF in Ditzingen dagegen ist vollständig aus Stahlblech konstruiert und setzt hierfür firmeneigene Laserschneide- und Schweißtechnologien ein. Es verweist gleich zweifach auf die eigene Konstruktion, indem es zum einen 20 Meter über die Straße auskragt, und zum anderen systematisch perforiert ist, um sein Gewicht zu reduzieren und so den statischen Anforderungen an seine eigene Länge gerecht zu werden.

Ein Gebäude in seiner Materialität und dem baulichen Entwurf als performatives Statement über Architektur einzusetzen, ist bereits eine bekannte Vorgehensweise von Barkow Leibinger, aber für eine Reihe jüngerer Projekte führen Analysen mit sozialgeschichtlichem Blick zu einem neuen, lohnenden, da noch unerforschten konzeptuellen Deutungsrahmen ihrer Arbeit. Viele der früheren Projekte des Büros befinden sich in der städtischen Peripherie, was den Entwürfen ein Maß an Freiheit, wenn nicht gar eine angemessene Gelassenheit im Umgang mit kulturellen Gegebenheiten erlaubt. Barkow Leibingers bereits erwähnte Pavillons befinden sich am Rand von Grüsch, einem Dorf im Prättigau-Tal in den Schweizer Alpen. Der Campus von TRUMPF liegt südlich des Ortskerns von Ditzingen – dahinter erstreckt sich bis zum Horizont Ackerland. Während diese Projekte – zusammen mit der festungsartigen Biosphäre in Potsdam (2001) und dem Betriebsrestaurant von TRUMPF mit seiner markanten wabenförmigen Kassettendecke – oft nach ihren formalen Attributen der baulichen Innovation und der Experimentierfreude in Bezug auf Materialien bewertet werden, offenbaren städtische Projekte wie die temporäre Installation *Loom-Hyperbolic* in Marrakesch (2012), das TRUTEC Building in Seoul (2006) und der Tour Total in Berlin (2012) die tiefgreifende, aber oft übersehene, gesellschaftliche Wirksamkeit im Schaffen des Büros. Entscheidend für diese Lesart ist eine genaue Analyse der Schnittstelle zum öffentlichen Raum, die jene Bauwerke entstehen lassen, sowie die physische und gesellschaftliche Auseinandersetzung mit dem Ort – und im Fall des Tour Total eine kleine Stadtgeschichte Berlins, der Stadt, in der Frank Barkow und Regine Leibinger 1993 ihr Büro gründeten. Ganz wie Yve-Alain Bois die großformatigen Arbeiten von Richard Serra als skulpturale Erfahrungen beschreibt, die von der Dialektik des Gehens und Schauens erzeugt werden, produzieren diese Gebäude Bedeutung durch unsere physische Begegnung mit ihnen – jedenfalls verlangen sie nach unserer tatsächlichen Anwesenheit, bevor sie uns in vollem Umfang ihr Beziehungsgeflecht zur Umgebung offenbaren.[4]

Bei *Loom-Hyperbolic,* Barkow Leibingers Beitrag zur 4. Biennale von Marrakesch 2012, ging es ebenso um die räumliche Performance von Material wie um die Verkörperung und den Ausdruck des lokalen kulturellen Kontextes.[5] Hier, mehr als ein halbes Jahrhundert nach Beginn der Unabhängigkeit Marokkos von Frankreich im Jahre 1955, sind die bildenden Künste, ihre Produktion, ihre Präsentation und der Zugang zu ihnen noch immer spannungsgeladene Themen. Maurice Tranchant de Lunel und Prosper Ricard, die ersten beiden Direktoren der Protektoratsverwaltung für bildende Künste im besetzten Marokko, gründeten Kunstschulen, um dort für Teppichweberei, Keramik, Seidenfärberei und Buchmalerei Produktionstechniken und Motive festzulegen.[6] Indem die Franzosen traditionelle Kunstformen derart institutionalisierten, und deren Produktion dabei häufig zu einem rein mechanischen Vorgang machten, konnten sie ihre westlichen Vorstellungen von marokkanischer Authentizität aufrechterhalten, während sie gleichzeitig die Sollvorgaben für Güter am französischen Markt erfüllten. Auf diese Weise wurden Marokkaner davon abgehalten, ihr eigenes kulturelles Erbe weiterzuführen. So ist in Marokko das Verhältnis zwischen den Künsten und ihrer technischen Produktion bis heute ein Thema, bei dem das Erbe der Kolonialzeit die politische Agenda beeinflusst.

Die gewonnene Inspiration durch marokkanische Webtechniken bei Recherchen in Marrakesch im Herbst 2011 fügten Barkow Leibinger mit Studien zum Moiré-Effekt und dessen Produktionstechniken in *Loom-Hyperbolic* zu einer architektonischen Erfahrung zusammen. Sie dokumentierten marokkanische Muster wie auch architektonische Formen in Marrakesch und ließen sie von einer Software algorithmisch verarbeiten, wodurch Konstruktionszeichnungen entstanden, die am Ende von Handwerkern aus Marrakesch umgesetzt wurden. Direkt neben der Koutoubia-Moschee inmitten der Medina installiert (auf einer 400 Quadratmeter großen Fläche mit den freigelegten Fundamenten einer früheren Moschee), sah *Loom-Hyperbolic* von Weitem wie eine ordentlich aufgereihte, weiße Zeltstadt aus, die gleich neben dem Minarett aufgeschlagen wurde. Trat man allerdings näher, lösten sich die Zeltflächen in einzelne Fäden aus weißem Garn auf. Eng über Reihen von hölzernen Pfählen gespannt, die Gipfel und Täler formen, tauchten die Fäden auf, bildeten Reihen und überschnitten sich – wie die Kett- und Schussfäden eines riesigen Webstuhls – wodurch unterschiedliche Transparenzgrade und Interferenzstreifen entstanden, während der Besucher durch die Installation und um sie herum ging. Unter den Gipfeln stehend hatte man das Gefühl, sich in einem durchsichtigen Zelt zu befinden. Und erst von oben betrachtet erschlossen sich die Einzelkomponenten der Struktur, deren Rhythmus mit dem der Moscheefundamente korrespondiert. Mit anderen Worten: Die Arbeit wechselte ihre Erscheinung grundlegend, je nach Standpunkt des Betrachters. Um ihre Logik zu verstehen, musste man sich in und um sie herum bewegen.

Die Koutoubia-Moschee ist eine der bekanntesten Sehenswürdigkeiten in Marrakesch; umgeben von fliegenden Händlern und Touristenbussen steht sie wie ein Fels in der Brandung, mitten in einem Strom von Menschen und Tieren, die aus den umliegenden Suks kommen und gehen. Die unverkennbare Gestalt des 77 Meter hohen Minaretts wird durch die städtische Bauordnung geschützt, die es verbietet, in der Nähe hohe Häuser zu errichten. Indem Barkow Leibinger ihre Installation direkt neben dieses Monument setzten, forderten sie Bewohner und Touristen gleichermaßen dazu auf, den öffentlichen Raum nicht nur als einen Ort für Kommerz und Unterhaltung zu sehen, sondern auch als Ort der künstlerischen Kontemplation und des Diskurses. Sich um *Loom-Hyperbolic* herum zu bewegen – dabei den Menschenmassen und dem Verkehr auszuweichen – hieß, der Ordnung der Stadt gewahr zu werden, die das Werk umgibt. Marokko hat keine Museen für zeitgenössische Kunst und die Galerien, die in Casablanca, Rabat und Marrakesch zeitgenössische Kunst ausstellen, sind heute genauso der ausländischen und marokkanischen Elite vorbehalten, wie sie es unter französischer Herrschaft waren. Kunst im öffentlichen Stadtraum Marrakeschs auszustellen, ist bereits ein Akt kreativer Transparenz und intellektueller Großzügigkeit, aber indem man zeitgenössische Werke von Ausländern so prominent im Stadtzentrum zeigt, übernimmt man eine gesellschaftlich herausfordernde Haltung, die offenlegt, wie und von wem und für wen kulturelle Teilhabe ermöglicht wird.[7]

Es geschieht nicht oft, dass Architektur so direkt und sichtbar an kulturgeschichtlicher Politik teilhat, wie es bei *Loom-Hyperbolic* der Fall war. Barkow Leibingers Büroturm in Seoul ist für seine kristallin facettierte Glasfassade berühmt und als eines der ersten Gebäude, das auf der Tabula rasa des neuen Stadtbezirks fertiggestellt wurde, scheint es auf den ersten Blick die neoliberalen Ideale zu bestätigen, die so viele der heutigen Stadterweiterungspläne befeuern, insbesondere in Asien. Und tatsächlich ist das TRUTEC Building ein Hochhaus mit einer glänzenden Vorhangfassade aus Glas – ein Nachfahre der Glastürme, die in den 1960er-Jahren als Echo auf die offenen Märkte der Wall Street entstanden. Während es sicherlich wichtig ist, jenen Verweis auf den ursprünglichen Typus des gläsernen Büroturms zu erkennen, offenbart sich das TRUTEC Building bei näherer Untersuchung geopolitisch als ein Projekt, dem man mit oberflächlichen Thesen nicht beikommt und das den Kontext scharfsinnig kritisiert, aus dem er erwachsen ist.

Ilhyun Kims Essay über den Standort des TRUTEC Building erinnert uns daran, dass Seoul von zwei gewaltigen Kräften des 20. Jahrhunderts geprägt wurde – Urbanisierung und Krieg.[8] Die Urbanisierung Koreas begann, nachdem das Land in den 1870er-Jahren seine Häfen dem Welthandel geöffnet hatte; ab Mitte des 20. Jahrhunderts, nach der japanischen Besatzung und dem Koreakrieg, war Südkorea fest entschlossen, auf urbanes und infrastrukturelles Wachstum zu setzen. Die Hauptstadt ging in die Höhe und Breite, und ihre Bevölkerung versechsfachte sich innerhalb von nicht einmal fünfzig Jahren, was zu massiven Infrastrukturproblemen führte.[9] Doch Urbanisierung führt zu Abfällen, und in den späten 1970er-Jahren, nicht weit südlich vom Standort des TRUTEC Building, wurde

Abfall auf Nanjido, einer Insel an der Mündung des Flusses Han, in solch rauen Mengen entsorgt, dass der Müllberg schließlich eine Höhe von über 100 Metern erreichte. Dieses intensive Wachstum wurde durch die wachsamen Augen Nordkoreas, nur wenige Autostunden von Seoul entfernt, überschattet. Obwohl die beiden Koreastaaten seit dem Waffenstillstand von 1953 durch eine 4 Kilometer breite demilitarisierte Zone (DMZ) getrennt sind, bleibt jene Grenze eine der am schwersten bewaffneten und unberechenbarsten weltweit. Einst als provisorische Verlegenheitslösung zur Unterbindung des gewaltsamen Konflikts geschaffen, ist die DMZ bis heute eine geopolitische Tatsache, die seit sechzig Jahren die Waffen schweigen lässt. In Seoul wird sie wie ein Dampfkochtopf wahrgenommen, den man auf dem Herd vergessen hat; sie ist Quelle anhaltenden Verdrusses, eine unerledigte Aufgabe, deren Lösung in gefährlichem Maß überfällig ist.

Die »Digital Media City«, kurz DMC, dagegen ist ein 570 000 Quadratmeter großer, trockengelegter Landstrich am nordwestlichen Rand der Stadt. Einst Teil der Müllhalde von Nanjido, verwandelte man die Gegend in einen nutzungsgemischten Stadtteil für Büros, Wohnhochhäuser, Geschäfte und diverse kulturelle Angebote, darunter auch ein neues Filmmuseum. Wie der Name DMC bereits vorgibt, setzt Seoul an dieser Stelle auf eine expandierende IT-Wirtschaft. Hier befindet sich auch der World Cup Park, die größte Grünfläche der Stadt; und genau in diesem techno-utopischen Kontext sollten Barkow Leibinger nun einen Büroturm errichten. Bis auf ihre Geschichte als trockengelegter Landstrich und ihren Neubaugebietsstatus bot die DMC keine Anknüpfungspunkte, da 2004, als Barkow Leibinger mit dem Projekt begannen, kaum jemand den ersten Spatenstich getan hatte.

Das TRUTEC Building ist ein 54 Meter hoher, Aufsehen erregender Büroturm, der seine Umgebung visuell fragmentiert. In der DMC sind gläserne Hochhäuser der Status quo; bei klarer Sicht wirkt die ganze Gegend vom Himmel, der sich in den Türmen spiegelt, wie von einem blauen Schleier überzogen. Das TRUTEC Building hüllt sich in eine silberfarbene Fassade aus spiegelndem Glas; die eine Hälfte der Oberflächen wirft sich in origamiartige Falten, wodurch alle umgebenden Gebäude auf der Fassade wie Picassos ihrer selbst aussehen. Wie in der kubistischen Malerei sieht man den Himmel, den Boden, die Umgebung und in Splitter zerlegte Teile seiner selbst – oben, unten, innen, außen, davor und dahinter, alles gleichzeitig; wie beim *Loom-Hyperbolic* verändert die Arbeit ihre Erscheinung je nach Standpunkt des Betrachters. Beim Umschreiten des Gebäudes blendet die von den Oberflächen reflektierte Sonne wie ein Paparazzi-Blitzlichtgewitter. Die Fassade des TRUTEC Building ist ein optisches Werkzeug, mit dem räumliches Verstehen verzögert wird, denn es verlangt Aufmerksamkeit statt flüchtiges Hinschauen und zwingt den Betrachter, seinen Blick zu fokussieren. Die gefalteten Glaspaneele folgen einem lockeren Muster, das ab und zu unterbrochen wird, was dem Bürobau einen Eindruck von Handlungsbewusstsein, Subjektivität und Zufälligkeit verleiht, der für diese Typologie ungewöhnlich ist. Es ist so vieles gleichzeitig sichtbar, dass die Entschlüsselung der Fragmente unmöglich wird. Wer den Schritt wagt, eine Spiegelfassade wie einen Juwel zu facettieren, erkennt an, dass die Idee der wahrheitsgetreuen Repräsentation immer eine Täuschung ist, und akzeptiert die Realität als etwas Unvollkommenes. Mit einem intuitiven Verständnis der latent vorhandenen geopolitischen Geschichte der DMC erklärte Frank Barkow, dass »eine verspiegelte Fassade niemals einfach nur flach, sondern immer in sich aufgebrochen sein muss«.[10] Diese Gegebenheit zum Entwurfsgegenstand des TRUTEC Building zu machen, deutet auf die bewusste Distanzierung von jeglicher Unternehmens-, Nachkriegs- und spätmodernistischen Ideologie hin.

2015 soll die DMC fertiggestellt werden, und wie ihr Name nahelegt, ist sie als urbane Antwort auf die ungreifbare, aber allgegenwärtige Präsenz digitaler Medien in den letzten beiden Jahrzehnten konzipiert. Ihrer Internetseite zufolge will die DMC zum Wachstum des Interesses an koreanischer Kultur, der sogenannten Korean Wave, beitragen.[11] Zwei Blocks westlich des TRUTEC-Turmes liegt der dreieckig angelegte Millennium Park, in dem 2010 die riesige Skulptur *Millennium Cell* der Künstler Soo Na, Young Ho Yoo und Bei Kyoung Lee enthüllt wurde. Wie die Fassade des TRUTEC Building ist auch diese Skulptur verspiegelt. Komponiert aus polierten Stahlbällen, die 23 Meter hoch gestapelt sind, fängt *Millenium Cell* die Welt in der »immerwährenden Essenz von Medien und Technologie« auf den Oberflächen seiner spiegelnden Sphären ein.[12] Am Fuße der Skulptur befindet sich ein 3 Meter breiter LED-Bildschirm, eingelassen in einen mauerartigen Sockel. Er zeigt rund um die Uhr den Himmel über der Stadt Montevideo, Uruguay, die sich genau auf der anderen Seite des Globus befindet. Angesichts einer solch ungenierten Darbietung von Erhabenheit, gepaart mit der selbstbestätigenden Behauptung technologischer Reichweite, erhebt das TRUTEC Building hier einen subtilen und dennoch wirkungsvollen Einspruch – seine Fassade wirft die geordnete Welt zurück, verwandelt.

Noch lassen sich keine Prognosen darüber stellen, ob es Seoul gelingen wird, seinen neuen Bezirk als Sitz von Koreas technologischer Zukunft zu etablieren. Gebäuden wie Schauspielern bestimmte Rollen zuzuschreiben, garantiert nicht, dass diese Rollen auch gespielt werden. Man denke nur an die vielen Rollen, die Berlin nach der Wiedervereinigung übernommen hat: der lange vermisste Cousin des Westens (Mitte), der Ex-Kommunist (Friedrichshain), der unkonventionelle Pionier (Prenzlauer Berg), der nostalgische Revisionist (Treptow), der Bohemien, arm aber sexy (Kreuzberg), und so weiter. Während des Kalten Krieges wurde Berlin zur Hauptbühne des ideologischen Wettrennens zwischen Ost und West. Als Ostberlin 1952 in der Stalinallee (heute Karl-Marx-Allee) mit dem Bau neoklassizistischer Wohnungen im Sowjetstil begann, antwortete der Westen 1957 mit den Wohnhochhäusern des Hansaviertels, entworfen von den Großmeistern der Moderne. Nachdem der Hamburger Mediengigant Axel Springer 1966 direkt neben der Mauer seinen Berliner Firmenhauptsitz – einen 78 Meter hohen Turm – erbauen ließ, konterte der Osten zwei Jahre später mit einer Reihe von Wohnhochhäusern (deren höchstes ebenfalls 78 Meter maß). In direkter Nachbarschaft zum Springer-Hochhaus erbaut versperrte dieser Wohnblock, die sogenannte Springer-Decke, die Sicht auf jenes Symbol westlicher Werte und der Pressefreiheit – die Fassaden zur Westberliner Seite hatten weder Fenster noch Balkone.[13] Das Park Inn Hotel wurde 1970 am Alexanderplatz, dem Zentrum Ostberlins, fertiggestellt, und ist mit seinen 125 Metern bis heute eines der höchsten Häuser der wiedervereinigten Stadt.[14] Im Vergleich mit Frankfurt oder anderen europäischen Hauptstädten wie London und Paris gibt es in Berlin nur wenige, relativ niedrige und über die Stadt verstreute Hochhäuser. Als Barkow Leibingers Tour Total 2012 direkt gegenüber dem Berliner Hauptbahnhof mit einer Höhe von 69 Metern fertig wurde, fügte er der langjährigen hitzigen Debatte um einen adäquaten städtebaulichen Maßstab für Berlin ein neues Kapitel hinzu.

Gleich nördlich des Humboldthafens, eines früheren Industriehafens, und des 2006 eröffneten Hauptbahnhofs liegt das urbane Entwicklungsgebiet der Europacity, deren Ausmaße etwa drei Viertel der DMC-Fläche erreichen, und für die ebenfalls eine durchmischte

Bebauung mit Wohnungen, Büros und Gewerbe geplant ist. Zu dieser Zeit war der Tour Total das einzige realisierte Projekt der Europacity. Bis dort andere Bauten entstehen, wird er alles sein, was die Besucher und Anwohner zu sehen bekommen, wenn sie den Bahnhof am Hauptausgang zur Invalidenstraße hin verlassen oder mit dem Auto aus dem Tiergartentunnel kommen. 17 Stockwerke hoch steht der Tour Total als weißer Betonkörper auf seinem von Kolonnaden gesäumten Sockel da; seine schlanke Höhe wird durch ein Raster aus langgestreckten Fenstern betont. Auf den ersten Blick sieht der Tour Total – eine Kiste, deren Oberfläche von gleichförmigen Fensteröffnungen durchbrochen ist – wie viele typische Berliner Gebäude der Nachwendezeit aus. Das 14-stöckige Motel One, 500 Meter entfernt gegenüber dem Bahnhof gelegen und 2011 fertiggestellt, hat eine ähnlich längliche Rasterfassade in weißem Beton – wie übrigens alle von Nalbach Architekten gebauten Motel-One-Gebäude in Deutschland. Seine schmalen, vertikal ausgerichteten Fenster lassen vage die Vergangenheit anklingen, indem sie auf Zeiten anspielen, in denen die industrielle Floatglasproduktion der 1950er-Jahre große Glasfassaden noch nicht möglich gemacht hatte. Als Hommage an die »Goldenen Zwanziger« sind die Türme des Beisheim-Center-Gebäudeensembles (2003) der Architekten Hilmer & Sattler und Albrecht wie auch Hans Kollhoffs Hochhaus in Backstein (1999) am Potsdamer Platz zu lesen; sie alle setzen vertikale Rasterfassaden ein, in denen die Formensprache der ersten Chicagoer und New Yorker Hochhäuser nachklingt, vielleicht um den Betrachter von erdrückenden Erinnerungen an die jüngere deutsche Geschichte abzulenken, ja vielleicht sogar, um derartige Gedanken im riesigen Ozean kollektiver Vorstellungen einer fernen Vergangenheit aufzulösen.[15]

Der zweite Blick auf den Tour Total offenbart hier einen frappierenden Unterschied. Die vorgefertigten Betonelemente der Fassade sind schräg abgefast und erzeugen durch die versetzte Anordnung ein diagonales Muster mit subtilem Kontur- und Farbspiel. Wie beim *Loom-Hyperbolic* und dem TRUTEC Building scheinen sich die physischen Eigenschaften des Tour Total zu verändern, sobald man ihn umschreitet. An einem bewölkten Tag frontal aus einiger Entfernung gesehen, scheint das Gebäude flach zu sein; nur seine subtil im Zickzack verlaufende Oberflächenstruktur unterscheidet es von den auf Leinwand gedruckten Fassadenattrappen, die in Berlin häufig an Baustellengerüsten hängen, um die Illusion eines fertigen Gebäudes zu erzeugen. An sonnigen Tagen, insbesondere aus einem schrägen Winkel gesehen, wirken die Vertikalen des Gebäudes wie in unterschiedliche Richtungen verzogen. Ein diagonales Muster aus dunklen, wellenartigen Bändern läuft über die Seiten; die dunklen Fensteröffnungen scheinen keine rechten Winkel zu haben; die weißen Betonvertikalen dazwischen weiten sich aus und ziehen sich dann wieder zusammen, wie die Vertikalen einer Schrifttype von Rudolf Steiner. Nachts, bei eingeschalteter Innenbeleuchtung, sieht der Tour Total mit seinem starren Fensterraster aus wie jeder andere Büroturm. Als zur Eröffnung auch noch eine Außenbeleuchtung eingeschaltet war, zersplitterte die Struktur in lange, facettierte Stäbe aus Schwarz und Weiß. Tritt man näher an das Haus heran, zeichnen sich die angeschrägten vertikalen Kanten noch deutlicher ab. Die zwei Stockwerke hohen Kolonnaden des Sockels scheinen anzuschwellen und sich zu biegen, während man um sie herum geht. Aus solcher Nähe wirkt der Tour Total wie ein Zerrbild des Motel One im Spiegelkabinett eines Jahrmarktes – die wahrgenommene Deformation verlangt nach einer Überprüfung dessen, was wirklich ist und was nicht.

Wenn das Motel One (und andere nahegelegene günstige Hotelketten im Trend der Rasterfassade, wie das InterCityHotel und das Meininger Hotel) die reflexartigen ökonomischen Zwänge widerspiegeln, die ein Vorhaben vom Maßstab der Europacity auslöst, dann ist der Tour Total deutlich als deren destabilisierende Kritik zu lesen. Und sollte er als kritische Wegmarke der Berliner Stadtplanung entwickelt worden sein, hätte es für diese Aufgabe keinen besseren Ort gegeben. Die Europacity befindet sich nur einen Block vom früheren Todesstreifen der Berliner Mauer, der befestigten Grenze zwischen Ost- und Westdeutschland, entfernt. Dieser Ort war einst der DMZ nicht unähnlich. Kraft seines Standorts, an der Grenzlinie zwischen den einstigen westlichen und östlichen Weltideologien, kann der Tour Total kaum anders, als den architektonischen Dialog weiterzuführen, der 1952 mit dem Bau der Stalinallee begann.

Von Stadtplänen aus der Mitte des 18. Jahrhunderts wissen wir, dass diese Gegend nie stark bebaut war, aber südlich der Invalidenstraße, wo sich heute der Humboldthafen befindet, sollte Adolf Hitlers Große Halle entstehen: das »achte Weltwunder« und der Gipfel seiner gigantomanischen Nord-Süd-Achse. 1937, vier Jahre nach der Machtergreifung der Nationalsozialisten, schmiedeten Hitler und sein Chefarchitekt Albert Speer Pläne, die Berlin in die neue »Welthauptstadt Germania« umwandeln sollten. Obwohl die Stadt

»reprovinzialisiert« werden sollte, waren monumentale Bauwerke, öffentliche Plätze und groß angelegte Achsen geplant, um die unermessliche Macht des Dritten Reiches vor der Welt und sich selbst zur Schau zu stellen. Die Ämter der neuen Metropole sollten sich, wie Perlen auf einer Schnur, als monumentale Granitpaläste an einer 5 Kilometer langen Allee aufreihen. Westlich des Flughafens Tempelhof beginnend sollte sich diese Achse nach Norden erstrecken, vorbei an Hitlers Reichskanzlei über einen riesigen Platz hinweg (der etwa 500 Meter breit und lang gewesen wäre), bevor sie die Große Halle erreicht hätte, einen gigantischen Kongressbau für 180 000 Menschen.[16] Die Große Halle war vom Pantheon in Rom inspiriert. Sie sollte an ihrem Scheitelpunkt 290 Meter hoch sein und sogar noch breiter – allein ihr 46 Meter weites Kuppelauge wäre größer als die gesamte Pantheonkuppel gewesen. Germania hatte mit Berlin weder im Maßstab noch in der Ausdehnung viel gemeinsam: Schon allein der 74 Meter hohe Sockel der Großen Halle hätte den Tour Total um 5 Meter überragt, und an die Stelle des gesamten Europacity-Geländes war ein riesiges rechteckiges Wasserbecken geplant, in dem sich die Große Halle spiegeln sollte.

Der Standort des Tour Total an der Heidestraße Ecke Minna-Cauer-Straße läge heute nur wenige Meter von der Nord-Süd-Achse entfernt, wenn diese in nördlicher Richtung weitergeführt worden wäre. Trotz der schlanken Fensteröffnungen geben die Büros in den oberen Stockwerken einen unverstellten Rundblick über Berlin frei. An der Spitze der geplanten Monumentalachse einer vergangenen Ära und angrenzend an die ehemalige Binnengrenze aus jüngerer Vergangenheit gelegen, ist die Aussicht vom Tour Total durch geschichtliche Ereignisse geprägt, die sich unauslöschlich in die Vergangenheit dieser Stadt eingeschrieben haben. Blickt man von hier nach Süden, sieht man das heutige Berlin – den Spreebogen, die Menschenströme rund um den Hauptbahnhof (mit dem Motel One auf der anderen Straßenseite), das dichte Grün des Tiergartens, den gläsernen Schimmer des Potsdamer Platzes – und wenn man sich einen Moment lang vorstellt, die Vision des Dritten Reichs wäre realisiert worden, wird all das, was nicht gebaut wurde, zum positiven Mahnmal dessen, was Berlin hätte sein können.

Im Februar 2009 eröffneten Barkow Leibiger eine Ausstellung in der Architectural Association in London mit dem Titel *An Atlas of Fabrication*. Auf der Webseite der Hochschule wird erklärt, wie das Berliner Büro mit 3-D-Lasern zugeschnittene Aluminiumrohre,

gesteppte Stahlblechschichten und Glasstücke unterschiedlicher Spiegelkraft ausstellte, um zu zeigen, »wie architektonische Ideen und Materialien untrennbar miteinander verbunden sind«.[17] Fügt man Barkow Leibingers Materialatlas jene geopolitische Dimension hinzu, die im kontextuellen Rahmen des *Loom-Hyperbolic,* des TRUTEC Building und des Tour Total zutage tritt, wird deutlich, dass nicht nur Materialien und architektonische Ideen miteinander verwoben sind, sondern auch dass architektonische Ideen, materiell manifestiert als Gebäude, aufs Engste am Einschreiben von Geschichte beteiligt sind.

1 Aaron Betsky, »From Field to Form, With an Attitude«, in: JaeHong Lee, *Barkow Leibinger Architects,* Seoul 2007, S. 16.

2 Anthony Vidler, »New Skins for a New Age. Class Culture in the Work of Barkow Leibinger«, in: Andres Lepik (Hrsg.), *Barkow Leibinger. Reflect,* Ostfildern 2007, S. 26.

3 Barkow Leibinger, »Barkow Leibinger in Conversation with Barry Bergdoll and Andres Lepik«, in: Lepik 2007 (wie Anm. 2), S. 67.

4 Yve-Alain Bois, »A Picturesque Stroll Around ›Clara Clara‹«, in: *October,* 29, Sommer 1984, S. 32–62.

5 Die 4. Biennale von Marrakesch wurde von Nadim Samman und mir kuratiert.

6 Katarzyna Pieprzak, *Imagined Museums. Art and Modernity in Postcolonial Morocco,* Minneapolis 2010, S. 5 f.

7 Bemerkenswerterweise eröffneten 1969 Kunststudenten der Akademie in Marrakesch eine öffentliche Malereiausstellung in der Djemaa el Fna.

8 Ilhyun Kim, in: Lepik 2007 (wie Anm. 2), S. 33.

9 1955 hatte Seoul 1,6 Millionen Einwohner; 1999 war die Zahl auf 10,3 Millionen angewachsen und ist seitdem ungefähr stabil geblieben. Seoul Metropolitan Government, *Seoul Statistical Yearbook,* Seoul 2000.

10 Lepik 2007 (wie Anm. 2), S. 72.

11 »Introduction. Meaning of the DMC«, online unter http://dmc.seoul.go.kr/eng/en_about/en_project/en_introduction/en_introduction.do (Stand: 31. Oktober 2013).

12 MillenniumEye, »Millennium Cell«, online unter http://millenniumeye.co.kr/en/cell.html (Stand: 31. Oktober 2013).

13 Jörg Niendorf, »Begehrte Platte«, in: *Frankfurter Allgemeine Sonntagszeitung,* 7.7.2013.

14 Die Treptowers wurden 1998 errichtet und messen dieselbe Höhe.

15 Claire Colomb, *Staging the New Berlin. Place Marketing and the Politics of Urban Reinvention Post-1989,* London 2012, S. 159–165.

16 Léon Krier, *Albert Speer. Architecture, 1932–1942,* New York 2013, S. 75–83.

17 Architectural Association School of Architecture, »An Atlas of Fabrication«, online unter http://www.aaschool.ac.uk/PUBLIC/WHATSON/exhibitions.php?item=23 (Stand: 11. Dezember 2012).

Liminal Façade/Deep Surface

Gebäudehüllen sind ein zwingender und zu bezwingender Gegenstand zeitgenössischer Architektur. Große Gestaltungsfreiheit entsteht immer dann, wenn die Hülle von Vorgaben zur nutzbaren Bodenfläche, dem Raumprogramm und mitunter sogar von Einschränkungen durch die Tragwerksstruktur losgelöst ist. Bestimmte Gebäudetypen unterstreichen diese Autonomie: So sind Büro- oder Industriebauten besonders auf den effizienten Umgang mit Licht und Luft angewiesen und benötigen außerdem Flexibilität und innere Wandelbarkeit. Aus diesem Grund verlangen gerade sie nach einer Neutralität, die stärker als andere Typen die Hülle vom Inneren des Gebäudes unabhängig behandelt. Durch ihre formalen und performativen Eigenschaften wird die Fassade zum Mittler zwischen außen und innen, zwischen öffentlichem und privatem Raum. Die Hülle reguliert maßgeblich den Einfall des natürlichen Lichts, die Belüftung und die Akustik. Sie ist daher die erste Schwelle, an der über die Nachhaltigkeit des Energieverbrauchs entschieden werden kann. Somit sind Fassaden Orte großer technischer und ästhetischer Verantwortung. Sie bilden (gemeinsam mit Maßstab und Kubatur) das entscheidende Element eines Gebäudes, um sich entweder in den baulichen Kontext einzufügen oder aber sich ihm zu widersetzen.

Die in diesem Kapitel vorgestellten Projekte zeigen ein breites Spektrum an Gebäudehüllen, von der Vorhangfassade über tragende Strukturen bis hin zu Mischformen. Diese Unterschiede manifestieren sich an den Gebäuden und werden an ihnen ablesbar, entweder indem das Innere mit einer Fassadenlösung zusammenwirkt oder die Fassade unabhängig davon existiert. Trotz der Unterschiede handelt es sich bei jeder Fassade um einen Ort des Übergangs, der körperliche Qualitäten besitzt: Die äußere Hülle ist ein Bereich, dem Raum gegeben werden muss, aber auch dessen Tiefe das Licht steuert und die Atmosphäre der Räume beeinflusst. Sie hat eine physische Präsenz, wie es bei den Betonfalten des Tour Total oder bei dem kaleidoskopischen TRUTEC Building deutlich erkennbar ist, dessen Fassaden verspiegelt sind – und zwar in Anlehnung an die Vorhangfassaden der 1960er-Jahre aus Stahl und Glas, die allerdings mit einer minimalen Tiefe auskommen und ihre Flächenhaftigkeit betonen. Beim TRUTEC Building sind die Fassadenelemente im Gegensatz dazu plastisch ausgebildet, sie haben Tiefe, sind als Volumen entwickelt, die in ihre Umgebung hineinwirken und sie kontrollieren.

Die Fassade wird als räumliche Schicht und als etwas Skulpturales verstanden, als dreidimensionale Oberfläche – raumgreifend, performativ und ikonografisch.

In solchen Hüllen manifestiert sich eine inhärente Umkehrbarkeit: Sie beeinflussen das äußere Erscheinungsbild eines Gebäudes als urbanes Objekt, und sie werden von innen als eine Art optische Linse erfahren. In den gezeigten Beispielen ist die Fassade Teil eines tektonischen Systems, das im ganzen Gebäude mitschwingt.

Nach oben schauen
Sarah Whiting

Wenn es um Architektur geht, kommen Decken meist zu kurz. Selbst Auguste Choisys in Froschperspektive gezeichnete, axonometrische Schnitte, anhand derer sich faszinierende und unerwartete Blicke nach oben ergeben, lenken ihr Augenmerk mehr auf raumgestalterische und bauliche Informationen als auf die Decke per se. Decken sind der Ort für all den Kram, der sich der Kontrolle der Architekten entzieht: Leerrohre, Rauchmelder, Sprinkleranlagen, Dämmplatten, Lichtgitter, Notausgangsschilder, Spinnenweben und Ähnliches. Sie sind der Ort des Pflichtprogramms, nicht des Erfindungsreichtums; und abgesehen von einigen wohl bekannten Ausnahmen – man denke beispielsweise an die Sixtinische Kapelle – wird man selten dazu ermuntert, nach oben zu schauen.

Fußböden, »floors«, müssen einige ganz ähnliche Anforderungen erfüllen – in Form von Entlüftungsschlitzen, Stufen, Schwellen, außerdem Zugängen und anderen Zweckmäßigkeiten – aber der Grundriss, der »floor plan«, ist das wichtigste Kontrollinstrument der Architektur. Dort findet die Definition des Raums durch das Einzeichnen von Wänden, Stützen und die Festlegung des Raumprogramms statt. Selbst der freie Grundriss, der »plan libre«, ist eine Form, Freiheit durch sehr bedachten Verzicht von Kontrolle zu gewinnen. Im Großen und Ganzen bewegt sich die Architekturgeschichte zwischen Entwürfen, die »definieren«, indem sie Räume für differenzierte Programme bestimmen, und Entwürfen, die »ermöglichen«, indem sie fast nichts festlegen, wie der plan libre, der Universalraum, Loftflächen und Ähnliches. Eben weil der Grundriss der Ort der Definition ist, sind Grundrisse die maßgeblichen Zeichnungen für das Verständnis eines architektonischen Raumprogramms. Im Vergleich dazu beschränkt sich die Gestaltung von Decken häufig auf die Darstellung als Deckenspiegel, die ausschließlich technische Funktionen beschreiben und denen über diese Notwendigkeit hinaus fast nie besondere Aufmerksamkeit geschenkt wird. Dächer hatten ihre Sternstunde in der Moderne, als man sie durch die Errungenschaft des Fliegens als »fünfte Fassade« zu begreifen lernte, aber Decken bekamen nie, was ihnen zusteht; oder vielleicht besser gesagt: bis jetzt nicht.

Im Laufe ihrer Karriere haben Barkow Leibinger eine einzigartige Beziehung zur Decke aufgebaut: Die meisten ihrer Projekte nutzen diese unterschätzte Oberfläche als ein Experimentierfeld der Architektur und nicht nur als einen Ort der technischen Pflichterfüllung: Ihre Decken definieren den Raum, sie inszenieren den Lichteinfall oder sind einfach derjenige Bereich, an dem ein gewünschter architektonischer Umgang mit einer Oberfläche so frei ausgelebt werden kann, wie er an einer Wand oder auf dem Boden unmöglich wäre. Dies gilt insbesondere für Projekte, die durch ihre Nutzungsanforderungen starken funktionalen Vorgaben unterliegen.

Zahlreiche Bauten von Barkow Leibinger haben einen Bezug zu industrieller Fertigung – einem programmatischen Milieu, das die Offenheit eines miesschen Universalraums bevorzugt: Es sind Produktionshallen, insbesondere für TRUMPF. Dabei verbinden Barkow-Leibinger-Projekte das Universale mit dem Definierten und sie erreichen dies, indem sie innerhalb vollkommen flexibler räumlicher Volumina die Decke als Ort der Definition nutzen. Viele ihrer Projekte nutzen die Decke als eine Oberfläche, die sonst anonymen Produktionshallen Charakter verleiht. In diese Gruppe von Bauten, deren Dächer und Decken durch die Tragstruktur und deren besondere Geometrie definiert werden, gehört die Laserfabrik in Ditzingen aus dem Jahr 2000, deren gefaltete Dachbänder in den Innenraum hineinwirken und ihn und seine gewaltigen Ausmaße gliedern. Dort, wo sich die Bänder in ihrer gegenläufigen Bewegung voneinander entfernen, belichten sie die Hallen über trapezförmige Fenster. Das vielleicht »reinste« Beispiel für eine Decke als gliedernde Tragstruktur ist die ebenso einfache wie elegante Installation *Loom-Hyperbolic* für die 4. Biennale von Marrakesch von 2012, bei der hyperbolische Räume aus Garn konstruiert wurden: eine filigrane, schwebende Fläche, Raum und Oberfläche zugleich. Weil die temporäre Installation keinen Witterungsschutz benötigte, formierten sich die filigranen Linien des Garns zu einer fast geisterhaften Hülle, in der Dach und Decke wirklich einmal eins waren.

Während in Marrakesch und bei der Laserfabrik jeweils nur ein einziges sich wiederholendes Muster zugrunde liegt, das auf diese Weise die Logik von Dach und Decke bestimmt, findet sich in anderen Projekten eine weitere Barkow-Leibinger-Strategie im Umgang mit Decken, die den miesschen Universalraum noch weiter aus seiner Komfortzone hinausdrängt. Hier wird die Decke dazu eingesetzt, auf einem freien Grundriss abgegrenzte Zonen zu schaffen. In der Montagehalle in Neukirch von 2004 verwendeten die Architekten einen Deckenrost aus Stahl, der mehr die Struktur eines Schachbrettmusters als die eines Schottenmusters aufweist. Die Decke erinnert dabei an eine Teppichstruktur (wie sie beim Erweiterungsbau der Freien Universität Berlin vom Architektenbüro Candilis – Josic – Woods und unter Mitarbeit von Manfred Schiedhelm konzipiert wurde), die aber nur in den schmalen Abschnitt zwischen Decke und Dach gepresst ist. Die oben angebrachten transparenten und opaken Rasterflächen beleuchten das Innere auf unterschiedliche Weise und zonieren so die riesige Halle, ohne sie dabei in tatsächliche Räume zu unterteilen. Im Betriebsrestaurant für TRUMPF in Ditzingen (2008) wird diese Strategie noch einen Schritt weitergeführt. Dieses Dach ist keine große zusammenhängende Fläche mehr, sondern setzt sich aus kleineren, dreieckigen und in Stahl eingefassten Feldern zusammen, die sich zu einer Grundform, einem beinahe unlesbaren Fünfeck, fügen. Jedes dreieckige Feld enthält wiederum eine unregelmäßige Ansammlung von tiefen polygonalen Holzwaben, von denen manche das Dach durchdringen und als Oberlicht fungieren. Das größere Fünfeck umfasst dabei alle Teile des Raumprogramms in einer einzigen räumlichen Einheit. Die Anordnung der Tischgruppen folgt der radialen Logik der Dreiecke, während der Bereich der Küche und Essensausgabe die polygonalen Formen wieder aufnimmt. Obwohl die geometrische Struktur auf dem Boden nur teilweise auftaucht, fühlt sich der Raum sehr viel strukturierter an, als er tatsächlich ist, da die Decke vollständig ausdifferenziert ist. Auf diese Weise erfährt der große »Einraum« des Restaurants eine behutsame Zonierung, ohne jedoch räumlich unterteilt werden zu müssen.

In den Decken ihrer Gebäude vermitteln Barkow Leibinger die gesamte Komplexität ihrer geometrisch-strukturellen Bestrebungen, während sie den Grundrissen – und damit dem Programm ihrer Gebäude – sehr viel mehr Spielraum einräumen. Anders gesagt, befreien diese Projekte nicht nur den Grundriss, sondern sie befreien die Architektur selbst, indem sie einen neuen Ort für architektonische Erkundungen etablieren. Wie andere zeitgenössische Büros legen auch Barkow Leibinger ihre architektonische Kernaussage in den Fassaden, Schnitten und Tragstrukturen ihrer Bauten an. Ein Grund mehr daran zu erinnern, nach oben zu schauen, wenn man das nächste Mal in einem ihrer Gebäude ist. Bei ihnen sind es die Decken, in denen Überraschendes zum Vorschein kommt. In einem Versuch zu beschreiben, was Kunst oder Poesie erschaffen, wenden sich Gilles Deleuze und Félix Guattari D. H. Lawrence zu, der einst schrieb: »Unablässig stellen die Menschen einen Schirm her, der ihnen Schutz bietet, auf dessen Unterseite sie ein Firmament zeichnen und ihre Konventionen und Meinungen schreiben; der Dichter, der Künstler aber macht einen Schlitz [*fente*] in diesen Schirm, er zerreißt sogar das Firmament, um ein wenig freies und windiges Chaos hereindringen zu lassen und in einem plötzlichen Lichtschein eine Vision zu rahmen, die durch den Schlitz erscheint [...].«[1] Der plan libre mag sicher der bekanntere Ort architektonischer Befreiung sein, aber wie erlösend ist es, Freiheit auch am Firmament zu finden?

1 Gilles Deleuze und Félix Guattari, *Was ist Philosophie?,* Frankfurt 2000, S. 241.

Ultra Structural

»Ultrastruktur: Eine biologische und besonders feine Struktur (wie die einer Zelle), die nur unter einem Lichtmikroskop sichtbar ist.«
Merriam-Webster Dictionary

Dieses Kapitel beschäftigt sich mit den geometrischen Organisations- oder Tragstrukturen, die so grundlegend und bedeutend sind, dass sie die Räume definieren, die innerhalb der Strukturen entstehen. Es geht also um Projekte, die im Wesentlichen von ihrem Innenleben bestimmt werden, und darüber hinaus um die Frage, wie Räume beschaffen sind, die durch solche Strukturen entstehen.

Die hier gezeigten Beispiele basieren auf Ideen von ausdifferenzierten zellularen Organisationsprinzipien, angelehnt an natürliche Formationen – Blätter, Schwämme, Äste –, oder beschäftigen sich mit dem Thema der Sammlung und Stapelung von Materialien. Im Ansatz geht es bei dieser Herangehensweise immer um die Addition gleicher Elemente. Asymmetrische ebenso wie symmetrische Organisationsprinzipien fördern die Ähnlichkeit mit natürlichen Systemen. Den Strukturen wird hier bewusst eine Materialstärke gegeben, die raumbildend wirken, den Lichteinfall lenken oder Tiefe erzeugen kann – und so wiederum bespielbaren Raum erschafft. Digitalen Herstellungstechniken und Arbeitsschritten fällt dabei eine Schlüsselfunktion zu, da sie die Fertigung komplexer und variierender Elemente erleichtern. Diese Techniken können auf alle Maßstäbe einzelner Gebäudekomponenten angewendet werden – seien es Tragstrukturen, Fassaden, Einbauten, Fliesen oder Betonfertigteile. Sie geben dem Architekten wieder die Freiheit, ein Gebäude als zeitgenössisches Gesamtkunstwerk zu denken – mit einzigartigen Lösungen für jedes individuelle Projekt. Dies ist eines der Arbeitsfelder, das am meisten von der Forschungsarbeit profitiert hat, mit der wir versuchen, den Standardbaukatalog zu überwinden. Dabei sind digitale Techniken die idealen Werkzeuge, da sich mit ihnen geometrische Fragestellungen auf der Basis gleicher oder variierender Komponenten am einfachsten lösen lassen. Muster sind zunächst einmal zweidimensionale Systeme, mit deren Hilfe sich aber Geometrien in dreidimensionalen Strukturen generieren lassen. Neue Softwareanwendungen wie das Scripting optimieren den Materialeinsatz und dessen Dimensionierung. Dennoch besitzt die digitale Fabrikation im Entwurfsprozess keine Exklusivrechte.

Vielmehr wird sie zusammen mit analogen und handwerklichen Techniken zu einem ganzheitlichen Entwurfsansatz kombiniert.

Gebäude wie das Betriebsrestaurant oder die Hauptpforte von TRUMPF haben uns erstmals die Gelegenheit geboten und Technologien den Weg geebnet, vorgefertigte Elemente in verschiedenen Maßstäben und aus unterschiedlichen Materialien so zu kombinieren, dass daraus ein selbstständiger Bau entsteht. Letztlich ermächtigt dies uns Architekten dazu, wieder beides zu definieren und zu kontrollieren: die Herstellung von Komponenten und die Umsetzung von deren räumlichem und tektonischem Potenzial.

Das Architekturdenken bei Barkow Leibinger
Brett Steele

> »Malen hat mit Denken nichts zu tun, das Denken beim Malen ist das Malen.«[1] Gerhard Richter

I. Die episodische Wirklichkeit der Architektur

Es ist das Wiederkehrende in einer Architektenlaufbahn, das sie am stärksten prägt; dies entspricht auch der Denkweise der Architektur. Das Lebenswerk eines Architekten ist episodisch: Sich stets wiederholend entfaltet es ein Projekt nach dem anderen; eins nach dem anderen, wieder und wieder, während der vielen Jahre, die eine Architektur-Laufbahn ausmachen. So betrachtet ist das Architekturdenken in Wirklichkeit ein Tun. In ihrer Arbeit sind sich Frank Barkow und Regine Leibinger dieser Tatsache bewusst und machen sie sich auf überraschende, beeindruckende und originelle Weise zunutze. Jede architektonische Karriere setzt sich mit einer Reihe unzusammenhängender und zufällig entstandener Projekte auseinander. Architekten wissen dies spätestens seit jener Zeit, als ein junger Römer namens Vitruv in einem einzigen Werk die mannigfaltigen Aufzeichnungen von Häusern, Brücken, Aquädukten, Säulenkapitellen, dekorativen Elementen, Militärgerätschaften und anderen Seltsamkeiten vereinte, die man später zur vitruvischen Architektur erklärte. »Die zufällige Serie von Aufträgen, von denen jeder Architekt abhängt, ist das Gegenteil einer klaren Agenda«, schrieb Rem Koolhaas in der Einleitung zu *Content,* einer 2004 erschienen Monografie über sein Werk. Ausgehend von dieser Beobachtung entwickelt Koolhaas die These einer Angst unter Architekten vor dem neuen Jahrtausend und sagt »Architektur ist zu langsam, [...] um auf die heutige Welt einzugehen.«[2] Der Gedankensprung von jener Verunsicherung zur gänzlichen Abberufung der Architektur als etwas Notwendigem ist von hier aus nicht mehr weit: »Architektur ist ein unscharfes Amalgam alten Wissens und moderner Praxis, eine unbeholfene Art, die Welt zu sehen, und ein inadäquates Medium, um in ihr zu funktionieren.«[3]

Im Gegensatz dazu fordert uns Barkow Leibingers Entwurf für ein Smart Material House (SMH) zu einem anderen Denken auf. An diesem Projekt wird offenbar, dass Architekturdenken, selbst wenn es in seinem engsten, traditionellsten und strengsten Sinn (als Arbeit an einem einzelnen, begrenzten Projekt) aufgefasst wird, alles andere als inadäquat ist; gerade wenn man sich mit einigen der größten

Herausforderungen unserer Zeit beschäftigt und sie nicht nur von außen betrachtet. Im Fall des SMH schließt dies so gewaltige, grundsätzliche und dringende Fragen ein wie die nach dem Umgang mit den schwindenden natürlichen Ressourcen unserer Welt. Hierauf findet das Gebäude vielgestaltige Antworten, so auch auf Ebenen, die man zunächst kaum wahrnimmt.

Das SMH entstand als Antwort auf einen einfachen, ja unspektakulären Wettbewerb. Dessen Hauptziel (zumindest in der Absicht der Auslober) darin bestand, ein energieeffizientes und bezahlbares Mehrfamilienhaus für die Internationale Bauausstellung in Hamburg zu entwickeln und somit zu thematisieren, dass solche Gebäude in der Regel einen unakzeptabel hohen Energieverbrauch haben. Der Wettbewerb schrieb sehr allgemeine Richtlinien zu Kosten, Grundstück, Bewohnern und Konstruktionsweisen vor. Das Projekt unterlag also nur wenigen Einschränkungen, abgesehen von einigen alltäglichen Vorgaben zu Wirtschaftlichkeit, Leistung und Realisierbarkeit (und natürlich der Phantasie der Teilnehmer).

Barkow Leibinger entwickelten ein Gebäude, das schon in der frühesten Entwurfsphase über eine schlichte Einzellösung hinausreichte, deren Sinn darin bestand und besteht, künftigen Energieverbrauch zu reduzieren. Besonders erfindungsreich ist das Gebäude dort, wo der niedrige Energiebedarf in Zusammenhang mit der gesamten Kultur des Bauens und Wohnens betrachtet wurde; also nicht nur im Hinblick auf eine spätere haustechnische »Performance«, sondern auch in Bezug auf die Herstellung, Anlieferung und Montage der beiden primären Konstruktionselemente. Dies wird auf unterschiedliche und bestechende Weise erreicht. Der Einsatz vorgefertigter Wandelemente aus Leichtbeton (so breit, dass sie wortwörtlich von allein auf den Geschossdecken stehen) ist eine von vielen smarten Maßnahmen. Der Energiebedarf für den Transport und die Anlieferung der Bauteile ist zudem durch die Materialeigenschaften stark reduziert (von der beachtlichen Wärmedämmfähigkeit aufgrund der Herstellung aus porösem, selbstisolierendem Material einmal ganz abgesehen), und, sogar noch erstaunlicher, als freistehende, selbsttragende Elemente fallen die beträchtlichen (immer gern übersehenen) Befestigungs- und Montagekosten sehr gering aus; Konstruktionshilfen und Baugerüste werden gar nicht benötigt.

Ich könnte noch viel ausführlicher wiedergeben, was die Architekten noch alles an haus- und bautechnischer Intelligenz in ihren schönen Prototypen haben einfließen lassen. Aber das Thema dieses Essays ist eine gänzlich andere Form des Energieerhalts. Hier geht es um die Art, wie das SMH von der Energie architektonischer Ideen, Konzepte und Lösungen anderer (früherer) Projekte zehrt. Im Sinne des SMH ist dies die wirklich nachhaltige Architektur unserer heutigen Welt: in der sich das Architekturfach über die Zeit selbst erhält, indem sich der Architekt auf intelligente Weise frühere Formen des Architekturdenkens zu eigen macht, sie anpasst, auf ihnen aufbaut und sie weiterentwickelt.

Wie das beim SMH geschieht, ist unerwartet und überraschend. Barkow Leibinger betrachten dabei einen der markantesten Prototypen moderner Architektur, Le Corbusiers Maison Dom-ino, und krempeln diese hundert Jahre alte Ikone regelrecht um. So wird Barkow Leibingers SMH ein vollkommen neuer Prototyp seines Jahrhunderts. Es ist ein Prototyp, der bewusst erschaffen wurde, indem man sich auf die Ursprünge des modernen Prototypen besann. Dementsprechend ist das SMH ein »disciplinary prototype«, eine Architektur, der es ausschließlich um die Architektur geht. Genau dieser Fokus ist es, der uns vor Augen führt, wie sich ein ernsthaftes Projekt heute in der Architektur behauptet, lebendig ist und sogar – und das überrascht vielleicht am meisten – die Projekte der modernen Architekturvergangenheit wie das Maison Dom-ino annehmen kann, das mit der gesamten Architekturgeschichte brechen wollte.

Barkow Leibinger durchdenken viele der wesentlichen Eigenschaften des Maison Dom-ino neu, von den Fundamenten aufwärts. Dom-ino ist ein auf ganz eigene Art maßgebendes Projekt, das sich als vielleicht berühmtestes Bild (einer ungebauten Idee) durch das gesamte 20. Jahrhundert zieht; ein Projekt, dessen Präsenz geholfen hat, die Identität der modernen Architektur zu formen. Für viele Architekten scheint das Dom-ino hundert Jahre nach seiner Entstehung einigermaßen erledigt, sogar irrelevant für das 21. Jahrhundert zu sein. Das SMH widerspricht allerdings dieser historistischen Wahrnehmung, verformt und dehnt Schlüsselelemente des Dom-ino, während es andere seiner Eigenschaften grundsätzlich ablehnt – nicht zuletzt seine frühmoderne Abhängigkeit von der unflexiblen Repetition. Dom-inos strenge, euklidische Gitterstruktur, seine identischen Stützen, sein unerbittlicher Fokus auf die Vertikalbewegung und seine uniformen Betondecken werden alle derart verbessert, dass ihr Ursprung fast unkenntlich wird und trotzdem immer noch durch das Beharren auf einer universell anwendbaren Elementbauweise präsent bleibt – eine Bauweise, deren Prinzipien und Eigenschaften sich aus der genauen Kenntnis heutiger Herstellungsprozesse ableiten. Während also das Material und die Komposition des Corbusier-Entwurfes fast bis zur Unsichtbarkeit manipuliert wurden, bekräftigt das SMH dennoch die schicksalhaften, universell wirksamen Impulse moderner Architektur, setzt sie auf neue und profunde, ja fast bewegende Weise um.

Das SMH verleiht seinen Bestandteilen eine neue Form, eine neue Bestimmung und Erscheinung, und zwar mithilfe neuester Materialien und Fertigungstechniken. Barkow Leibinger lockern das Raster von Le Corbusiers minimalistischem Stahlskelett in Kombination mit Betonfertigteilen (und erlauben so die subtile Ausbildung einer nicht-repetitiven Anordnung von Vertikalelementen). Das Projekt mildert Dom-inos Abhängigkeit von der reinen Wiederholung und schafft abwechslungsreiche Innenräume durch verschiedene Kombinationsmöglichkeiten der drei Hauptbauelemente, aus denen das System besteht (dieselben drei Elemente wie beim Dom-ino: vertikale Stützen, horizontaler Wohnraum und vertikale Zirkulation). Die geschwungenen vertikalen Betonscheiben müssen nicht exakt übereinander positioniert werden (sie brauchen nur so viel Überschneidung, dass die Last des Gebäudes durch alle Stockwerke in den Boden abgeleitet werden kann). Auch die Treppen können an verschiedene Stellen des Grundrisses verschoben werden, entgegen Le Corbusiers Beharren auf einer immer gleich platzierten Erschließung an derselben trennenden oder tragenden Wand. Und die monolithischen, massiven Bodenplatten bestehen nicht etwa aus Beton, sondern sind, unglaublicher Weise, aus Brettschichtholz hergestellt. So fügen sich die drei Schlüsselelemente des Systems auf grundlegend neue und didaktische Weise zusammen. Der Effekt ist erstaunlich.

Was bei Dom-ino ein System gleicher Vertikalelemente war, einheitlich verbunden durch monolithische Geschossplatten, wird im SMH zu einem neuen Kombinationssystem, das innerhalb gewisser Grenzen immer wieder neu arrangiert werden kann und so in der Lage ist, eine ganze Welt unterschiedlicher Wohneinheiten zu generieren, umschlossen von einer nichtrepetitiven Hülle, deren Innenräume sich subtil voneinander unterscheiden. Das verblüffende Ergebnis ist, dass hier zwei normalerweise konkurrierende Materialsysteme miteinander interagieren und so die bisher stillschweigend vorausgesetzte Materialeinheit von Stahl und Beton aushebeln, die zum einen ein Vorgriff Le Corbusiers war, zum anderen auch dessen Vermächtnis in Form von bis heute geltenden Konstruktionsideen. Wie bereits erwähnt, handelt es sich beim ersten dieser Materialsysteme um die leichtgewichtigen, konkav und konvex geschwungenen Betonscheiben (die im Vergleich zum Dom-ino den Platz der undifferenzierten und undefinierten Säule einnehmen). Das zweite ist eine massive, solide und schwere Bodenplatte aus Brettschichtholz, die als Einzelkomponente hergestellt wird. Der Kombinationseffekt dieser beiden ungleichen Elemente und damit der gewählten Materialwelten, ist beeindruckend. Denn wir erkennen nicht nur ein neues universelles Architektursystem, sondern auch ein Mittel, das uns Dom-ino (genau wie eine Reihe gleichgesinnter Experimente) neu sehen und verstehen lässt.

Besonders trifft das auf die plastisch geformten Betonwandscheiben zu; seltsame Bauteile, die gleichzeitig als Säule und Wand fungieren. Diese geschosshohen Elemente sind modular, regelmäßig geformt, durch und durch modern und (Dank ihrer vertikalen Anordnung) taktil, sie muten fast wie korinthische Säulen an. Sie werden industriell vorgefertigt, in einem Umfeld, in dem das Material getestet und in einem integralen Prozess hergestellt werden kann. Sobald sie auf der Baustelle angekommen sind, können sich schnell und ohne aufwendige Befestigung montiert werden. Hergestellt werden sie mithilfe einer leicht steuerbaren Maschinenrobotik durch Betonguss in vertikalen Formschalungen. Sind sie an ihrer Position aufgestellt, sind sie dort ohne weitere Befestigung stabil und bilden die vertikale Struktur des Hauses, das sie als thermische, strukturelle und raumbildende Elemente prägen.

Leichte Granulate mit dämmender Wirkung (Ton oder Schaumglas) werden mit Zement gemischt. Zusammen mit technischen Installationen (wie Heiz- oder Kühlleitungen) und der Bewehrung, welche die Elemente selbsttragend macht, entsteht so ein Hybrid aus Baustoff und Gebäudesystem – und zwar einer mit einer beachtlichen inneren Logik, Energie- und Kosteneffizienz. Dies wird besonders offensichtlich, wenn man dieses vorgeformte, präzise System mit den tendenziell eher schlampig und ungenau ausgeführten Stahlbetonkonstruktionen vergleicht, wie sie heutzutage üblicherweise auf Baustellen entstehen. Die Wandscheiben sind tragend, raumbildend und gleichzeitig umhüllend, formen also auch die Fassade. Wie bereits erwähnt, stehen sie direkt auf der Bodenplatte aus Brettschichtholz. Die Umkehrung des gewohnten Materialnutzungsverhaltens –

indem große, relativ schwere Betonelemente auf vorgefertigte Holzgeschossplatten gestellt werden, die sie gleichzeitig tragen – ist in sofern genial, da hier mit dem jahrhundertealten Glauben aufgeräumt wird, ein monolithisches Betongerüst sei die unerlässliche Tragstruktur, die letztlich mit Holz oder anderen Materialien ausgeschmückt, zu einem architektonischen Objekt würde. Mit dem SMH wird diese Logik – wie so viele andere aus Le Corbusiers Maison Dom-ino – auf vielen Ebenen gründlich umgekehrt oder weiterentwickelt, dass wir in ihm als Projekt eine sehr effiziente Plattform erkennen.

II. Das Projekt als Plattform

Die Arbeit des Büros Barkow Leibinger ist so organisiert, dass ganz bewusst Freiräume für Forschungstätigkeiten bestehen. Hierzu gehört nicht nur das stetige Experimentieren mit neuen Baumaterialien und Fabrikationstechniken, sondern inzwischen auch eine moderne Ahnenreihe von Projekten und Prototypen, die dieser selben Absicht folgen. Dieser Teil des Schaffens von Barkow Leibinger war bereits Gegenstand verschiedener Publikationen, Ausstellungen und Installationen und steht aus diesem Grund nicht im Mittelpunkt dieses Essays.[4] Das Büro testet, kartiert und untersucht den freien Fluss von Ideen und architektonischem Denken nicht nur innerhalb ihres eigenen Archivs, sondern auch innerhalb des Erbes von Experimenten der Moderne, aus denen frühere Architekturbeispiele hervorgegangen sind. Hier werden die Umrisse des Architekturdenkens von Barkow Leibinger erkennbar; eine Welt der Erkundung, in der jegliche Konzepte von der Verwendung eines Baumaterials, einer Struktur, eines Herstellungsprozesses, einer Form oder einer Funktion alles andere als abstrakt ist. Für sie sind Konzepte nur echt, wenn sie beobachtbar ist: Es sind Qualitäten, nicht nur Einschränkungen oder Möglichkeiten, die durch die genaue Untersuchung früherer Episoden und Projekte erschließen – sowohl ihrer eigenen als auch der von anderen.[5]

Ich habe schon an anderer Stelle über Barkow Leibingers elegant facettiertes TRUTEC Building geschrieben (fertiggestellt in der Digital Media City in Seoul, Korea, 2007). Im Kontext dieses Essays kann das Hochhaus als ein weiteres Beispiel dafür herangezogen werden, wie die Architekten systematisch nach Wissen suchen und Erkenntnisse gewinnen. Trotz seiner nahezu gegensätzlichen Erscheinung zum SMH in Form, Materialwahl, geografischer Lage und Funktion stellt auch das TRUTEC Building eine Verbindung zwischen sich selbst und einer anderen Ikone der Moderne her, Mies van der Rohes 1921 entworfenem Hochhaus für die Berliner Friedrichstraße. Im Falle des TRUTEC Building ist dieser Bezug eine hochentwickelte digitale Technologie des CNC-Fräsens, die dazu verwendet wurde, eine delirierende, sich zwar systematisch wiederholende, aber doch nicht repetitive, plastisch geformte gläserne Hülle herzustellen und zusammenzufügen, die dasselbe mit Mies' Hochhaus tut, was das SMH mit dem 1914 entstandenen Dom-ino getan hat.

Ich habe diesen Exkurs zum TRUTEC Building auch noch aus einem weiteren Grund unternommen: um zu zeigen, wie Barkow Leibinger stets in engem und bewusstem Zusammenhang zu anderen Projekten vorgehen. Gerade in den vielen Gegensätzen zwischen TRUTEC und SMH, in der bewussten Unterschiedlichkeit, mit der die Architekten hier vor allem die äußere Erscheinung gestalten, aber auch in Bezug auf den Bauprozess, die Geografie, Nutzung und das Raumprogramm lässt sich erkennen, dass etwas Größeres ihre Arbeit antreibt. Barkow Leibinger sind Architekten, die völlig ohne Vorliebe für bestimmte Gewohnheiten oder einen bestimmten Stil mit ihrem Architekturdenken auskommen – jenen Richard-Meier-esquen Versuch, das Äußere eines Œvre zu vereinheitlichen, also wiedererkennbar zu sein, von einem Projekt zum nächsten. Nicht so Barkow Leibinger – indem sie ihre beiden aktuellen Projekte in Relation zu früheren (jetzt sogar schon ein Jahrhundert alten) Entwürfen stellen, werden Formen der Kontinuität und Diskontinuität erkennbar. Dieses Vorgehen überrascht in einer Zeit, in der es heißt, Architektur müsse sich über ihre bekannten Grenzen hinauswagen, wenn sie in einer Welt globaler Unsicherheit weiter relevant sein wolle.

III. Wissen innerhalb eines erweiterten Architekturfeldes

Rem Koolhaas' bereits erwähnte Beobachtung in Bezug auf die begrenzten Fähigkeiten der Architektur, in einer größeren, komplexeren Welt zu bestehen, verleitet ihn zu einem houdiniartigen Fluchtversuch aus den engen Grenzen der Disziplin: »Architektur muss von der Pflicht zu konstruieren befreit werden«, schreibt er, »damit sie ein Mittel werden kann, über irgendetwas [...] über alles nachzudenken.«[6] Wir leben heute in einer Zeit, in der nahezu jedes erdenkliche kulturelle, kommerzielle oder intellektuelle Projekt mit allem möglichen »vollgestopft« wird (vom Wired-Magazin über die »Cultural-Studies«-Stundenpläne und Design-Studiengänge für Graduierte bis hin zu zahllosen

Silicon-Valley-Businessplänen), was zu immer unklareren, verschwommeneren Grenzen führt. Heute, da interdisziplinäre Kulturwissenschaften und sonstige »Promiskuitäten« der meisten Forschungsuniversitäten schon die bloße Idee einer klar abgegrenzten, stabilen und sinnvollen »Fachdisziplin« fast undenkbar machen, bietet das Architekturdenken von Barkow Leibinger ein seltenes Beispiel von Beständigkeit. Ihr Denken steht im Kontrast zu einem generalisierten Architekturexpansionismus, zu dessen Haupteigenschaften wohl die beschleunigte Globalisierung der Architektenprofession zählt.

Ein jüngst erschienenes Kompendium von 2014 illustriert diese globale Expansionstendenz sehr gut. In seinem Vorwort zu *Forensis. The Architecture of Public Truth* (ein Buch, das, wie sein Autor behauptet, den »globalen Konflikt ästhetisieren« will, was auch immer das bedeuten mag) erklärt Eyal Weizman, dass Architekturdenken eher ein Blickwinkel (soweit es heute noch so etwas gibt) als eine Arbeitsweise oder ein Erfahrungswert sei. Es ist in seiner Wahrnehmung ein »Werkzeug«: ein »Ansatz« um auf andere Dinge oder die Welt zu schauen. Sicherlich kann Architektur auf diese Weise genutzt werden; es fragt sich nur – im Sinne der Architektur – warum? Und noch wichtiger die Frage: Kann die Architektur sich durch diese Verschiebung selbst neu erfinden? Der Ruf nach einer Architektur, die »sich nicht nur mit Gebäuden beschäftigt, sondern mit einem sich ewig wandelnden Beziehungsgeflecht zwischen Menschen und Dingen, vermittelt von Räumen und Strukturen in multiplen Maßstäben«,[7] setzt natürlich voraus, dass es möglich sei, Gebäude ohne diese gedachte Vermittlung zu entwerfen und zu bauen. Weizman – wie Koolhaas zehn Jahre vor ihm – erklärt das fachliche Wissen der Architektur für unzureichend, um auf eine größere Welt zu schauen: »Die Architektur hat bescheiden begonnen: Sie wurde inspiriert von der anspruchslosen Arbeit Bausachverständiger.«[8] Das Ziel ist also, einfach gesagt, die Domäne des Architekturdenkens zu erweitern, bis es in der Architektur gar nicht mehr um deren Ausführung geht und sie zu einer Art Ansichtssache geworden ist.

Dieser architektonische Expansionismus findet sich auch im Titel eines anderen Artikels, 2004 von Anthony Vidler unter dem Titel »Architecture in an Expanded Field« veröffentlicht. Im Essay heißt es, dass nach »einigen Dekaden der selbstauferlegten Autonomie« die Architektur kürzlich »erwacht« sei; nicht so sehr durch neue Ideen wie durch »neue formale und programmatische Inspiration in einer Reihe von Disziplinen und Technologien, von der Landschaftsarchitektur bis zur digitalen Animation«.[9] Während Vidler es in Bezug auf eine Belebung »der Disziplin« rumoren hört, ist seine und die Aufmerksamkeit des Essays ganz woanders, nämlich bei den sozialen, materiellen oder ökologischen Aufgaben »außerhalb« der Architektur, die nach seinem Verständnis so wichtig sind, dass Architekten ihr Bewusstsein erweitern sollten, um sie zu meistern.[10]

Architekten haben lange darum gekämpft, das Wesen, die Grenzen und die Gründe für ihr Wissen zum Ausdruck zu bringen, mit einer ihnen eigenen Art zu denken, die sie selbst und ein gleichgesinntes Publikum weiter als Architektur ansehen. Zwei Jahrtausende nachdem Vitruv sich abmühte, diesem Denken in seinen *Zehn Büchern* Form und Namen zu geben, griff Le Corbusier diesen Impuls in der Moderne mit seinem Buch *Towards a New Architecture*[11] auf. In seiner zusammenfassenden Darlegung richtet Le Corbusier seine ungeteilter Aufmerksamkeit auf die grundlegenden und materiellen Eigenschaften als die Mittel um (sogar seine moderne, revolutionäre) Architektur dingfest zu machen: »Masse und Oberfläche sind die Elemente, in denen sich die Architektur manifestiert.«[12] Wie sich diese Elemente in einer modernen Welt festlegen lassen, ist für Barkow Leibinger die entscheidende Frage, die sich auch Le Corbusier stellen musste. In einem frühen Akt moderner Rebellion und architektonischer Vorahnung in Bezug auf den wachsenden Einfluss fremden Wissens auf das moderne Wissen stellt Le Corbusier an anderer Stelle in *Towards a New Architecture* fest, dass »amerikanische Ingenieure mit ihren Berechnungen unsere veraltete Architektur überwältigen«.[13] Ein Jahrhundert nach dieser etwas merkwürdigen Befürchtung Le Corbusiers, und nachdem er durch den Fokus auf das Bauingenieurwesen sein Maison Dom-ino zur Waffe machte, mit der die Architekturgeschichte ausgelöscht werden sollte, kehren Barkow Leibinger die Formel des Dom-ino auf überraschende, paradoxe und unerwartete Weise um. Indem sie sich ihre eigenen Gedanken zur Neuerfindung dieses immer mehr in die Historie gehörenden Projektes machen, unternehmen sie eine Art von Revanche, die jedem wahrhaftigen architektonischen Streben innewohnt: die Möglichkeit, sogar den revolutionärsten Impuls moderner Architektur zu etwas Historischem werden zu lassen. Die Arbeit und das Denken von Frank Barkow und Regine Leibinger erinnern daran, dass das stabilste und haltbarste Baumaterial von allen die Beziehungen sind, die jedes Projekt zwischen sich und jenen

herstellt, die ihm vorangegangen sind. In einer Zeit wie der unseren, die vom grenzenlosen Glauben an eine immer vagere Zukunft dominiert wird, könnte sich die episodische Wirklichkeit der Architektur, ihre Abhängigkeit von dem, was vorher da war, als wertvoller den je erweisen.

1 Gerhard Richter, »Notes [1962]«, in: *Gerhard Richter: Text, Writings, Interviews and Letters. 1961–2007,* hrsg. von Gerhard Richter, Dietmar Elger und Hans Ulrich Obrist, London 2009, S. 15.

2 Rem Koolhaas, »Contents«, in: *Content,* Köln 2004, S. 20.

3 Ebd.

4 Siehe dazu ein Statement der Architekten über die Rolle von Langzeitforschung in ihrem Büro in »An Atlas of Fabrication«, in: Frank Barkow und Regine Leibinger (Hrsg.), *Barkow Leibinger. An Atlas of Fabrication,* London 2009.

5 Brett Steele, »Atlas-Tectonics«, in: *Barkow Leibinger. Bricoleur Bricolage,* London 2013, S. 1 f. Ein als Atlas für Designforschung ausgelegtes Buch von Barkow Leibinger und eine Sammlung, die auf eines der einflussreichsten Kunstprojekte unserer Zeit Bezug nimmt (Gerhard Richters *Atlas),* liefert die Erklärung, warum ich das Epigramm auswählte, mit dem ich dieses Essay hier ein Jahr später eröffne.

6 Ebd., S. 20.

7 Eyal Weizman, »Introduction«, in: *Forensis. The Architecture of Public Truth*, hrsg. von Forensic Architecture, Berlin 2014, S. 13.

8 Weizman fährt fort, einen solchen Blickwinkel für seine Zwecke einzunehmen, und dokumentiert ihn in seinem Kompendium, das angeblich nur versucht, »eine Materialgeologie zeitgenössischer Konflikte« zu verzeichnen, die laut Weizman möglich gemacht wurde, indem man wie ein Architekt denkt, um diese »Geologie« aufzudecken. Ebd., S. 13 f.

9 Anthony Vidler, »Architecture's Expanded Field. Finding Inspirations in Jellyfish and Geopolitics«, in: *Artforum,* 2004, S. 142.

10 Ebd., S. 143.

11 Le Corbusier, *Towards a New Architecture,* englisches Vorwort von Frederick Etchells, London 1931, S. 21–31.

12 Ebd., S. 26.

13 Ebd., S. 31.

Makeover

Unabhängig davon, wie viele Bedeutungen dem Begriff Nachhaltigkeit zugesprochen werden, besteht immer mehr Einigkeit darüber, dass vorhandene Substanz (sei sie architektonischer, infrastruktureller, urbaner oder landschaftlicher Art) ein wertvolles Gut ist. Der Architekt Sverre Fehn sprach einst vom »Tanz um tote Dinge« und bezog sich damit auf die Interaktion eines Museums mit seinen Ausstellungsobjekten, also historischen Artefakten, Kunstwerken oder anderen Exponaten. Fehns Aussage könnte jedoch ebenso darauf angewandt werden, wie Architekten mit dem umgehen, was man allgemein als »Bestand« bezeichnet. Der Terminus »Makeover« beschreibt keine Restaurierung im eigentlichen Sinne einer historisch akkuraten und pflichtbewussten Rückkehr zum Originalzustand (man denke an die Villa Tugendhat von Ludwig Mies van der Rohe), sondern umschreibt die Idee, Vorhandenes in etwas Neues zu überführen, das über die ursprünglich zugewiesene Bestimmung hinausweist. Unter einem Makeover, einer gründlichen Veränderung, verstehen wir hier Projekte, die bereits existierende Dinge erneuern, ergänzen, verändern oder transformieren.

Makeover ist eine Strategie, die auf Beobachtung, Wertschätzung und Weiterverwertung basiert und dabei einen Dialog zwischen Bestehendem und neu Entstehendem herstellt. Künstlerarchitekten wie Gordon Matta-Clark oder Carlo Scarpa haben hier (räumlich wie syntaktisch) neue Wege beschritten, indem sie alten Gebäuden radikal neue Nutzungen zugewiesen haben. Dabei tritt das bestehende Gebäude wie eine Art Gastgeber auf, das durch eine nutzungsverändernde Choreografie wiederbelebt wird.

Aber welche Kräfte sind eigentlich am Werk, wenn es um die Sanierung oder Verjüngung eines Gebäudes oder sogar eines städtischen Kontextes geht? An erster Stelle steht das Gebot der Funktionalität, ob nun im Sinne einer programmatischen Neuorientierung, der zeitlichen Abfolge einzelner Bauphasen oder technischer Fragen: Es geht immer um eine Erneuerung, die das unausweichliche Altern, den Verfall eines Gebäudes, verzögern oder aufhalten soll. Bei der technischen Ertüchtigung geht es auch um die »Performance« eines Gebäudes – um seinen Energieverbrauch, die Umweltfreundlichkeit, den Umgang mit Lichtverhältnissen und klimatischen Bedingungen, um die Be- und Entlüftungsmöglichkeiten sowie um die Akustik – kurz, um die Frage, wie sich Nutzerkomfort erzeugt lässt.

Die Performance eines Gebäudes ist aber nicht die einzige Motivation für einen Makeover. Formale Ambitionen schließen die Transformation von Räumen und ihrer Dichte, von Tragstrukturen und Materialien mit ein, und zwar in Hinblick darauf, wie sie die vorgefundene Bausubstanz durchdringen und so das Vorgefundene erneuern. Makeovers gewinnen immer mehr an Gewicht, da die Verknappung von Ressourcen, die wachsende Bedeutung von Nachhaltigkeit, der (Weiter-)Nutzungswert einer Substanz und wirtschaftliche Beschränkungen in unseren heutigen Städten und Industriegebieten (anders als die Tabula rasa der Nachkriegszeit) uns dazu drängen, »tote Dinge« wiederzubeleben und ihnen eine zeitgemäße neue Vitalität einzuhauchen.

Iwan Baan: Der lässige Beobachter

Die Gebäude auf dem TRUMPF-Campus in Ditzingen bei Stuttgart sind über die Jahre hinweg von mehreren international bekannten Fotografen dokumentiert worden. Dabei lag ihr Fokus üblicherweise auf dem jeweils gerade fertiggestellten Einzelgebäude. Zweifellos immer ästhetisch ansprechend zeigen diese Aufnahmen die Gebäude doch fast ausschließlich als solitäre Objekte, mit wenig Aufmerksamkeit für die weiteren Zusammenhänge und dafür, wie der gesamte Komplex Tag für Tag von den dort arbeitenden Menschen genutzt wird.

Da der Campus, dessen Ursprünge in den 1970er-Jahren liegen, nun weitgehend vollendet ist, wurde Iwan Baan gebeten, das Areal für diese Publikation noch einmal ganz neu fotografisch zu untersuchen und die Gebäude deutlicher in einen Zusammenhang zueinander zu stellen – so wie sie im Alltag von den Angestellten (ob nun im Blaumann oder Anzug), Besuchern und Kunden bevölkert sind. Er sollte auf diese Weise dokumentieren, wie Menschen den Ort nutzen und die Gebäude durch ihre Anwesenheit beleben. Seine Arbeiten zeigen, wie die Architektur die unterschiedlichen Arbeitswelten umrahmt, die Produktion in den Fabrikhallen ebenso wie den Alltag in den Büros und an allen sozialen Treffpunkten (wie im Betriebsrestaurant oder im Park). Zu sehen ist ein Umfeld, das für die deutsche Industrielandschaft kennzeichnend ist und eines, das zeigt – und das ist vielleicht generell noch nicht oft genug der Fall –, wie Architektur zur Produktion, zur Entstehung und Entwicklung neuer Ideen beiträgt. Eine Fabrik ist keine utopische Stadt. Sie bleibt immer unfertig, ist immer im Werden, wird ständig überarbeitet. Dieser Umstand erfordert eine heterogene, weiche Planung, ein Patchwork von Räumen und Nutzungsarten, die sich über die Zeit durch Wachstum oder Schrumpfung des Unternehmens verändern können.

Iwan Baan zeigt die Gebäude nicht als autonome Objekte, sondern als Teile eines sich entwickelnden, ausdifferenzierten Industriecampus, der wie eine kleine Stadt funktioniert. Wir werden vom Blick des beiläufigen Beobachters auf das Geschehen gelenkt und daran erinnert, dass diejenigen, die in einem Gebäude Tag für Tag leben und arbeiten, allzu oft die vom Planer intendierte Nutzungsweise unterlaufen. So lässt uns diese Fotoreportage ermessen, wie Gebäude von ihren Nutzern angenommen und verändert werden, und sie zeigt gleichzeitig, wie sie sich über die Zeit entwickeln.

Unsere Hoffnung bestand darin, durch jene Art der fotografischen Dokumentation die zuvor beschriebenen Dynamiken sichtbar und nachvollziehbar zu machen. Aus der großen Fülle an Bildern musste letztlich eine sehr kleine Auswahl getroffen werden, die die Erfahrungen des lässigen, aber am Ende doch sehr scharfsinnigen Beobachters transportieren.

Site Specific

Der Terminus »site specific«, ortsspezifisch, umschreibt die Idee, dass Architektur aus vorgefundenen Bedingungen, aus der gebauten Umgebung, erschaffen werden kann. »Site-specific art« – im klassischen Sinne eine Installation – wird für einen ganz bestimmten Ort geschaffen. Sie weist auf den Ort hin, wird aber auch durch den Ort geformt, an dem sie ist. Sie steht also nicht einfach nur an irgendeinem Platz, sondern ist aus diesem entsprungen und kann nirgendwo anders sein.

Während sich das Kapitel Makeover mit den Gegebenheiten eines bestimmten existierenden Gebäudes beschäftigt, geht es im Kapitel Site Specific um den Raum im weiteren Sinne, um den Kontext, um dessen Grenzen und die Frage, wie er ein Gebäude formt und beeinflusst. Die spezifischen Charakteristika eines Ortes sind zwar häufig nur latent spürbar, aber kraftvoll genug, um ein Projekt vollkommen zu prägen. Die notwendigen Fähigkeiten, damit umzugehen, sind Beobachtungsgabe, Entschlossenheit und die Fähigkeit, bestimmte Einflüsse auszuwählen und den Schwerpunkt gegebenenfalls zu verlagern.

Die entscheidende Frage ist stets, was den Kontext eigentlich ausmacht und wie er das Ortsspezifische an einem Gebäude generiert. Im Allgemeinen beschreibt das Wort kontextuell, wie ein Teil zum großen Ganzen in Beziehung steht; in architektonischer Hinsicht geht es wohl mehr um eine syntaktische Zuordnung als um eine visuelle oder tektonische Verwandtschaft. Für Barkow Leibinger erschließt sich ein Projekt zu weiten Teilen durch die Frage nach dem Kontext: Welches sind die entscheidenden Merkmale eines Ortes und wie können sie genutzt werden, um ein Projekt zu konzipieren? Hierbei kann mit Kontext die historische Identität eines Ortes, einer Stadt, eines Viertels oder einer Straße, gemeint sein, aber ebenso abstraktere Aspekte, die ebenso wichtig sind: die Beschaffenheit einer Landschaft, die Geometrie und der Maßstab angrenzender Gebäude, ortstypische Materialien, das Klima, geologische Prägungen und vieles mehr.

Was das Ortsspezifische zu solch einem andauernden und beherrschenden Thema für Barkow Leibinger macht, ist die absolute Einzigartigkeit eines jeden Bauplatzes und die daraus resultierenden einzigartigen Anforderungen an ein Projekt. Sie birgt die Chance, jedes einzelne Bauvorhaben autonom von allen anderen Werken im Büroportfolio zu entwickeln. Dadurch wird das Architekturschaffen zu einer sich immer wieder erneuernden und verändernden Arbeit – angetrieben von jeweils anderen zeitlichen, räumlichen und subjektiv wahrnehmbaren Einflüssen.

Während die Baukonstruktion und Materialität ein übergreifendes Interessenfeld bilden, ist es doch vor allem die Reaktion auf einen Ort, die das Gebäude ausdifferenziert und seine Einzigartigkeit hervorbringt. Dieser Ansatz gilt zwar nicht für alle Projekte, dennoch ist der Ortsbezug ein gutes Mittel, nicht in die Falle eines selbstbezogenen Formalismus zu tappen, der, um es mit den Worten Richard Serras zu sagen, »ortsangepasst« ist, ohne in direkten Dialog zur Umgebung zu treten.[1]

Durch ortsspezifische Architektur wird der bauliche Kontext als komplexe, subjektiv wahrnehmbare Umgebung gelesen, die fruchtbar und bestimmend auf das Architekturschaffen einwirkt. Entscheidend ist es dabei, sichtbare oder auch verdeckte Muster zu erkennen und sie so einzusetzen, dass etwas Neues entstehen kann.

1 Yve-Alain Bois, »A Pituresque Stroll around Clara-Clara«, in: *October,* 29, Sommer 1984, S. 39.

Contributor Biographies Autorenbiografien

IWAN BAAN is a Dutch photographer known primarily for images that narrate the life and interactions that occur within architecture. Iwan grew up outside Amsterdam and studied at the Royal Academy of Art in The Hague. Baan's work is characterized by the portrayal of people in their architectural surroundings and by rendering visible the social context and broader environment linked with architecture. His images appear frequently in magazines and exhibitions worldwide. In 2010 he received the Julius Shulman Photography Award and in 2012 the Golden Lion at the Venice Architecture Biennale.

CARSON CHAN is an architecture writer and curator, pursuing a PhD in architecture at Princeton University. After working for Barkow Leibinger and the Neue Nationalgalerie's architecture exhibitions department in Berlin he founded PROGRAM, a noncommercial initiative for art and architecture collaborations. His writing on art, architecture, and contemporary culture appears in books and periodicals worldwide, including *Kaleidoscope,* where he is a contributing editor, and *032c*, where he is editor-at-large. Chan cocurated the Marrakech Biennale 2012 and was executive curator of the Biennial of the Americas 2013 in Denver, Colorado. Also in 2013, he co-organized the conference Exhibiting Architecture: A Paradox? at the Yale School of Architecture.

HAL FOSTER teaches twentieth-century art and theory at Princeton University and writes regularly for *October, Artforum,* and *the London Review of Books*. His recent books include *The Art-Architecture Complex* (2011) and *The First Pop Age: Painting and Subjectivity in the Art of Hamilton, Lichtenstein, Warhol, Richter, and Ruscha* (2012).

BRETT STEELE directs the Architectural Association School of Architecture in London, where he founded and directed the AADRL Design Research Lab. He has taught and lectured at schools throughout the world and is the editor of numerous books, including *Supercritical* (2010), *0-14: Projection and Reception* (2012), and *Networks: An Anthology of Distributed Design Cultures* (2014). Steele's articles, interviews, and lectures have appeared in various architectural journals and newspapers and on television. He is the founder and series editor of *Architecture Words,* which since 2009 has published the critical writings of Denise Scott Brown, Rem Koolhaas, Peter Eisenman, Max Bill, Kengo Kuma, Toyo Ito, and others; and *Agendas,* a series of books documenting the work of AA students and units.

SARAH WHITING is William Ward Watkin Professor and Dean of the School of Architecture at Rice University. She is also a founding partner, along with Ron Witte, of WW in Houston, Texas.

IWAN BAAN ist Fotograf, bekannt vor allem für seine erzählerische Art der Architekturfotografie, mit der er Leben und Interaktion im gebauten Kontext zeigt. Der Niederländer wuchs in der Nähe von Amsterdam auf und studierte an der Royal Academy of Art in Den Haag. Typisch für seine Arbeiten ist es, Menschen in ihrer architektonischen Umgebung zu porträtieren, gesellschaftliche Zusammenhänge und das weitere Umfeld um Architektur herum sichtbar zu machen. Iwan Baans Bilder werden weltweit veröffentlicht und in Ausstellungen gezeigt. 2010 erhielt er den Julius Shulman Institute Photography Award, 2012 den Goldenen Löwen der Architekturbiennale in Venedig.

CARSON CHAN ist Architekturkritiker sowie -kurator und promoviert an der Princeton University. Er arbeitete für Barkow Leibinger und die Abteilung für Architekturausstellungen in der Neuen Nationalgalerie in Berlin, bevor er PROGRAM gründete, eine nichtkommerzielle Initiative für Kooperationen der Bereiche Kunst und Architektur. Seine Texte zu Kunst, Architektur und zeitgenössischer Kultur erscheinen weltweit in Büchern und Zeitschriften wie *Kaleidoscope,* für die er als Redakteur tätig ist, und *032c,* für die er als Auslandsberichterstatter arbeitet. Chan war Ko-Kurator der Marrakech Biennale 2012 und leitender Kurator der Biennial of the Americas 2013 in Denver, Colorado. Ebenfalls 2013 war er Mitorganisator der Konferenz »Exhibiting Architecture. A Paradox?« an der Yale School of Architecture.

HAL FOSTER lehrt Kunst und Theorie des 20. Jahrhunderts an der Princeton University und schreibt regelmäßig für *October, Artforum,* und die *London Review of Books.* Zu seinen neuesten Büchern zählen *The Art-Architecture Complex* (2011) und *The First Pop Age. Painting and Subjectivity in the Art of Hamilton, Lichtenstein, Warhol, Richter, and Ruscha* (2012).

BRETT STEELE ist Direktor der Architectural Association School of Architecture in London, wo er das Architectural Association Design Research Lab gründete und leitete. Er unterrichtet weltweit, hält Vorträge und ist Autor beziehungsweise Herausgeber zahlreicher Bücher, darunter *Supercritical* (2010), *0–14. Projection and Reception* (2012) und *Networks. An Anthology of Distributed Design Cultures* (2014). Steeles Artikel, Interviews und Vorträge erscheinen in vielen Architekturmagazinen und Zeitungen oder werden im Fernsehen ausgestrahlt. Er ist Gründer und Herausgeber der Reihe *Architecture Words,* in der seit 2009 Aufsätze von Denise Scott Brown, Rem Koolhaas, Peter Eisenman, Max Bill, Kengo Kuma, Toyo Ito und anderen publiziert wurden, sowie von *AA Agendas,* einer Buchreihe, die die Arbeit der AA-Units und ihrer Studenten dokumentiert.

SARAH WHITING ist William-Ward-Watkin-Professorin und Dekanin der Fakultät für Architektur an der Rice University in Houston, Texas. Gemeinsam mit Ron Witte leitet sie das Architekturbüro WW, ebenfalls in Houston.

Thanks to all Barkow Leibinger team members who contributed to the projects shown in this book

Ayax Abreu Garcia
Michael Ahlers
Justin Allen
Matthias Anke
Paulo de Araujo de Guzman
Anika Arndt
Meredith Atkinson
Sebastian Awick
Matthias Graf von Ballestrem
Peter Ballman
Derek Bangle
Frank Barkow
Stefan Barme
Hans-Georg Bauer
Julie E. Bauer
Martina Bauer
Natacha Bauer
Frédérik Beaupère
Konstanze Beelitz
Dietrich Bernstorf
Marian Beschoner
Larissa Böhler
Michael Bölling
Jörg Boettger
Giuseppe Boezi
Markus Bonauer
Pia Brückner
Franz Brunnert
Didier Callot
Daniel Carlson
Jeremy Carvalho
Filipa Leal de Carvalho
Nina Cattaneo
Carson Chan
Woonghee Cho
Matthew Christensen
Joel Cichowksi
Christian Coburger
Sonia Cohan
Thomas Day
Patrick Delahoy
Michael Deutschmann
Joanna Doherty
Daniel Dratz
Gustav Düsing
Mascha Egberts
Stephan Egert
Christina Eichmeier
Larissa Eichwede
Michael Eidenbenz
Sebastian Ernst
Stefan Felber
Fabian von Ferrari
Ana Filipovic
Andreas Friedli
Ulrich Fuchs
Mari Fujita
Douglas Gauthier
Elisabeth Gellein
Clemens Gerritzen
Johannes Gestering
Cynthia Grieshofer
Antje Grossmann
Paul Grundei
Pierre Guérin
Mathias Gussmann
Ralph J. Habbel
Dörte Hanisch
Josephine von Hasselbach
Kevin Jin He
Philipp Heidemann
Christian Helfrich
Philipp Heydel
Jana Hildebrandt
Zachary Hinchliffe
Felix Hoepner
Caspar Hoesch
Enlai Hooi
Jerome Hord
Shoko Hoshino
Andrea Houghton
Andrea Hronjec
Ariel Huber
Shusuke Inoue
Gian-Marco Jenatsch
Nadja Jeske
Michael Johl
Bernd Jürgens
Stephanie Kaindl
Jakob Kartenbeck
Christine Kehlenbeck
Brendan Kellog
Christopher Coryn Kempster
Daria Khapalova
Ki Jun Kim
Yen Sun Kim
Jan Kircher
Clemens Klein

Jonathan Kleinhample
Fabian Koch
Martina Kohler
Henrike Kortemeyer
Hartmut Kortner
Carsten Krafft
Heiko Krech
Charlotte Krefeld
Nina Küpers
Jan-Oliver Kunze
Jeanette Kuo
Andreas Lamprecht
Andreas Lang
Mark Lauener
Corinne Lehner
Regine Leibinger
Wiebke Lemme
Arne Löper
Philip Loskant
Martin Lukasczyk
Arne Maibohm
Lisa Manns
Michael Meier
Carlo Mellis
Zsofia Mester
Michael Metzger
Ulrike Meyer-Hanschen
Heike Michel
Simon Mildner
Christina Möller
Julien Monfort
Elizaveta Mosina
Jürgen Müller
Aki Nagasaka
Hiroki Nakamura
Oliver Neumann
Volkmar Nickol
Claus Nieländer
Nicole Nuñez
Michel Obladen
Karin Ocker
Anne Marie O'Connor
Mathias Oliva y Hausmann
Christian Pälmke
Matthew Peddie
Reto Pedrocchi
Dagmar Pelger
Andrea Pelzeter
André Perret
Nora Peyer
Fabian Pfeiffer
Katja Pfeiffer
Hermann Plöckl
Almin Prsic
Phillip Raum
Matthias Reese
Ina Reinecke
Klaus Reintjes
Julia Renfer
Peter Rieder
Esther Righetti
Ruwen Rimpau
Maria Rook
Susann Ross
Christian Rudolf
Karsten Ruf
Anna Saeger
Vincenzo Salierno
Tanja Salomäki
Sonia Sandberger
Jason Sandy
Ushiro Sayaka
Roger Schaerer
Sonja Schellenberg
Jakob Schemel
Veronika Schmid
Michael Schmidt
Konrad Scholz
Julia Schüler
Henrik Schulte
Morihide Seki
Richard Sharam
Christopher Sklar
Lance Wilson Smith
Astrid Smitham
Kasper Spange
Elke Sparmann
Katharina Specht
Steffen Sperle
Marion Spillmann
Elisabeth Srajer
Constanze Stark
Antje Steckhan
Florian Steinbächer
Thomas Strebel
Bogdan Strugar
Tyler Swingle
Pearl Tae Kang
Gabriel Tamez
Ian Thomas
Erika Tillberg
Jonas Troescher
Ulrich von Türckheim
Alexandra Ultsch
Patrick Unger
Tim Unnebrink
Ludwig Uphues
Blake Villwock
Katrin Voermanek
Daniela Voss
Annette Wagner
Zherui Wang
Gabriel Warshafsky
Lukas Weder
Cirsti Weich
Marlen Weiser
Veronika Weisner
Tobias Wenz
Jens Weßel
Maik Westhaus
Jörg Wich
Sara Wiedenbeck
Ariane Wiegner
Leonie Woltermann
Dylan Woock
Dylan Marx Wood
Alexander Wright
Kent Wu
Yasuaki Mori

Please visit our full archive with all projects, additional project information, and a comprehensive list of project partners and collaborators at *barkowleibinger.com*

Barkow Leibinger
Spielraum

With a foreword by Hal Foster and contributions by Iwan Baan, Carson Chan, Brett Steele, and Sarah Whiting

Editorial Team
Frank Barkow, Regine Leibinger, Katrin Voermanek and Nicole Nuñez, supported by Elisabeth Gellein, Kira Grimm, Christina Jentsch, and Mirjam Thomann.
Special thanks to Oliver Elser for his editorial advice

Copyediting
Joann Skypzak-Davidsmeyer (English); Charlotte Neugebauer, Annerose Bach, Hatje Cantz; Katrin Voermanek; Eva Zimmermann (German)

Translations
(English–German)
Wilhelm von Werthern, Zweisprachkunst;
Eva Zimmermann

Graphic design
Zak Group

Typeface
HaasUnica

Production
Katja Jaeger, Hatje Cantz

Reproductions, printing, and binding
DZA Druckerei zu Altenburg GmbH, Altenburg

Paper
LuxoArt Samt, 100 g/m^2

Published by
Hatje Cantz Verlag
Zeppelinstrasse 32
73760 Ostfildern
Germany
Tel. +49 711 4405-200
Fax +49 711 4405-220
www.hatjecantz.com

A Ganske Publishing Group company

Hatje Cantz books are available internationally at selected bookstores. For more information about our distribution partners, please visit our homepage www.hatjecantz.com.

ISBN 978-3-7757-3666-4

Printed in Germany

Cover illustration
Corinne Rose
Illustration pp. 18–19:
Exhibition view, *Atlas of Fabrication,* Gallery 032c, Berlin, 2009

Image credits
Iwan Baan: pp. 53–55, 104, 111, 114–15, 121, 160, 163–64, 172, 173 top, 174–75, 186, 257 left, 282–313; Amy Barkow: pp. 24, 29, 84–85, 91 top left, bottom left, 262 top left and right; Barkow Leibinger: pp. 22–23, 27, 35, 70 bottom right, 78, 87 center left and right, bottom left and right, 100 top left, 127 bottom, 150 bottom left and right, 170, 173 center left and right, bottom left and right, 184 top left and right, bottom left and right, 188, 190, 195–96, 219 center left and right, bottom left and right, 226, 229, 249 center left, bottom left and right, 276 top left and right, center left, 278, 318, 323 top left and right, 334 center left and right, bottom left and right, 344, 347, 349, 356 top, 359; Valerie Bennett / Architectural Association Photo Library: p. 243; Zooey Braun: pp. 128, 130 top, 133–36, 139–41, 176; Andrea Compagno: p. 100 top right; Uwe Dettmar: p. 38 top; Jockel Finck: p. 272; Johannes Foerster: pp. 48, 51 bottom left and right, 81, 354, 356 bottom, 360–61; David Franck: pp. 110, 116, 118, 167–69, 179, 182–83, 187, 218, 219 top, 254, 256, 257 right; Heiko Haberle: p. 198; Lutz Hannemann: pp. 319–21; Werner Huthmacher: pp. 35, 112, 171, 181, 191–93, 222, 227, 250–52, 258, 263, 323 center left and right, bottom, 325 top, 327–29, 362, 367; Roman Keller: p. 100 center left; Linus Lintner: pp. 261 bottom, 262 bottom; Robert Mehl: p. 76; Philip Meuser: p. 70 bottom left; Stefan Müller: pp. 26, 200, 203–04, 210, 212–15, 246, 249 top, 253; Nicole Nuñez / Barkow Leibinger: p. 77 top, 350; Ina Reinecke / Barkow Leibinger: pp. 40, 43, 80, 130 bottom, 132, 142–45, 147, 216, 220; Christian Richters: pp. 91 top, 93, right, 162; Corinne Rose: pp. 18–20, 30, 32–33, 44, 46 top left, 47, 68, 71–73, 75, 77 bottom, 82, 87 top, 90, 94, 184 center left and right, 185; Margherita Spiluttini: pp. 96, 98, 100 bottom, 103, 106–09, 206, 208–09, 316, 324, 325 bottom, 326; Sprüth Magers: p. 261 top (Exhibition view, Sterling Ruby, *I Am not Free Because I Can Be Exploded Anytime,* Sprüth Magers, Berlin, 2011) Hagen Stier: pp. 36, 38 bottom; Paul Warchol: pp. 330, 332–33, 336–39